SINGLE TRACK OBSESSION

A Book of Extraordinary Railway Journeys

ROB SISSONS

Order this book online at www.trafford.com
or email orders@trafford.com

Most Trafford titles are also available at major online book retailers.

Print information available on the last page.

ISBN: 978-1-4251-6239-9 (sc)

Trafford rev. 02/29/2020

 www.trafford.com

North America & international
toll-free: 1 888 232 4444 (USA & Canada)
fax: 812 355 4082

To My Father

ROBERT JAMES SISSONS

(1914 - 2006)

To whom I owe my love of travel

CONTENTS

Introduction   7

European Journeys and Maps   13

1)   *And do you STILL wish that the French ran our railways?*   15

2)   *The White and Silver Railway (Le Blanc-Argent)*   21

3)   *A Priest in a Peugeot, and a Trip behind a Tracteur*   27

4)   *In the Footsteps of Bryan Morgan (the Vivarais and the Velay)*   31

5)   *A Cab Ride in a Caravelle, and train-driving lessons for senior citizens*   37

6)   *Escape from Saint-Geniez-d'Olt*   44

7)   *Travels With My Mother: The Line That Had Three Lives*   49

8)   *The Chemins de Fer Corses and a Quartet of Corsican Cats*   53

9)   *A Train Ride with a Tibetan, and Trouble with a Tram*   58

10)   *The Beautiful Brünigbahn and the Miniscule MIB*   63

11)   *Saved by the FART: the Glacier Express that wasn't*   69

12)   *The Train in Spain that stays mainly in the Plain*   74

13)   *Deep-Freeze in Finse and on the Flåmsbana*   83

14)   *An overnight ride to Russia*   86

15)   *Steam trains, a Soaking in Stiege and a Stasi Cat*   90

North American Journeys and Maps   95

16)   *Across the roof of Canada*   97

17)   *After a night with Marty, I ride the Rails from Durango to Silverton*   102

18)   *Across America by Song Title*   106

19)   *From the Pacific to the Atlantic by way of Paradise (and Liverpool)*   112

South American Journeys and Maps   121

20)   *Rails Through Deepest, Darkest Peru*   123

21)   *The Great Paraguayan Train Robbery*   130

22)   *The Railway at the End of the World*   136

Asian and African Journeys and Maps   141

    23)   *Going Japanese: Fast and Slow Lines in Japan*   143

    24)   *Jabalpur to Shimla: Monkey business in India*   148

    25)   *The Living Portion of the Death Railway*   153

    26)   *The Art of Travelling Graciously: Singapore to Kuala Lumpur*   157

    27)   *Pardon Me Boy, Is That The Outeniqua Choo-Tjoe?*   162

    28)   *South African Contrasts: The Game Train and the Apple Express*   166

Australasian Journeys and Maps   173

    29)   *Crossing the Outback with Sissy*   175

    30)   *The Land of the Long White Cloud (and long-lost railways)*   179

British Journeys and Maps   189

    31)   *The Prehistoric Railway from Andrew's House to the Causey Arch.*   191

    32)   *A Pass, a Petition, a Blonde in Blaenau and a Diesel around the Deviation*   194

    33)   *Riding the Ghost Train*   200

    34)   *Don't Look Back in Ongar*   203

    35)   *A Beautiful Berkshire Branch Line - and Cakes with the Women's' Institute*   206

    36)   *Blame it on Miss Bessemer: A Birthday Brake-Van Ride on the Bluebell*   209

    37)   *The Rails I have ridden more than any Others*   214

    38)   *A Railway Revival in the Rother Valley*   221

    39)   *No More Bloomers: I molest a Maiden on the Marsh Link*   226

    40)   *The Little Train That Takes Me Home Past Many a Garden Gnome*   234

The Ethereal Railway   239

Ode to a Country Railway   242

PRAYAS   243

Appendix I - Squashed Pennies   244

Appendix II - Songs for a Railway Journey   245

Bibliography   247

Index   250

A note about the maps in this book

Maps are not drawn to scale, and the length of some shorter lines has been exaggerated so that they can be shown more clearly. Major stations are shown as black squares; many intermediate stations have been omitted for clarity. Lines travelled on by the author and described in the text are shown as solid lines; some disused or freight-only lines mentioned in the text are shown as dotted lines.

INTRODUCTION

The love-hate relationship between human beings and railways is rather like that between the English and the French. While a fair proportion of English people claims to despise all things French, an equally large proportion buys vast quantities of French cheese and wine, copies Parisian fashion and Provençal cooking, spends every holiday in France and saves up for a cottage in the Dordogne. Similarly, we complain about trains when they run late or are cancelled, we hate the daily trek to London and, when in a car, we grumble about being held up at level-crossings. Yet why do so many of us flock to preserved railways to ride behind a steam engine, go on a day trip to Paris or Brussels on the Eurostar or take our partner for a romantic weekend on the Orient Express? Why did the closure of so many of Britain's branch lines in the 1960s by Dr Beeching arouse such intense opposition, even from those who seldom used the railways? It appears that trains have a universal emotional appeal.

Railways have fascinated people for years. The 'Newcastle Roads', as the pioneering colliery lines in North-East England became known in the eighteenth century, attracted artists, writers and travellers from far away. The development of the network and the introduction of the steam locomotive brought admiration and criticism alike. J M W Turner was fascinated by the power of the railway engine in his 1844 painting *Rain, Steam and Speed*, whilst that same year William Wordsworth sent a poem to the Prime Minister to protest about the proposed construction of the line from Kendal to Windermere. Charles Dickens was an enthusiastic railway traveller (until his train was involved in a notorious accident at Staplehurst in 1865!) but his novels generally hark back to the stage-coach era of his childhood, although he uses a railway to great effect as the setting for his spooky 1866 short story *The Signalman*. By this time, Thomas Cook had organised his first railway tour (from Leicester to Loughborough in 1840), and thousands of ordinary people had travelled by train to London for the Great Exhibition. As railways expanded to cover most developed countries, the train journey became less of a novelty and more of a way of life. When we think how computers have changed our lives in the last 30 years, we should reflect on how the iron roads transformed much of the world between 1830 and 1860.

Anybody can enjoy train travel, or admire the beauty of a curving stone viaduct or the power of a fine locomotive, but railway enthusiasts in Britain are predominantly male. I have never quite understood why. Are the *Thomas The Tank Engine* stories read only to little boys? Do little girls' parents 'condition' them at a young age by buying them dolls as presents rather than train sets? Or is it the sheer male illogical stupidity of laying down sleepers, spiking down two long iron rails 4 feet 8½ inches apart and then building something to run along them? One cannot help thinking that a woman would have found a much easier solution to our mass transport problems! (It is strange how the steel wheel on the steel rail has remained dominant for 200 years. In the Beauce, south of Paris, the concrete viaduct built for the futuristic *Aérotrain* monorail system in the late 1960s stands unused and unloved, while the TGV Atlantique trains race by on a conventional railway track that would have looked familiar to George Stephenson).

Yet the female rail enthusiast can be found in greater numbers overseas. Women contribute many of the articles and photographs in the French railway magazine *Voie Etroite*, and I have met quite a few female railfans in France - including teenage girls! When the preserved Vivarais railway recently ceased operations, a rail enthusiasts' website set up a page where readers could voice their opinions. I looked at this after a couple of weeks and saw that about half the comments had been posted by women. I wonder what the 'gender split' would be on a British website discussing the closure of a preserved steam railway?

I would urge any single women looking for a caring, sensitive male to join their local railway preservation society! And, although you *may* find some of the classic stereotypes with the anorak and the glasses held together with sticking-plaster, you will probably be in for a very pleasant surprise.

Like many railfans, I had a train set when I was young (I would not be so presumptuous as to call it a model railway). This started life as a simple oval of track on my bedroom floor, with a little blue tank engine called *Nellie* and four goods wagons. Gradually this expanded and eventually became a twin-track layout in the loft, which I named the *Little Kenton, Abton & Bletchley Railway*. (Bletchley was the name on one of my plastic Airfix or Hornby model stations). I was more interested in the scenery and buildings than in the trains: I loved making churches, castles and cottages out of cardboard and brown sticky tape and placing them alongside the tracks, together with some rather unconvincing trees! One of the favourite games I played with friends consisted of putting tiny Tri-ang model figurines in open goods trucks, sending them off at high speed around the track behind *Nellie*, and seeing who survived in the event of a derailment. Many unfortunate passengers disappeared down a dreaded gap in the baseboard by Little Kenton station. Luckily for the safety of rail transport, the LKA&BR came to an ignominious end when the Sissons family moved house and no room could be found for it in our new abode: it was later acquired, lock, stock and barrel, by my elder brother who incorporated it into his own far more professional layout.

A rare view of the LKA&BR

I still find the journey (and the scenery) more interesting than the actual train. Whilst I definitely prefer trains that have windows you can open, and I love ones where you can sit at the front and watch the track ahead (as on the Docklands Light Railway or the modern Montreux-Oberland-Bernois units in Switzerland), I really don't mind too much what the locomotive and rolling stock look like. It is the feeling of anticipation when you step into that bizarre shared space, watching the landscape roll by and perhaps interacting with strangers whom you would never otherwise have met. In a car you are trapped in your own hermetically-sealed bubble; on a bus you might talk to the person in the next seat, but a railway carriage is like a small world on wheels, conveying you from one part of the Universe to another but remaining essentially unchanged for the duration of its voyage.

I have enjoyed some wonderful conversations on trains. I remember speaking to some Bulgarians once on a train in France - they were among the first people I ever met from beyond the Iron Curtain - and once from Didcot to London I shared my compartment with a charming young lady of about 16 who told me she was absconding from her public school and was going to elope with her boyfriend in London! But striking up conversations on trains is getting more and more difficult, thanks to the invention of the personal stereo. First the Walkman, then the personal CD player and now the iPod have given every rail passenger the chance to cocoon himself in his own soundtrack. Still, if you cannot beat them you might as well join them. The iPod can be a boon when I wish to cut off the foul language of the teenagers two rows behind, the interminable chatter of the girl on her mobile phone or even the two train spotters opposite discussing every locomotive they have seen… A few suggestions of appropriate songs for a railway traveller's iPod (or cassette player) will be found in Appendix Two.

Victorian station canopy

Many people say that rail travel is not what it was. I am inclined to agree. Although I would not want a wholesale return to the days of steam, I cannot help thinking that many aspects of a train journey were rather more agreeable a few decades ago. The welcoming station with its friendly staff has all too often become an unstaffed halt; delicate Victorian awnings with their cast-iron supports have been demolished and replaced with plastic pseudo-bus shelters. The reduction in staffing has resulted in an epidemic of weeds, litter, vandalism and graffiti. It is all very well for the railway companies to say that there are CCTV cameras everywhere, but this does little to reassure the traveller boarding or alighting late at night at a station where the ticket office is closed. Whereas trains should be providing a safe and convenient way to travel, many people are quite simply too scared to use them after dark. It is not that rail travel is truly dangerous: it is the perception that it has become so. If someone has the time to deface a railway carriage or an embankment wall with elaborate graffiti, then someone also has ample time to mug or rape a fellow passenger or to plant a bomb. And if a railway company doesn't seem to care that their trains are 'tagged' and vandalised, and that there are litter and weeds all over the track, then how bothered will they be if one of their so-called 'customers' is attacked, robbed, injured or blown up?

Hardly any railway seems to be entirely free of graffiti these days: I was quite upset recently to see that a model railway exhibitor at Alexandra Palace had included some 'scale model' graffiti on his modern-image OO-gauge layout! The SNCF in France seems to be one of the worst affected: virtually every catenary support, signal box and lineside structure along the approaches to Paris-Nord has been liberally coated in tags. On a recent visit to the Toulouse area I was shocked at how many trains were running in service covered in graffiti. The Rome Metro seems to have given up altogether; the official Rome public transport map shows a heavily-graffitied metro train on its cover, as if that were its normal fleet livery, and there is so much etching on the windows that it is difficult for a metro traveller to read the station names!

An all-too-common sight on trains today

Some people call this 'art', but to me it is simply vandalism. It can even be dangerous when it affects signals or equipment, and I wonder why more action is not taken against it. There *is* a successful remedy. In the mid-1980s the New York subway system was dirty and dangerous, and large numbers of trains were covered in unofficial paint. The new Transit Authority president, David Gunn, declared war on graffiti, and announced a 'zero tolerance' policy: any car would be taken out of service for cleaning as soon as it was defaced, no matter how slightly. Mr Gunn believed that graffiti artists would become disheartened if they saw less of their work traversing the city, and he was proved right. By 1990 the entire fleet was graffiti-free, and it has largely remained so.

I should add that some of the uninspiring new liveries that have appeared in the last few years just seem designed to attract graffiti - especially when there is a lot of blank white paint. I can't imagine graffiti on an old Great Western chocolate-and-cream carriage or on a Southern Railway malachite green locomotive.

Not so very long ago all trains in Britain were grey and blue, and that wasn't very interesting either. But at least we had a national railway system, where tickets were issued 'via any suitable route' and where the track, trains and stations were all managed by the same company. The Beeching years showed what happened when you let a railway be run by accountants, but the legacy of John Major's government is a fragmented system run seemingly for the benefit of its fat-cat managers. We have seen hundreds of stations repainted and fitted with new nameboards bearing the logos of their private operators - and then repainted and 're-nameboarded' a few years later for another operator. Ticket prices have risen unbelievably, although such are the pricing policies that it is impossible to know how much your ticket is going to be. In Switzerland (despite a multitude of operators) you simply turn up at the station, pay the fare and get your ticket; in the UK, you have to plan ahead to be sure of the best price.

BR had its critics, but it was a *national* network. If one main line had to close temporarily, long-distance trains would be diverted via another route. Nowadays that often cannot happen, as all routes are in the hands of separate private operators. I recently witnessed scenes of complete chaos at Nottingham when hundreds of travellers to Manchester, unable to travel via the West Coast Main Line owing to engineering works, got off a London train and then tried to cram onto a local two-car diesel unit. Nobody had foreseen the problem and no-one had considered putting on extra trains. Virtually all trains now are multiple-units, and there is no longer a stock of spare carriages that can be coupled on in times of high demand. In the old days, if a branch line in Cornwall needed extra capacity in the summer when the tourists came, a train could be borrowed, say, from a line in the industrial north-west, where it might be surplus to requirements during the school and factory holidays. Now the lines are run by different Train Operating Companies, the trains are leased from separate proprietors and a charge would be imposed by Network Rail to move them from one area to another. It is hardly surprising that the extra passengers on the Cornish train find there is standing room only. (I should add that the private railway companies have many hard-working, devoted employees, and there has been considerable investment in new rolling stock).

The break-up of British Rail has led to huge increases in costs, as every organisation involved in running the system has its own staff and management, and even a simple repair to a piece of infrastructure can run into millions. In the Railway Development Society's book *A-Z of Rail Reopenings* (1992), the cost of restoring passenger services to the 6-mile branch from Stirling to Alloa was stated to be £1,100,000, and it was planned to re-open the line in 1994. The Alloa branch was ultimately reopened... in May 2008, at a cost of £85,000,000! The figures quoted in railway magazines for the reopening of simple village halts lead me to believe that their platforms must be constructed of solid gold ingots under a thin layer of concrete!

At least lines *are* reopening in the UK. In some countries the spectre of Beeching is alive and well. New Zealand and Costa Rica, both popular 'eco-tourism' destinations with strong environmental policies, have lost the majority of their rail passenger services in recent years. National networks all over Africa and Latin America have simply collapsed through lack of investment. Mexico withdrew virtually all its passenger trains overnight in January 2000.

Of course there are countries all over the world where railways are flourishing: India, China, Japan and Switzerland come immediately to mind. Even in the USA the anti-rail tide seems to be turning, with the Amtrak network remaining remarkably intact despite numerous threats of cuts and closures.

The Cuckoo Trail in East Sussex

Derelict railways have a fascination all their own. There is something very special about exploring a disused line, standing on the platform of a former station and hunting for relics such as old sleepers and the cast-iron 'chairs' that once held the rails. The first abandoned railway I remember walking along was the old Great Eastern line between Great Dunmow and Braintree - the ballast was still intact and a number of recently-felled telegraph poles were lying in the undergrowth by the line - I wish I had unscrewed one of the ceramic insulators as a souvenir! The former Heathfield - Polegate line in East Sussex has been converted to a wonderful footpath and cycle route, called the 'Cuckoo Trail'. Walking is now the only way that an enthusiast can experience the landscapes of once-busy lines such as the Great Central London Extension, the Somerset & Dorset or the Waverley Route from Edinburgh to Carlisle.

Closure is not the only way a beautiful railway journey can be destroyed. Some lines have been the victims of insensitive, though necessary, modernisation. I have seen a number of photographs of a charming rural narrow-gauge railway that once served Alcorcón, Móstoles and a number of townships to the west of Madrid. This area has since been greatly built-up, and there is now a double-track, broad-gauge electric line served by ugly multiple unit trains. One of my favourite journeys in the past was the Southern Region line from Tonbridge to Redhill, which runs dead straight through glorious countryside. Built as part of the main line to Dover, it was bypassed when a new route was opened via Sevenoaks, and reduced to the status of a branch. For many years it was served by weird hybrid diesel-electric units that had the nickname 'Tadpoles', as they were formed from a full-width motor car hauling two narrower trailer coaches from redundant Hastings line trains. (The London - Hastings line for many years had special narrow-bodied stock owing to the limited clearance in its tunnels). The Tonbridge - Redhill was a line of great character where the staff always had a friendly word, although it had a poor reputation for punctuality! Now it has been modernised and electrified so that it can be operated by standard rolling-stock; all of the intermediate stations have had their buildings demolished and replaced by 'bus shelters', and it is just another Southern electric line.

How about preserved railways? The best of them provide an incomparable travel experience and many of them are described in this volume. Some (especially in France) are really just 'grown-ups playing with trains' - get an engine, attach a couple of carriages, and see if anyone wants to come along for a ride. Others are now fully-restored and give their passengers a genuine feeling of what travel was like many years ago, although sometimes they can be just that little bit *too* serious. I like the ones that serve the local community as well as tourists and enthusiasts, and those that try to involve the younger generation with family days and 'Thomas' events. It is wonderful that volunteers have been able to rescue so many little railways from dereliction. But once a line has been preserved, there is no guarantee that it will remain so, as I have discovered on more than one occasion.

Not every railway journey is memorable. Many are simply dull and some can be quite unpleasant. I have stood like a sardine between Bromley South and Victoria, and I have endured a melancholy trip on the flat, featureless Cambridge - Newmarket - Ipswich line, with a train full of threatening-looking teenagers that paused at stations long since gone to seed. Underground railways can be particularly terrifying: Line 4 on the Paris Métro seems to attract the city's fattest and smelliest residents, and its trains creep along at such a slow pace that one emerges at the terminus gasping for fresh air.

In this book I have grouped together 40 of my favourite train journeys. Some of these were once-in-a-lifetime experiences; others are trips I have taken many times. On some occasions the scenery was the main point of interest; on others the quaintness of the rolling-stock or the architecture of the stations; sometimes it was the fellow-travellers who made the ride so memorable. You will find the world's oldest railway here, in addition to the world's highest standard-gauge passenger line, the steepest adhesion-only line and the first railway to have an automatic train control system. Some of these lines are well-known and feature in many books on railways; others are so obscure that most local residents are probably unaware of their existence. Some are efficiently-run and some simply disastrous; half a dozen have closed, either in entirety or partially, since I first rode on their rails. But they all had their little quirks and eccentricities, and I loved them all.

EUROPEAN

JOURNEYS

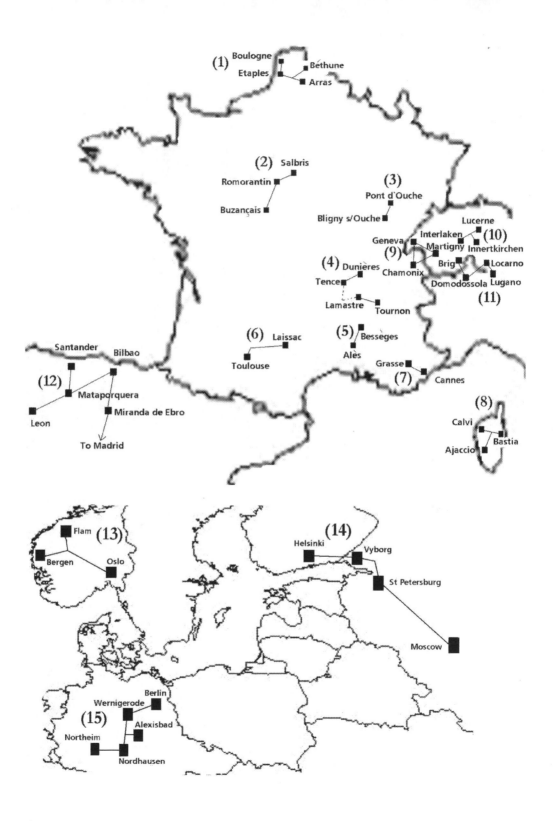

1. *And do you STILL wish that the French ran our railways?*

1978 - 2007: Pottering around the Pas-de-Calais

I can still remember listening to a phone-in programme on BBC Radio Kent (it may even still have been called 'Radio Medway' in those days), in which various callers were complaining about how bad our local train services were. "We should get the French to run them!" one woman said. "The French really know how to run a railway".

I would have liked to have deposited that woman on the platform of Gravelines station, barely 25 miles across the Channel, to see what she thought of her wonderful French railways. Gravelines is quite a large town mid-way between two busy ports, Calais and Dunkerque, in one of the most densely-populated and industrialised parts of France. Just how many trains do you think run on the Calais - Dunkerque line? An hourly service? Perhaps one train every half-hour? Well, no. There are five up trains and four down trains *daily* from Monday to Friday, and three up trains and two down trains on Saturdays. Nothing on Sundays.

I love France and its railways, but I am often annoyed when ill-informed people tell me how much better things are over there than back home. It is true that the French have many more high-speed lines, their fare structure is refreshingly straightforward, and between their capital and certain lucky large provincial cities their rail service is unparalleled in the world. But on other routes trains can be slow and infuriatingly infrequent. The British always seem to compare the shabbiest outer suburban service in the UK with the newest and smartest TGV route. One could equally well show a Frenchman a photo of a filthy old stainless-steel Parisian *rame de banlieue* and a brand-new *Virgin Pendolino* and ask him whether French or English railways are better. One day I was sitting on an ordinary electric train on the way from Ashford to London. A group of young French people got on and I heard one of them exclaim "Tiens! C'est meilleur que la SNCF!" (It's better than the SNCF) as they settled into their seats. An article in a recent French railway magazine described a visit to Cornwall, and the author was full of praise about the county's branch lines with their comfortable modern trains and frequent services! However, I have never actually heard any French person say that they wish the British would run *their* railways.

The best way to compare the two systems is simply to get a ferry to Calais, take the shuttle-bus to Calais-Ville station, opposite the great Flemish town hall, and go down to the platform. If there is no train scheduled for Dunkerque (and that is not an outstandingly picturesque route anyway), you still have two other directions in which to travel: south-east to Hazebrouck, or south-west to Boulogne.

For a more interesting and attractive journey, take a train to Boulogne. Although the railway runs slightly inland for much of the journey, at Wimereux it crosses a dramatic viaduct, with fine views on the right-hand side over the little resort and its beaches.

Boulogne used to have four SNCF stations. The boat-trains left from Boulogne-Maritime, whilst Boulogne-Aeroglisseurs provided a connection with the ephemeral hovercraft service. Nowadays only the main-line stations remain. The train from Calais halts first at an old-fashioned station near the Old Town, the delightfully-named Boulogne-Tintelleries, before continuing across the rooftops of the New Town to the 1960s monstrosity that is Boulogne-Ville.

It is normally necessary to change trains at Boulogne if one wishes to continue south to Etaples. The local trains are a mixture of railcars and locomotive-hauled stock. I remember the stainless-steel-and-orange TER units being introduced in 1978, with posters and leaflets at the stations proclaiming 'Votre prochaine voiture - le train!' and 'Fini le temps des banquettes en bois!' (Your next car - the train! No more wooden seats!) Nowadays the same trains are in a pitiful state, covered with graffiti inside and out, with the inevitable etching on the windows.

Modern TER train at Calais-Ville

The Boulogne to Etaples section has the air of a main line that has somewhat gone to seed. It is still double-track and retains its telegraph poles, but the little wayside stations look shabby and most trains pass straight through them. At Hesdigneul, the old line to Desvres and St-Omer branches off; part of this, from Lumbres to Arques, is run by a preservation society as the *Chemin de Fer de la Vallée de l'Aa*. Hesdigneul is also the site of the bumpiest level-crossing I know. Whenever my parents drove over it in our Dormobile, on our way to a camping-site somewhere in the south, the cutlery drawer would always shoot out and scatter its contents all over the floor!

Etaples is a large station that also serves the resort of Le Touquet. The platforms have huge awnings and the buildings are maintained in good condition. It is the junction for the line to Saint-Pol, which I rode frequently in the late 1970s.

While the double-track ex-main line continues south to Amiens and Paris, the Saint-Pol train heads east along the valley of the River Canche. It is a beautiful journey. The first stop is at Montreuil-sur-Mer, where the station is down by the river, below the historic fortified town. Although it is manifestly *not* on the sea, Montreuil is one of the loveliest small towns in France, and it is well worth breaking your journey here, as long as you check the time of the next train. Although well-served compared to many French secondary lines, the running is very patchy, with, for instance, no up train between 9.50am and 1.10pm. Montreuil was formerly also served by a narrow-gauge line from Aire-sur-la-Lys to Berck-sur-Mer, closed in 1955. A journey on this long-lost railway is described in the opening sentences of the French chapter of Bryan Morgan's wonderful book *The End of the Line*.

Montreuil has some fine old houses and a 15th-century church dedicated to Saint-Saulve. The town was visited by Laurence Sterne on his *Sentimental Journey* in 1765, and 150 years later served as the HQ for General Haig during the First World War. When I walked around the town in the late 1970s I remember being intrigued by the sight of an old medieval chapel that had been converted to a fire-station, with its huge wooden doors flung open to reveal bright scarlet fire engines standing under a Gothic vaulted roof.

From Montreuil the railway continues east along the Canche Valley. The village of Beaurainville marks the end of the salty plains and the start of the long slow climb towards Saint-Pol. Beaurainville station had been rebuilt in a modern style by the time I first travelled on this line; the station building has now been sold off as a private dwelling. From here onwards, most of the original stations still stand, dating from the opening of the line in 1878, and ranging from well-cared-for structures still offering ticket sales to derelict shells long past their prime.

The line continues past ponds and fields, still flanked by its traditional telegraph poles, to Hesdin. This ancient and pretty town has an old church and a huge bell-tower. The next station, Auchy-les-Hesdin, was lovingly-maintained when I first travelled on this line, with beautiful flowerbeds, but it is now an unmanned halt. The countryside around here is delightful. The Canche River has now left us and the line is following the valley of the Ternoise.

Anvin, where I once had a glass of Kronenbourg in a café on the station square, was formerly the junction for a narrow-gauge line to Calais. In the late 1970s the station booking office had a display of photographs showing this old line, in addition to others of steam trains on the standard-gauge line. On my last trip I was saddened to see that the station had become unstaffed, its ground-floor windows and doorways all boarded over.

The château at Monchy-Cayeux

Beyond Anvin there is a curious sight. As the train goes through the small hamlet of Monchy-Cayeux, a once-magnificent château, now falling into decay, is passed on the left. An avenue of trees leads down from the château towards the railway… and continues on the other side! Evidently when the Compagnie du Nord built their line, they had no compunction about driving it right through the line of trees.

After passing the pretty village of Wavrans, the train stops in Saint-Pol-sur-Ternoise. This is a junction with three possible directions of travel: west to Etaples, south-east to Arras and north-east to Béthune. Formerly there was a fourth line, heading south-west to Abbeville, but by the time I discovered Saint-Pol this line stopped at Frévent and was freight-only. I often wondered how easy it would be to change the points and send an autorail through to Frévent instead of Etaples! Sadly, such a fanciful diversion would no longer be possible, as the rusting rails curving towards Frévent have now been lifted.

Rebuilt after the Second World War, Saint-Pol is rather a dull little town, although it does have a bizarre modern church with an unusual open-fretwork bell-tower.

For a pretty journey finishing in a beautiful city, the line to take from Saint-Pol is the one to Arras. This railway passes through the Scarpe Valley, with the pretty villages of Aubigny-en-Artois and Frévin-Capelle, while the final few kilometres into Arras are unusual, as, rather than approaching from the west, which would be logical, the line makes a great semicircle around the city and enters the station from the south, meeting up with the main route from Amiens. There are risks, however, in travelling this section of line on Friday evenings, when it seems to be taken over by noisy university students playing practical jokes.

Autorail in the Ternoise, 1979

When I was working and living in this area, *my* local line was the one from Saint-Pol to Béthune. The first part of the journey is pleasant and pastoral. The first station out of Saint-Pol in those days was Brias, an unbelievably decrepit and dilapidated structure right by a level-crossing: it was a request stop and I remember signs at Béthune and Saint-Pol saying that passengers wishing to alight there should inform the guard, not that I ever saw anyone using the station. During my period in France there was an incident when a motorist, assuming that the line was disused, parked his car on the level-crossing; it was hit by a train and the accident was reported in the local paper. To this day I wonder why he chose to park directly *on* the level-crossing rather than just beside it. (There was also once a story in the local press about a jealous husband who caught his wife *in flagrante delicto* with her lover, and tied them both down to the Abbeville - Eu railway. I can't remember what actually happened, but I suspect that the unfortunate couple died of boredom or starvation, such is the infrequency of services on that line!)

Bours, beyond Brias, had a tiny halt with just a nameboard and platform. I would get off here sometimes to visit friends who lived in the nearby village of Marest. When I asked the conductor-guard on my train how to reach Marest from Bours station, he told me to walk to the end of the platform, continue along the railway track for a kilometre and then scramble down the embankment at the next road bridge!

Such invitation to trespass may give you the impression that the Béthune - Saint-Pol line was carefree and casual, but this is far from the truth. I have never had my tickets checked as assiduously anywhere by the SNCF as on this short stretch of track. The conductors seemed to take pleasure in finding something wrong with everyone's ticket and getting them to pay a supplement of some sort! And I cannot imagine the train crew inviting a passenger for a cab ride, as happens sometimes in the south.

Bours has a medieval château - to be honest, just a keep - which is clearly visible from the train. The next station is Pernes-Camblain, one of those double-barrelled stations that is halfway between the two villages whose name it bears. Pernes is quite a sizeable place. There were always a few goods wagons in the yard at Pernes, but they were probably just for show, as they never seemed to move from one week to the next!

Castle keep and church at Bours

At Pernes I would normally be getting ready to leave the autorail, as my station was next. Calonne-Ricouart marks the start of the Pas-de-Calais mining area, and the station serves the conglomeration of Calonne, Auchel and Marles-les-Mines. Calonne itself has quite an attractive, tree-lined main square with an absurdly pompous neo-Classical town hall; sitting there with half a baguette on a summer afternoon one could imagine oneself in Provence. Marles consists mainly of grimy red-brick terraces of former miners' cottages, all in neat estates with names such as 'Cité No. 5'. I visited an elderly couple in one of these houses and was astonished that they were still using an earth closet in 1978. The headgear of one mine in Marles has been preserved as a memorial.

Auchel, where I worked, was the main shopping centre of the three towns; it is now twinned with West Malling on the Victoria - Maidstone East line! On November 11th, 1978, I attended the Remembrance Day ceremony at Auchel cemetery, and was moved almost to tears by the passionate anti-war speech by the young socialist mayor. His words echoed in my mind for many months afterwards, and I am sure that they had something to do with me deciding to join CND. Many years later, I met the same mayor at a Malling / Auchel Twinning Association dinner. I told him of the great effect his speech had had on me back then. "Oh, that old rubbish!" he said, "I used to churn out the same thing every year!" Another illusion of my youth was shattered.

The last few kilometres from Calonne to Béthune are of interest only to the dedicated industrial archaeologist, with the remains of various spurs and former mine sidings in a blighted landscape of overgrown slag-heaps, before the branch joins the main Calais - Hazebrouck - Arras line at Fouquereuil, just before Béthune.

Béthune has little to detain the visitor, but its main square, rebuilt after World War I around the surviving medieval belfry, is not without charm. For the railway enthusiast, a visit to the shopping centre near the station has to be recommended - it has been converted from the former locomotive roundhouse! And the *Friture de la Gare* in the station forecourt sells the finest chips in France!

Journey's end at Béthune station

The medieval belfry still towers over Béthune

2. The White and Silver Railway (Le Blanc-Argent)

May 25, 1980: I fall in love with a French narrow-gauge line

It was only in the late 1970s that I started to take a real interest in railways. Before then I had certainly enjoyed train travel as a means of transport, but had never gone out of my way to travel on a particular line just for the sake of it. I can firmly lay the blame for my enthusiasm on a French singer called Alain Souchon.

From October 1978 to June 1979 I worked as a classroom assistant in France as part of my university degree course. I developed quite a liking for French pop and rock music and bought several albums during this period, including one called *Bidon* by Alain Souchon. One of the tracks on the album was *Calin-Caline*, a gentle lament about lost teenage love. At first I did not especially like the song, but it was sandwiched between my two favourite tracks, and in those pre-CD days it was quite fiddly to lift off the stylus and put it back down again a quarter-of-an-inch later.

After a few months the lyrics of *Calin-Caline* were imprinted on my brain. The song mentioned a trip to the Loire Valley in the summer of 1960, a place called Romorantin, and a narrow-gauge railway. So what? The Loire was a popular holiday destination and I could well imagine such a tourist trap having its own equivalent of the Romney, Hythe and Dymchurch.

Some months later, I was back in the UK, searching the University library for a book connected with my degree course. My eyes fell on a book a little further along the shelf, called *French Minor Railways* by WJK Davies. I opened the book and glanced through it, hoping perhaps to find something on the Béthune - St Pol line that had provided my regular transport during my months in France. Instead I discovered a whole new world of narrow-gauge, independent and idiosyncratic railways whose existence I had never suspected. But, alas, many of them probably no longer existed - the book had been printed in 1965.

Leafing through *French Minor Railways*, the name *Romorantin* leaped from a page. Where had I heard that name before? Of course, in the song by Alain Souchon! And here it was: a description of the amazing metre-gauge Chemin de Fer du Blanc à Argent, which meandered for 102 kilometres through the Loire Valley between the towns of Salbris and Buzançais, passing through the quaint old town of Romorantin.

I was instantly hooked and simply had to get the book out and read it from cover-to-cover. But there was little opportunity for further research. This was long before the World Wide Web. British railway magazines practically never carried articles on foreign lines. A glance at a mid-1970s Michelin map (sheet 64) showed the track still in place, but that meant little: railways are about the last thing to be updated on maps, and even if the rails were still in position, the line may well have been disused or open only for freight.

French Minor Railways did point me in the direction of another, very interesting railway book - Bryan Morgan's inimitable *The End of the Line*. This is undoubtedly one of the finest railway books ever written, but sadly had little useful information on the Blanc - Argent line; it proved to be one of the few in France that the author had not travelled on!

21

The railway's name, incidentally, has nothing to do with its trains bearing a white and silver livery! When originally opened at the start of the 20th century, it went from a town called Le Blanc to another called Argent, a distance of some 190 kilometres. By the mid-1950s the northern and southern extremities had been closed, reducing it to the central section from Salbris to Buzançais.

After my Finals in May 1980 I armed myself with a seven-day *France-Vacances* rail pass, and took the ferry to Boulogne and an express train to Paris. Spending the night in the capital, I headed for the Gare d'Austerlitz the next morning. In those days most French railway stations actually had paper timetables for the relevant region on display. I found the appropriate table - number 431 - and my heart leaped as I saw it was headed AUTORAIL - a railcar. Many French branch line services were actually operated by bus.

A soulless stainless-steel electric suburban train took me to Salbris, a rather pleasant little town that is, appropriately enough, twinned with Dymchurch! Getting off the train, I looked for the narrow-gauge line. At last I found a sign 'Direction Romorantin'. The arrows pointed to a separate platform with a small concrete shelter, where a small, elderly red-and-cream railcar was waiting. I took my seat inside. The railcar was well-filled and was soon off into the woods and thickets of the marshy Sologne, the driver sounding his horn repeatedly as we approached the numerous ungated level-crossings.

The railcar awaits at Salbris

We stopped at several small, picturesque stations: La Ferté-Imbault, Selles-St-Denis, Loreux and Villeherviers. The stations were of a distinctive design with a large goods shed attached to the main building; most had brightly-painted shutters and colourful window boxes. Some of the sidings were full of ancient, miniature goods wagons. The railcar generally took the passing loop whenever we went through a station: it was essential to hold on tight here as the car negotiated the sharp curves. For the first but not the last time I wondered why French metre-gauge railcars were not equipped with seatbelts!

At one point in the journey a little boy opposite me pointed out of the window and shouted "Un chevreuil!" I looked up and saw a reddish-brown roe deer running away from the train, its white rump clearly visible.

I had decided to break my journey in Romorantin, the major town served by the line, 29 kilometres from Salbris. The large SNCF station building here seemed out of scale for the diminutive metre-gauge railcar. I chatted with the station-mistress, who knew the song *Calin-Caline* and said that Alain Souchon did indeed travel on the line. She was quite happy for me to walk across the tracks and take some photos in the station yard. As I examined an elderly locomotive, I heard a friendly "Miaow" and was greeted by a longhaired black cat. It walked with a strange, hoppity gait - I soon found out that this was because one of its front legs was missing. Whether it lost its leg to a metre-gauge train I will never know.

Romorantin station in 1980

Romorantin is not only a perfect little 'railway town': it is also one of the most remarkable places in France. Mention its name to any group of Frenchmen and you will usually hear a chorus of sniggers. It is the ultimate 'trou de province', the little French provincial town *par excellence*. Like Tunbridge Wells it has been the butt of music-hall and television comedians' jokes. Yet at one time it could have become the capital of France. King François I commissioned Leonardo da Vinci to plan a new town and build an enormous château by the River Sauldre. Sadly Leonardo's death in 1519 at the age of 67 put an end to the king's projects, and François I turned his attention to Chambord.

Romorantin faded into obscurity, with its half-timbered houses, ancient inns and the remains of its medieval castle, stuck forever on a branch line. Apart from the three-legged cat, my sightseeing included a visit to an art exhibition (disappointingly, no railway paintings), and museums dedicated to the history of the Sologne and to Matra racing cars, which, surprisingly, were manufactured here (as, later, were the *Renault Espace* people-carriers).

My train to Buzançais was due to leave at 16.52. Getting back to Romorantin station around 4.30pm, little activity seemed to be in progress. The grand total of three other passengers got into the tiny railcar with me, and we all took seats at the front - a novel experience that enabled me to look ahead at the track in the direction of travel. I introduced myself to my fellow passengers, a couple with a young son. They were from Valençay and had come to Romorantin on the train because they enjoyed it and it made a day out for the boy.

The line changed in character south of Romorantin. It left the wild woods of the Sologne behind and entered the valley of the Cher. The first few kilometres were actually quite dull, as the railway followed a main road and passed alongside a large military camp, before entering the picture-postcard country station of Pruniers. Next came the extraordinary junction of Gièvres, where, with much lurching and grating, the metre-gauge railcar joined and then ducked underneath the SNCF standard-gauge line from Tours to Vierzon. No-one got on or off here. A spectacular steel girder bridge across the wide River Cher followed, and we were soon at a station called Chabris. Now we had left the département of the Loir-et-Cher and entered the Indre, and the station buildings were different! It appears that different contractors were responsible for each section of the line, and although they followed the same basic specification, they had a free hand in determining the final design.

The quality of the ride was definitely worse after Chabris. This section of track appeared to be in need of maintenance, and the little train that featured in a French pop song really did 'rock and roll' as it hurtled towards the next station at about 70kph (which felt like over 70mph!) Looking ahead, I could see only the tops of the rails through the weed growth. No passengers were waiting at the delightfully-named station of Varennes-sur-Fouzon, where the station-mistress (this railway seemed to be staffed largely by women) waved us through without stopping. A long straight stretch followed, and my travelling companions pointed out the domes and towers of Valençay Castle in the distance.

Avenue leading to Valençay Castle

The château of Valençay was built in 1540, but its most famous owner was the great statesman Talleyrand, who somehow managed to hold top jobs from the reign of Louis XVI to the late 1830s, despite the numerous and often bloody changes of regime during this period. Talleyrand's nephew, who inherited the castle, was given the title of Duke of Valençay by Louis XVIII, and castle and title have remained with the family ever since. When they drove this new-fangled narrow-gauge railway through Valençay in 1902, the Duke insisted that the local station should match his château. Thus Valençay acquired one of the finest station buildings in France - a bijou Renaissance palace in miniature. Fortunately both castle and station are maintained in superb condition.

My travelling companions left me at Valençay, and for the remaining 39 kilometres I had the train to myself, chatting with the driver and guard. At La Gauterie, Luçay-le-Mâle and Terre-Neuve, we slowed down for the station stops but no-one was waiting. We paused in the former junction at Ecueillé, where once another narrow-gauge line joined the Blanc-Argent. We continued through gentle farming country, passing through Heugnes, Pellevoisin, Juscop and Argy, before the little railcar finally let its motors die by a deserted platform on the far side of Buzançais station. The insignificant village of Buzançais saw its moment of glory long before it became a railway junction: in 1412, during the Hundred Years' War, an important treaty was signed here.

Elegant station at Valençay

If my experience was typical, it is surprising that the passenger service on the southern section of this line lasted as long as it did. One English student could hardly have constituted a profitable load for one of the two journeys of the day. I did not realise at the time that the southern 35 kilometres were living on borrowed time - closure to passengers came four months later, on September 24, 1980.

When I alighted at Buzançais station, I could still feel the rhythm of the rails from the one-and-a-half-hour journey I had just undertaken on the narrow gauge. But what followed was an anticlimax. Buzançais station is on the standard-gauge SNCF line from Tours to Châteauroux, but the section from Loches to Châteauroux had been closed to passengers some years previously and replaced by a bus service. "C'est un bus orange", the train driver had said, puffing on his Gauloise as he pointed the way to the bus-stop.

Rush hour at Buzançais station!

I had awful thoughts of being stranded in Buzançais, but, amazingly, the orange bus appeared within a few minutes. I showed the driver my *France-Vacances* pass and clambered aboard. The road followed the freight-only railway to Châteauroux. We even stopped at a couple of stations where the stationmaster came out to check the time of the bus and collect tickets from alighting passengers. The bus deposited me in the forecourt of Châteauroux SNCF station, where I had a date with the overnight express to La-Tour-de-Carol, in search of another narrow-gauge line - the famous *Petit Train Jaune*.

When I first travelled on the Blanc-Argent, it was a typical French secondary railway of the early 1950s preserved in aspic, its elderly De Dion and Verney railcars plodding along in their old-fashioned livery. Since then much has changed. The line now runs for just 67 kilometres, from Salbris to Luçay-le-Mâle, and the rolling-stock consists of smart new articulated diesel units. But the countryside is just the same, the stations are still well-maintained, and good old traditional telegraph poles - with those peculiarly French 'curly bits' that hold the insulators - still run alongside the line. South of Luçay-le-Mâle, all is not lost, for a preservation society has taken on the line as far as Argy, and runs trains on summer Sundays. I hope they carry more passengers than my train did in May 1980! In June 2007 they even borrowed a steam engine from another line for a 'Fête du Train'. They have built up an impressive collection of stock at Ecueillé station, including some of the railcars formerly used on the line.

Strangely, the last few kilometres of the line, from Argy to Buzançais, were a victim of their own success: this section of track carried so much freight that it was converted to standard-gauge. It has seen the odd passenger 'special', but never again will a metre-gauge railcar pull up at Buzançais station.

New railcar on the BA in 2007

I have good reason to be grateful to the Blanc-Argent - and to Alain Souchon. Although *French Minor Railways* was not the book I had intended to borrow from the University library, it was more beneficial to my future than the volume of Proust or Baudelaire that I was probably looking for. On the notice-board at the Students' Union I saw an advertisement for a travel courier to take people on tours of French preserved railways. A knowledge of French and of French railways was essential. I phoned a London number, was offered an interview and got the job. This was my first step on a very enjoyable career in travel.

Ironically, despite having escorted groups subsequently on many other French railway lines, I have never actually taken any tourists on board the Blanc-Argent.!

3. A Priest in a Peugeot, and a Trip behind a Tracteur

August 20, 1985: In deepest Burgundy, I take drastic measures to join a narrow-gauge train to the middle of nowhere

In the summer of 1985 I escorted several departures of a coach tour around France. The tour was advertised in the brochure as 'Summer Wine', and that summed it up quite nicely; visits to vineyards and châteaux from the Champagne country to Bordeaux, passing through Burgundy on the way down and the Loire Valley on the way back.

Whilst most of the tour was on the hectic side - 'if it's Tuesday, this must be Epernay' - there was one surprise. When we got to Burgundy, we had *two full days* in Beaune. I imagine that the extra day was to comply with the EC regulations on drivers' working hours, or possibly the tour operator just happened to get a very good deal at the hotel in Beaune - a gloomy, side-street establishment run by a father-and-son team who would not have looked out of place in *The Munsters*.

Our first day in Beaune was always taken up with visits to vineyards and a wine-tasting. The following morning I would normally offer to take my passengers on a tour of the Hôtel Dieu, the beautiful old medieval hospital with the multicoloured roof that is the town's main tourist attraction. The afternoon was, according to the brochure, 'at leisure'.

The Hôtel Dieu at Beaune

I would often use these off-duty afternoons as an opportunity to catch up with some paperwork, or have a swim in the *Piscine Municipale*. But after several free afternoons in Beaune on successive tours, I wondered if there were any railways nearby that were worth a visit. Looking at my guide-book, I saw that the Chemin de Fer de la Vallée de l'Ouche was located only 20 kilometres from Beaune, and that there were daily trains in July and August. I headed off to Beaune tourist office to see if there was any transport between Beaune and Bligny-sur-Ouche, where the railway was based.

"Pas d'autobus" I was told at the tourist office. The prospect of a train ride looked dim. A taxi would be horrendously expensive, and cycle hire didn't seem a practical proposition - imagine being stuck with a puncture - or worse - on a rural road miles from anywhere! When I stayed in Blois, the waitress at the hotel would lend me her Renault 5, but here in Beaune the hotel staff would be more likely to loan a hearse hauled by spectral horses. "So how can I get to Bligny-sur-Ouche?" I asked. "Auto-stop!" was the reply.

I am not a very experienced hitchhiker. It is far more socially acceptable in France than in the UK, but even so I found the prospect of hitching on my own a bit daunting. The last time I had hitchhiked was six years previously, when I had been fortunate enough to be accompanied by a very attractive French girl! Still, if the official advice of the French tourist board was to hitchhike, that is what I would do.

Returning to the Spartan comforts of my hotel room, I packed a quick picnic and made two card notices, one saying 'Bligny-sur-Ouche' and the other 'Beaune'. Keeping my fairly smart work-clothes on, I looked on the map to see which road led towards Bligny, and then set off. Just in case anyone from the tour group was around, I walked a couple of kilometres out of town before pulling out the card and sticking out my thumb.

Bligny-sur-Ouche station

I only had to wait about 15 minutes. An old black Peugeot 403 pulled over, and the driver reached across and opened the passenger door. I got in and pulled it shut as I sank into the worn leather seat. I then said "Bonjour!" to my chauffeur, who was a Catholic priest, probably in his sixties. He had a jolly smile and wore a soutane just like priests in old photographs. Yes, he knew where the railway station was at Bligny-sur-Ouche. He hadn't heard of the tourist railway but he could definitely take me there.

We made a steady if unspectacular progress across the Côte D'Or, passing hundreds of acres of vines and climbing a hill that was so steep I was glad I hadn't hired a bicycle. We talked about the Church, about the differences between the Catholic and Protestant faiths, and about why so few young men were being ordained these days. After about half-an-hour I was dropped at Bligny-sur-Ouche station.

The station was a typical SNCF country building and was deserted. Both the main building and a shed, that looked as if it might contain a locomotive, were firmly closed. The timetable on display showed that the first train of the afternoon ran at 2.30pm, so I had nearly an hour to kill. I sat down on the edge of the platform and had my picnic - half a baguette, some fruit, a small bar of chocolate and a bottle of *Orangina*.

The Chemin de Fer de la Vallée de l'Ouche is a narrow-gauge railway laid on the trackbed of a closed standard-gauge line. Such lines are quite common, both in the UK and abroad. Examples include the Bala Lake Railway in Wales, the South Tynedale in Northumberland, the Kirklees Light Railway in Yorkshire and the Bure Valley and Wells & Walshingham in Norfolk. Although some purists might disapprove of these lines, they have the special appeal of the narrow gauge, and they are also generally less expensive to construct and maintain than a full-size railway.

CF de la Vallée de l'Ouche

In France there is a long history of standard-gauge railways being rebuilt as narrow-gauge lines, but not for pleasure purposes! During the First World War, when vast areas of the north-east of the country were laid waste, many main-line railways were completely wrecked. Military engineers would frequently lay portable 60-centimetre gauge 'Decauville' field railways on the trackbeds of the destroyed lines. After the war, the Ministère des Régions Libérées took over many of these army railways and ran them as a form of public transport until the main lines were rebuilt. Appropriately enough, the 'new' Vallée de l'Ouche line has been laid to the gauge of 60 centimetres, a gauge once used by many secondary and industrial lines in France. The line has an excellent pedigree, as the trackbed it occupies was one of France's oldest railways, opened in 1830 to haul coal trucks from the mining town of Epinac to the Canal de Bourgogne at Pont D'Ouche. It was later extended to Dijon and eventually became part of the SNCF, closing in the 1960s.

Around 2.15pm a couple of cars pulled up in the station forecourt, and someone opened the station building. A rake of open-sided bogie coaches known as *baladeuses* was extracted from the shed, together with a diminutive diesel locomotive of the sort that the French call a *tracteur*. It looked quite like a tractor, despite its smart, almost Southern Railway livery. I wandered over to buy a ticket, only to be told that they were sold on the train.

A few well-fed French families with children appeared from nowhere and boarded the train. Perhaps they had been staying in a nearby camping-site. We left about ten minutes late and set off along the old line in the direction of Dijon.

The track was well-laid and the train was exceptionally smooth-riding. The staff were friendly and quite casual as is the norm on French preserved lines: they were intrigued that I came from England. The line ran roughly alongside the River Ouche, but only occasional glimpses of the river were possible from the train.

In fact, at the time of my journey, the vegetation on each side was so high that one had the impression that the little train was running through an impenetrable jungle.

The Terminus in 1985!

We crossed a minor road, where there was a typical French *maison de garde-barrière* - the two-storey crossing-keeper's cottage that can be seen all over France. The line carried on, with no further signs of human habitation, until it came to a sudden halt in the middle of nowhere, in a cutting apparently called Les Cudilles. Here someone had had the foresight to lay a passing loop, so the *tracteur* ran around the train, and coupled itself onto the rear coach. We passengers had a few minutes to inspect the terminus and its exceedingly limited range of facilities before setting off again for Bligny-sur-Ouche.

On returning to Bligny, I made a few enquiries among the detraining passengers to see if anyone was heading back to Beaune, but they were all off in other directions. I had no option but to get out my card marked 'Beaune' and stick out my finger. I got a lift almost immediately. A bright orange cement-mixer, looking just like a large version of a Dinky Toy I once had as a boy, pulled up and the driver motioned for me to get in. It was quite a climb to the passenger seat. The driver was quite interested when I said I was English, but expressed no interest whatsoever in narrow-gauge railways. Seeing his collection of cassettes, I switched the conversation to music. He turned out to be a fan of Michel Sardou, and we had an animated discussion as to which of that singer's songs was the best: I preferred *La Maladie d'Amour* but he was more keen on *Etre une femme* and *Les Années Trente*.

I was dropped off just down the road from the hotel, and had plenty of time before joining my group for our set meal of *Boeuf Bourguignon*. This was never particularly good, and I am sorry to report that one member of my group was heard to remark "Now I think I know what happened to Shergar!"

I have never revisited the Chemin de Fer de la Vallée de l'Ouche, but it remains fresh in my memory as one of my favourite French tourist train rides. Since 1985 a steam locomotive has been restored to working order, and the tracks have now been extended to La Garenne, giving the railway a respectable length of seven kilometres. The extension includes a high embankment and an ex-SNCF bridge across the river, so views from the *baladeuses* will now be more spectacular than formerly.

4. In the Footsteps of Bryan Morgan (the Vivarais and the Velay)

September 2005: A tale of one réseau and two preserved lines

The Réseau du Vivarais was one of the greatest of the French narrow-gauge networks. It was developed in the 1890s in the rural Ardèche département, which, with its mountainous interior and lack of large centres of population or industry, held little interest for the big 19th-century railway companies. The PLM (Paris-Lyon-Mediterranée) main line from Lyon to Marseille ran along the left bank of the Rhône to the east, whilst the Cévennes railway between Langogne and La Bastide passed just to the west, leaving the département unserved.

The local Compagnie des Chemins de Fer Départementaux (CFD) started construction work in 1886 and, after five years of work, opened the line from Tournon to Lamastre on July 1, 1891. All construction was done by hand, and cuttings were blasted through the rocks with gunpowder. In 1898 the line was extended to Le Cheylard. When completed, the Vivarais network had four lines with a total length of over 200 kilometres, centred on the small town of Le Cheylard and linking the Loire and Rhône rivers with termini at Dunières, La Voûte-sur-Loire, La Voulte-sur-Rhône and Tournon.

The Vivarais system was first brought to the attention of the British railfan by Bryan Morgan in his delightful book *The End of the Line* in 1955. At that time the network was still largely complete. The railways also featured in Morgan's travel book about the Massif Central, *Fastness of France*. Sadly, even in the mid-fifties, Bryan Morgan predicted that the lines would soon be closed. The railcars and steam locomotives were showing their age, and the handful of new diesel locomotives were too underpowered to be of much use. The network was eventually closed entirely on November 1, 1968.

During its final months of operation, the Vivarais network had been visited by thousands of people and a number of special trains had been operated. This gave local enthusiasts the idea to save a section of the route as a tourist railway. The section from Tournon to Lamastre was chosen, because it had good road access, it linked two pleasant towns that were already tourist attractions, and it enjoyed superb scenery along the Doux Valley.

The preservation group that took over the Tournon - Lamastre line was called CFTM. They had been in existence since 1961, and operated a narrow-gauge tourist railway they built from scratch in the suburbs of Lyon - the *Chemin de Fer Touristique de Meyzieu*. However, by 1968 this line was suffering because the surrounding area was rapidly becoming built-up and unattractive. The group moved their operations to the Tournon - Lamastre line, keeping the same initials (CFTM) but changing their name to *Chemins de Fer Touristiques et de Montagne* (Tourist and Mountain Railways). They were able to obtain financial assistance from the Département of Ardèche to help purchase the line. It is said that sceptical councillors were persuaded of the potential of a tourist railway when the chairman of the group showed them photographs of the Ffestiniog Railway in Wales, with crowds of people waiting to board steam trains!

One of the few French preserved railways to run several trains daily in summer and at weekends for much of the year, the Vivarais could have become just a slick tourist operation, but in fact it retained much of the atmosphere of a real working metre-gauge railway. Nothing was over-restored; much of the original rolling-stock was still operated, and the piles of rusting locomotives and carcasses of carriages that form part of the stock-in-trade of any preserved line were hidden out of sight in a depot behind Tournon station. My train was hauled by one of the famous Mallet compound locomotives, with four cylinders and an 0-6-6-0T wheel arrangement. The first three axles of these locos are on an articulated chassis, enabling them to negotiate tight curves with ease. The railway also has a whole fleet of the diminutive but bulbous diesel railcars built by Billard of Tours in the 1930s. Although primarily a tourist railway, it still ran a weekly railcar in the summer of 2005 to enable the locals to go shopping in Lamastre market!

Train at Tournon station

Tournon was the starting point of my journey. The Vivarais station is alongside Tournon SNCF station, which is closed to passengers. Leaving Tournon, the train headed north for two kilometres along the SNCF freight-only Lyon-Nîmes line. The metre-gauge train could run along this section of track thanks to a third rail placed inside the standard-gauge track: one hoped nothing was coming along in the opposite direction! There is a 600-metre tunnel on this mixed-gauge section, and a metal viaduct over the River Doux. Reaching the junction, the metre-gauge train left the main line and passed through the station and village of St-Jean-de-Muzols. The line here is fairly level and passes houses, vineyards and a camping site.

When I rode the train in September 2005 we had an enthusiastic local guide in our carriage who pointed out some of the sights in fairly good English. One of the first points of interest is a medieval bridge with an immense arch that crosses both the railway and the river. A little further on, our guide showed us a pillar in the middle of the river: all that survives of a Roman bridge.

At Douce-Plage we were treated to the sight of a few topless sunbathers on the riverbank, as the train started climbing high above the River Doux. After passing through a disused station at Troye we crossed the Doux on a fine curved masonry viaduct, after which our guide pointed out a hydro-electric power station at Mordane. This was followed by a short tunnel and a bridge over a dam. The river gorge here makes this the most scenic stretch of the railway.

We stopped at the charming station of Colombier-le-Vieux-St-Bartélémy-le-Plein, which has the longest station name in France! It is situated roughly halfway between the two villages whose name it bears, not especially convenient for either of them. Scenes from the BBC Television adaptation of *Clochemerle* were filmed here in the 1970s, and there is a bar by the station where I enjoyed a pastis with the train crew!

Local wine and cheese producers were exhibiting their wares at the station, and it was possible to taste their wine and cheese and make purchases. Most passengers left the train and walked happily around on the tracks, many of them posing for photos by the locomotive. The driver blew the whistle when it was time to get back on board.

A well-earned stop

The next station was Boucieu-le-Roi, where we stopped to let off a pre-booked party. A large building above the village is a former convent. On the right-hand side of the line after the station is a fortified manor-house known as the Château de Chazotte, still inhabited by a count. It has become customary for the engine to whistle when passing the château, as the late countess, who died in 1981, was a great supporter of the preserved railway.

After the disused halt of Tincey, our guide showed us a rock precariously balanced over the line on the right-hand side. Called 'La Pierre qui Vire', this rock is supposed to rotate once every hundred years! There is a particularly scenic stretch of the line after this, when the train crosses the Arlebosc viaduct and runs north of the river for a few kilometres, crossing it again on the Garnier viaduct. The railway then remains on the south bank as far as Lamastre, and the countryside gets tamer. There are large numbers of chestnut trees here (chestnuts are something of a speciality in the Ardèche), and brown-and-white cows in the fields that watch the trains go by.

At Monteil the line crosses the 45th parallel, the midway point between the North Pole and the Equator and the start of the French 'Midi'. Shortly afterwards, our train arrived in Lamastre, 33 kilometres from Tournon. The journey had lasted two hours, but it was worth every minute.

Lamastre is a pleasant small town in the hills, with the remains of a castle destroyed in the Wars of Religion. There are several notable restaurants in the town (including a buffet at the station) and most travellers leaped off the train to head for the nearest restaurant to enjoy a long leisurely French lunch before getting the train back to Tournon. Some preferred to picnic by the river.

Lamastre was originally a through station. It has a larger station building than usual, a small locomotive shed and a turntable. Beyond the station a bridge has been demolished and a few hundred metres of embankment levelled to make way for an access road and car park. But just past this is the site of an old level-crossing, and here I joined the trackbed of the old line for a short walk towards Le Cheylard.

Lamastre station

There are no rails left in Le Cheylard, although the old station building remains intact and in service as a bus station: one can even still purchase tickets in the ticket office! But travel north from Le Cheyland to St-Agrève and the metre-gauge track starts again. It was here that I took my party for a ride on the second and lesser-known surviving section of the Réseau du Vivarais.

Encouraged by the success the CFTM group had with the Tournon - Lamastre line, a group of local enthusiasts calling themselves the CFR (Compagnie de Chemins de Fer Régionaux) took over the St-Agréve - Dunières section in 1970. Unfortunately they did not prosper as well as the pioneers. For one thing the journey is not as scenic, being mostly on a high plateau, and the railway is more difficult to access both by road and by public transport. Another problem was that the CFTM group, being first on the scene, had taken all the best locomotives and rolling stock.

The CFR initially had to face a lack of co-operation with the CFTM. Rather than marketing their railways together as part of the same former network, the CFTM at first opposed any attempts to revive another section of the old Vivarais system.

The poor CFR tried to offer its passengers more of a folklore experience than just a preserved railway, with a brightly-coloured train named *La Galoche du Plateau* evidently aimed at the younger visitor. However, services were suspended in 1986 and the line became derelict for a second time. The luckier bits of rolling stock found homes on other preserved metre-gauge lines, while the less fortunate items were left rusting on sidings to become targets for local graffiti artists.

Since 1995 the line has been revived by a new organisation, VFV (Voies Ferrées du Velay). By 2005 they were making a brave attempt but as yet it did not come close to the Tournon - Lamastre experience.

Our train consisted of two second-hand Swiss carriages, still in their original owners' liveries, hauled by a small diesel locomotive dating from the 1940s. Although we had been basking in the sun in Lamastre only two days earlier, it was now only two degrees Celsius! For those of you thinking of buying a holiday home in the Ardèche, a few kilometres can make all the difference!

While we were travelling across the high Ardèche plateau towards Tence, it started raining - that kind of near-horizontal rain that soaks everything and chills you to the marrow. The few brave souls who had been standing with their cameras on the open balconies of the coaches soon came in. Not that this was much better: there was no heating of any sort, and icy-cold water started dripping through a hole in the roof!

The VFV diesel train

Tence is the largest town on the line, and has a modern purpose-built depot where the VFV house their rolling stock. Here we stopped, and the engine driver and his wife climbed onto the carriage roof to fix the hole while we looked for something to eat. Don't go to Tence for the gastronomy - it's a far cry from Lamastre: the only restaurant we could find open served microwaved frozen pizzas! Even Bryan Morgan, for all his love for the railway, was not impressed by these sleepy market-towns on this northern branch of the Vivarais.

About half the passengers left the train at Tence, and the crew decided to detach one of the coaches and leave it here. I helped them push it over a rusty turntable into a shed.

Old rolling-stock at Tence

Leaving Tence after what was only two hours but seemed much longer, the train headed north through pleasant pasturelands. We passed through the amusingly-named halt of Trifoulou and stopped briefly at Raucoules-Brossettes, which was the junction of the line to La Voûte-sur-Loire. The station is in an isolated position and its sidings were full of superannuated goods wagons and railcars, most of which looked as if they could not possibly ever run again.

Montfaucon, the next town, is 930 metres above sea level according to the obligatory survey mark that is found on almost every French station building. During our brief stop, I thought the town itself looked about equally as interesting as Tence, but the toilets in the refurbished station were superb.

Several of my passengers were treated to cab-rides in the diesel locomotive on the return trip; it was definitely the warmest part of the train. We coasted gently downhill through a pine forest to reach Dunières-Ville station, where the wc facilities were unreconstructed rural French in style. There was quite a long stop here as we lost a few passengers, but my party was determined to stick it to the end of the line. The last kilometre or so was quite fun, as our unlit single-coach train went through a longish tunnel to emerge again at Dunières SNCF station.

Dunières-Ville station

Dunières SNCF station has both standard- and narrow-gauge tracks. At one time there were SNCF branches to St-Etienne (via Firminy) and to Annonay. The Annonay branch has been closed and lifted and the line to Firminy replaced by buses; the station buildings are boarded-up and derelict. Here the train crew waved goodbye as they reversed back up the line to put away their loco and remaining carriage.

In 2005 the Tournon - Lamastre line was a French icon while Dunières - St-Agrève was a struggling upstart. But appearances can be deceptive. In April 2008 the CFTM suddenly suspended all operations. The track was in urgent need of repair, no steam engines were serviceable, and the SNCF had given the railway three years' notice to quit the station site at Tournon, as they intend to restore passenger trains to the Lyon - Nîmes line and could well do without ancient steam trains sharing their track.

I cannot believe that either the local authorities or enthusiasts will allow the Tournon - Lamastre line to go under: in any case, many items of its stock and parts of its infrastructure are protected as *monuments historiques*. But at the time of writing the only way to experience a ride on Bryan Morgan's 'Marvel of the Midi' is to ride one of the VFV's ramshackle trains along the windswept rails of the high Ardèche plateau.

5. *A Cab Ride in a Caravelle, and train-driving lessons for senior citizens*

September 2005: High jinks on the Alès - Bessèges line

There is something very special about a rural branch line, leaving the main line at a junction station and meandering across open countryside to its terminus. Perhaps it is because most such lines in Britain were closed by Dr Beeching that the rare survivors have such an appeal.

France never was a very good country for proper *rural* branch lines. You find them in the Paris suburbs, in the mountains and at the seaside, but true dead-end branches were never that common in lowland France. Even a map of the French railway system in 1930 doesn't have as many as one might expect. During the great years of railway expansion, the French loved extending their country branches to create vast inter-linked networks. Even the narrow-gauge railways were joined up to make extensive systems, creating a whole labyrinth of little secret passages across the country.

Many of the apparent branch lines on the current SNCF passenger map - Le Buisson to Sarlat, Tours to Loches, Carcassonne to Quillan and Le Havre to Rolleville, for instance - are not true branches but are the truncated remnants of former cross-country routes.

One genuine inland branch that has, surprisingly, survived to celebrate its 150th birthday, joins the busy town of Alès, about fifty kilometres north of Nîmes, to the village of Bessèges. I cannot understand how it has been allowed to retain a passenger service when many places of national importance elsewhere in France lack any kind of railway. But I am very pleased that it has.

Amazingly, a book has been published on the history of this line, and it is really quite interesting. The late 1840s and early 1850s saw the development of coal mines between Bessèges and St-Ambroix, of which not a trace survives. In 1854 an independent company, the 'Bessèges à Alais', started constructing a line to link the collieries to the main line at Alès. In 1855, before it was completed, they handed it over to the Chemin de Fer du Midi. The branch was opened to traffic on December 1, 1857. The initial timetable showed just three return passenger trains daily between Alès and Bessèges: this level of service has remained unchanged for 150 years! In its heyday the line's passengers were a strange mixture of grubby coal miners bound for Molières-sur-Cèze or Bessèges, and rather posh holidaymakers taking the waters at a spa called Les Fumades, which was linked by horse-drawn buses to the stations of St-Julien and St-Ambroix.

In 1871 a branch-of-a-branch line was opened from the intermediate station of Robiac to Gagnières in Ardèche. This was extended in typically French fashion in 1876 to Vogüé, eventually creating a very slow, roundabout single-track route across rural Ardèche that allowed through trains from Valence to Nîmes. Bessèges always remained a dead-end terminus. The Robiac -Vogüé line was closed in 1969, restoring the Alès-Bessèges railway to its original condition.

I first became aware of the existence of this line in the early 1980s when I read an article in *La Vie du Rail*. At that time it was one of the last stamping-grounds of the celebrated *autorails panoramiques,* those elegant 1½-decker diesel railcars with a first-class observation compartment raised above the roof, like the dome cars on Canadian trains. Sadly I did not travel on the line in those days. But one day in 1997 I found myself driving through the pleasant tree-lined main street of Saint-Ambroix, and came to a railway bridge and a battered sign pointing to 'La Gare'. I knew this had to be the Alès-Bessèges line. I turned off, out of curiosity, and parked in the station's vast but empty car park. The large station building was boarded up and obviously disused. An inspection of the platforms revealed a similar air of dereliction; there were weeds and litter on the track and the top surface of the rails was dull and brown. No timetable of any sort was on display, and the self-service ticket-machine looked as if it had been broken for years. Convinced I had left things too late, I returned sadly to my car and drove to Alès, intending to stop for lunch there.

Saint-Ambroix station in 1997

It was pure luck that the first parking space I found in Alès happened to be right opposite the railway station. I took my camera and went in, hoping there might be a train of some sort due. To my surprise and delight I found that a train to Bessèges was due in ten minutes! After checking at the ticket office that it definitely *was* a train and not an SNCF replacement bus, I bought a return ticket and walked through to the platform.

It was a hot day and was around noon - any sensible French person would be just sitting down to lunch. A handful of passengers were waiting for the Bessèges train: a young woman with a pushchair, an older one with a suitcase. The train was one of the classic 1960s red-and-cream articulated railcars that are officially 'Class 4500' but are affectionately known as 'Caravelles'. It was in a vehicle identical to this that I had made my very first French railway journey over 20 years earlier.

The Caravelle hooted and set off along the main line, then curved off sharply to reach the branch. Beyond Salindres, which is quite an industrial place with lots of sidings, the scenery was attractive and unspoilt, and ever-so-slightly wild. We passed through a tunnel, over the D904 road and then between the derelict-looking platforms of Saint-Ambroix. From here the line became really scenic, with tight curves, a few lovely curving stone viaducts and some great stone embankments as we followed the course of the River Cèze. We stopped at Molières-sur-Cèze, where a few people got on and off. An old photograph in the history book shows this as a large and busy station, with an impressive building and smartly-uniformed staff, but now it was just a single-platform unmanned halt.

The station of Robiac, however, had much to excite the industrial archaeologist. It once boasted a water tower, signal box, locomotive depot, a large station building and an extensive goods yard. The main station building was alongside the Vogüé line. There was now just a single through line and a small concrete platform with a shelter, but it was easy to make out the former junction, and most of the buildings were still standing, albeit in a state of decay.

Caravelle at Alès for Bessèges

Bessèges station was a pleasant surprise. It still stood as a rare and complete example of a French country terminus, with sidings and a goods yard, and the station building was still manned and maintained in good condition. Stepping inside was like travelling back in time, with its old-fashioned ticket windows marked 'Billets - Bagages' and 'Marchandises'.

The timetable only allowed me a few minutes' stop at Bessèges. Only a couple of passengers boarded the train, and the crew seemed surprised to see me getting back on. I explained that I was an 'amateur de chemins de fer'. They immediately insisted I rode in the cab all the way back to Alès! Folding down a brown vinyl *strapontin* between the two crew seats, they gave me a wonderful commentary as I enjoyed a fantastic panoramic ride through cuttings and tunnels and over embankments and viaducts back to the main line. Along the way, they pointed out disused sidings, sites of former collieries and the place where one of the viaducts was repaired after damage in the Second World War. At the junction, they asked me to keep my head down, just in case anyone was looking! Shaking hands with my guides at Alès, I told them that it was one of the most incredible journeys I had ever undertaken, and long afterwards I thought of Bessèges and wondered if ever I would ride the line again.

Eight years later I was staying in the Ardèche, taking a group of British railway enthusiasts on a tour around French preserved lines. We had already travelled on the two Vivarais lines and the pleasant Cévennes railway from Anduze to St-Jean-du-Gard. Our final trip should have been with the 'Viaduc 07' group on their ex-SNCF railcar set that runs on part of the Vogüé - Le Teil line. Unfortunately, when I telephoned Viaduc 07 to confirm our reservation, they told me that their *autorail* had just suffered a serious breakdown and would be out of action for the rest of the week.

Consulting my employers, they were happy to leave it to me to sort out the problem. Ideally I should find a railway journey of similar interest and duration, and no more expensive than the proposed trip, and offer it as an alternative to my passengers. I thought immediately of the Alès - Bessèges line. A call to Alès SNCF station revealed that the train times were much as they had been in 1997. To simplify coach transfer arrangements, I decided we would start our railway journey by boarding the 'up' lunchtime train at Saint-Ambroix, riding to the terminus at Bessèges. The coach driver would drive from Saint-Ambroix down to Alès SNCF station and we would ride the whole length of the line back to meet him there.

As on my previous visit, it was a glorious sunny day when we got off the coach at Saint-Ambroix. My 25 or so customers were almost all senior citizens, mostly married couples plus several single men and two single ladies who said "they just happened to like railways". Arranging to meet them all at the station, I gave them free time to purchase lunch or have a picnic. A small flea-market was taking place under the plane trees in the main square, and this proved a delightful way to while away the time until the 12h36 to Bessèges.

A view from the driving cab

When we all assembled at the station, the general view of most of my group was that there surely couldn't still be a passenger service operating on this line. Saint-Ambroix station looked even more forlorn than in 1997, graffiti-artists having added over the years to the general air of dereliction. The ticket-machine had disappeared altogether, but an A4-size photocopy of the appropriate SNCF timetable page had been stuck on one of the boarded-up windows. Apart from my group, the only other person at the station was a beautiful, smartly-dressed young black woman, aged about 20, who was stretched out on the seat on the disused 'down' platform. She was poring over an immense text-book, and there was a bag of other books by her side. I assumed she was a foreign student who had probably come to the station to do her studying, as it is usually one of the quietest places in town.

The peace and quiet of Saint-Ambroix station, already disturbed by a score of British enthusiasts clicking their Nikons and Pentaxes, was soon shattered altogether by a two-tone horn. Someone shouted that a train was coming. We saw the headlights in the tunnel, and then a brand-new *autorail* scurried into sight, crossed the D904 road bridge, and, hooting furiously, came to a halt at the station. The driver's expression changed from curiosity to wide-eyed amazement when he realised that we were all actually getting on the train!

After what must have been the nearest thing to a rush-hour that Saint-Ambroix had experienced for decades, we set off along the sylvan rails to Bessèges. Apart from the train itself, everything about the journey was just as I remembered. I explained to the driver that I had brought a 'groupe d'amateurs anglais de chemins de fer', and he obligingly left the glass door to his compartment open so those with camcorders could come to the front and film through the windscreen.

Bessèges station in 2005

Meanwhile, I bought our tickets from the *contrôleuse*, a petite and unforgettably pretty blonde. I showed her the book on the history of the line, which I'd brought with me, and she was most interested, especially in the 1857 timetable showing the same three daily trains as in 2005. She did point out, however, that timings had improved: our equivalent train 148 years ago, the 11h10 from Alès, took 50 minutes to travel from Saint-Ambroix to Bessèges! Our train was timetabled to cover the 12 kilometres in 21 minutes - still not exactly a fast service in the land of the TGV!

Station interior, Bessèges

One of the few 'regular' passengers on the train was an elderly lady with a small dog. I showed her the old photos in the book, and she was amused to read that back in 1857 dogs were only admitted on trains if they were muzzled, and even then they were accommodated in a separate van!

I was surprised to see the lovely black girl from Saint-Ambroix station among the passengers on the train. Why on earth was a sophisticated person like her going to Bessèges? I just had to know. She was still immersed in her text books; the complicated symbols and formulae meant absolutely nothing to me. She smiled broadly when I said "Excusez-moi, mademoiselle?" and explained that she was only going *unintentionally* to Bessèges! She was a university student, living in Saint-Ambroix and studying in Nîmes, and habitually got a bus to Nîmes, but today had missed it. She had checked on the internet and found that there was this train that connected at Alès with another to Nîmes. So she had gone to Saint-Ambroix station for the first time in her life. Determined not to miss the train, she had arrived early. When the Bessèges-bound railcar had come along, she had not unnaturally assumed that it was the train to Alès, and had hopped on. The guard fortunately did not charge her for the return trip to Bessèges!

While most of the male passengers were filming and taking photos, the majority of the females were enjoying the comfort of the *autorail's* luxurious interior, most of them commenting that it was much better than their local trains back home. Even the lavatory, accessed by an amazing curved sliding door, came in for favourable comments, especially when compared to some of the very primitive facilities we had endured on the preserved lines!

Arrival at Bessèges came all too soon. Most of 'my' passengers detrained to take photos; I went into the station building and found the *guichets* still in their perfect time-warp, and chatted to *charmante* Alison, the *chef de gare*. I was informed that a locked goods shed at the station housed a small steam locomotive, being restored by a group called *Vapeur Val-de-Cèze*. If the SNCF does close the line, their aim is to step in and run it as a tourist steam railway.

Nearly time to leave Bessèges

The 51-minute return trip to Alès was great fun. The cab became a driving school, as members of my party were encouraged to sit in the co-driver's seat and try the controls - the horn proved especially popular. When we crept back into Saint-Ambroix, the guard persuaded one of my passengers to deliver a station announcement in English! Many photographs were taken of British senior citizens, including a retired Church of England clergyman, at the controls of a modern state-of-the-art French train. I let all my group have a go before taking the controls myself. The railcar needed little encouragement as it left Salindres and made its way towards the junction with the main line. As we reached the curve, I thought it was best to hand back to the SNCF crew, and I marshalled my flock for the imminent arrival in Alès.

We were honoured with a special fanfare on the two-tone horn as we got down from the railcar. There was much shaking-of-hands with the crew, and the young black woman flashed us a stunning smile as she crossed the platform for the Nîmes train. Counting my party to make sure no-one was left on the *autorail*, I led them out to the station forecourt where our coach was waiting.

Out of all the journeys we did in France, I am sure that this is the one that will remain the freshest in the mind of the group of railfans. Even a few days later it all seemed like a dream: had I really been seated at the controls of a brand-new, scheduled passenger train on what is generally considered Europe's most up-to-date and civilised railway system?

Perhaps the SNCF keeps this line open just to entertain the occasional foreign traveller who fancies a spot of train-driving, or perhaps their head office staff in far-off Paris have simply forgotten that it exists. Or is there some historic Act of Parliament, like that which temporarily saved the Bluebell Railway, whereby the *Bessèges à Alais* railway company, and their successors, guarantee to run three passenger trains each way, daily, in perpetuity?

On a more serious note, my journeys in 1997 and 2005 show that merely introducing brand-new rolling stock, without making any other improvements to the service, does not increase patronage. By all rights, Saint-Ambroix should be a railhead for the northern Gard and the whole of the southern Ardèche, with its station selling thousands of tickets to everyone living in the catchment area. Three trains a day at inconvenient times may not have bothered the prospective rail traveller of 1857, but surely a far better service is required today if one wishes to tempt the average citizen of Bessèges out of his Renault, Citröen or Peugeot and onto the train. Even employing the best-looking *contrôleuse* in Europe doesn't help.

The chef de gare, Bessèges

6. Escape from Saint-Geniez-d'Olt

May 21, 1992: A chance trip on an elusive French line

My time spent working in the travel industry has been divided almost equally into office work and coming face-to-face with customers, working either as a tour manager or a local guide. There have been several occasions when I have been asked to leave the office and 'take out' a tour at very short notice.

One example was in May 1992, when the sudden illness of one of our tour managers meant that I was unexpectedly asked to go to Dover to take out a tour called 'Hidden France'. I had barely half-an-hour to pack my bags before a colleague whisked me off to Dover Eastern Docks where I met up with my coach and party. We overnighted at Beuvry, near Béthune, and spent the next two nights in Chalons-sur-Saône, then heading south to Joyeuse in the Ardèche, where the hotel proprietors fortunately were personal friends of mine.

The old station at Florac

By the time I was in Joyeuse the original tour manager was feeling better, and my bosses were quite anxious for me to get back to my work in the office. I would happily have completed the tour, but the fax came through confirming that the tour manager would be rejoining the group at Saint-Geniez-d'Olt, our next stop, and I had been booked a flight from Toulouse to Gatwick the following day.

On a rather wet May the twentieth I escorted my group from Joyeuse through the Causses and the Lozère, stopping for coffee at Florac, where the parking area for tourist coaches is in the forecourt of the former railway station! When we got to Saint-Geniez-d'Olt I handed over the reins to my replacement, who didn't require much of a briefing as he was one of the 'regulars' on that tour.

I now had the problem of how to get to Toulouse airport for a flight that left at 5.20pm the next day. I asked the charming hotel receptionist, who told me to go to the Café du Pont. The café proprietor knew all about transport. He even sold SNCF tickets, she explained.

The Café du Pont was one of those relaxed establishments where no business got done without a drink of some kind being ordered. I sipped on my *pastis* while the café proprietor pored over timetables and looked up something on the *Minitel* - the amazing French information service that predated the World Wide Web by many years.

"Il y a un train à 8.25 à Laissac" he finally said. "Laissac, c'est pas loin".

Further enquiries revealed that the train got to Toulouse at 10.57, which gave me plenty of time before my flight. Only having the vaguest idea of what route this train could possibly take, I handed over the francs and got my ticket.

Back in my hotel bedroom, with my Michelin map of the area unfolded on the bed, I realised that I was about to take quite an exciting journey. Laissac station was halfway along the line from Séverac-le-Château to Rodez, and I had read an article about this railway a couple of years earlier. For this is one of a handful of French railways to have been closed to passengers and then re-opened.

The SNCF implemented a kind of mini-Beeching Plan in 1980, withdrawing supposedly uneconomic passenger services from about 900 kilometres of track. In a few cases the closures were to be temporary: the short line from Mulhouse to Chalampé, near the German border, was revived after a few months, thanks to a subsidy from the local authority. Another line, from Tours to Chinon, reopened in 1982, partly due to the local député successfully lobbying François Mitterand's new pro-rail Minister of Transports, Charles Fitterman.

The fate of the Rodez - Séverac line was bizarre to say the least. Although closed to regular passenger services from September 28, 1980, it was reactivated the following summer for a daily Toulouse - Lyon express and for a weekends-only Paris - Millau sleeper. The Millau train was withdrawn in 1983 and the last of the seasonal Lyon trains ran in August 1988; the line was then completely abandoned.

Waiting at Laissac…

The story then should have been… tracks disappearing under a blanket of weeds; level-crossings buried in tarmac, signals dismantled, station buildings falling into dereliction and the track eventually being lifted. But for some extraordinary reason the SNCF decided to reopen the line in September 1989, creating a new service between Millau and Toulouse. This train ran only once daily, giving the people of Millau the opportunity to spend just three hours in the regional capital.

On May 21 I had an early breakfast. The coach driver had agreed to take me to Laissac, and the hotel proprietor let us use his car, which had been parked on the square overnight with the keys in the ignition (well, it was rather an old Lada!) I loaded my bags in the car and we set off for Laissac. Once we got there, we looked for some evidence of the railway. Nothing obvious was visible. Seeing a group of teenagers standing at a bus-stop, we pulled in and I asked them "S'il vous plait, où est la gare?" They all started laughing and pointed down a narrow, pitted alley that led off the main road.

Denis, my driver, was convinced that the youngsters were having us on. He continued along Laissac's single main street until we came to a *Boulangerie*. I went in and asked there. I was given the same directions: the station must indeed lie down that rutted track.

Gingerly, we headed down towards the station. It looked as though very few motor vehicles ever came this way. Eventually we came to a tall, shuttered station house. There was no ticket office or waiting room. Moving onto the platform, all was desolation. There was a broken clock and a damaged nameboard, whilst weeds were sprouting between the sleepers. The track, incidentally, was of the old-fashioned 'bullhead' variety, held down to the sleepers by great cast-iron chairs stamped with the old railway company's name.

Denis was all for turning back. But at that moment a window in the station building creaked open and an old, mad-looking woman peered out.

"Vous attendez le train pour Toulouse? Hier il n'est pas passé!" (Are you waiting for the Toulouse train? It didn't come yesterday!)

This was not good news. I asked our informant if there was any way of telling if the train was running. She said there was a telephone on the platform, and I should pick it up and ask someone.

I had not noticed the telephone. It was inside a grey metal box, and was obviously for railway workers rather than for passengers. But there was a reassuring buzz when I put the receiver to my ear. Feeling rather stupid, I spoke into the mouthpiece "Je suis à la gare de Laissac. Y-aura-t-il un train pour Toulouse à 8h25?" The reassuring reply was "Oui, Monsieur!"

The railcar arrives!

Denis insisted on waiting until the train actually came. Around 8.20 I thought I heard a distant two-tone horn. And five minutes later, dead on time, the train came in. I was in for a treat, for this was a real vintage SNCF diesel railcar from the 1950s. I signalled to the motorman, making it clear I wanted to get on. Denis helped me on with my luggage. I waved him goodbye and had a look at my surroundings.

The railcar's interior was a perfect period piece, with brown vinyl seats and overhead nets to hold the luggage. The contrôleur checked my ticket and I settled back to enjoy my two-and-a-half hour ride. There were about eight other passengers.

The first station after Laissac was Bertholène, where there was a large building and several sidings. A recently-lifted line could be seen curving away to the north: this was the Espalion railway, opened in 1908 and closed to passengers only 30 years later. Goods services were withdrawn in 1987 and an attempt to preserve it as a tourist line sank without a trace.

The stations at Gages and Canabois were deserted, but a fair number of people were waiting at Rodez, a magnificent station with a great overall roof. Now we would be joining the line to Albi, which, though not exactly a busy trunk route, did have a regular passenger service from Toulouse.

A plump, middle-aged Frenchwoman sat next to me and we started chatting. When I explained that I had never been on this line before, she said that I mustn't miss the Viaduc du Viaur. This is a great steel cantilevered bridge, built between 1895 and 1902, that carries the line 116 metres above the river. The rail passenger comes upon it completely by surprise: one moment you are on a level, rural line crossing gentle farming country, the next you are suspended on a huge steel necklace above a vast chasm. It is much easier to take a photograph of the viaduct from the nearby road than from a train crossing it.

Albi is one of the most beautiful cities in France, and I was delighted that the train passed right through the centre, giving wonderful views of the great fortified Gothic cathedral, looking for all the world like an elegant brick radiator. Under normal circumstances I might have broken my journey here, to revisit the cathedral and the Toulouse-Lautrec Museum. But I had a plane to catch.

From Albi the station buildings and crossing-keepers' cottages were all subtly different. For this line was formerly part of the Paris-Orléans Railway, whilst Séverac - Rodez - Albi was built by the Chemin de Fer du Midi. The smaller wayside stations on the Paris-Orléans line were quite plain and basic, but at Tessonnières, where the Albi branch joined the Capdenac - Toulouse main line, the main building was larger, with an elegant *oeil-de-boeuf* window above the eaves. From here the line followed the broad, flat valley of the River Tarn.

Viaur Viaduct

The railcar was quite full now, with passengers getting on at every station. This was one of the busiest stretches of single track in France and there had been many proposals to double it, especially after 1950 when 19 people were killed in a head-on collision between two trains at Lisle-sur-Tarn, the second stop after Tessonnières. From Saint-Sulpice station, a little further on, the railway assumed a distinctly suburban character, before finally calling it a day at the grandiose Matabiau station in Toulouse.

The majestic SNCF station at Toulouse

I bid goodbye to my neighbour and disentangled my bags from the netting above. It had been one of the most picturesque journeys I had ever made. I deposited my bags in the *consigne automatique* and went on a leisurely exploration of the city, with its magnificent arcaded squares and Romanesque churches. I did a little shopping and had lunch before returning to the station and catching the 3pm bus to the airport.

My flight to Gatwick was with Dan-Air, and in retrospect was quite historic as it would be the last time I ever flew with that airline. Six months later British Airways acquired the assets of Dan-Air for just £1. I reckon that no more than 2p of this could have been for their in-flight catering.

I had one other beautiful railway journey to come. It was a lovely evening when I landed, and I got the front seat of a diesel multiple-unit for a fantastic panoramic ride between Redhill and Tonbridge, passing through gorgeous English spring countryside. From Tonbridge one of the old Southern slam-door electrics took me home and it seemed incredible that I had set out from Laissac's desolate station only that morning.

Surprisingly perhaps, the SNCF's half-hearted gamble seems to have paid off. The 2008 timetable shows three daily trains in each direction on the Séverac-le-Château to Rodez line, all stopping at Laissac. The service has reverted to that of a normal SNCF branch line, although to reach Toulouse from Laissac one now has to change at Rodez.

7. *Travels with My Mother: The Line That Had Three Lives*

October 8, 2007: I take the train from Juan-les-Pins to Grasse

The beautiful old city of Grasse stands on a hilltop some 25 kilometres inland from the Côte d'Azur. It is extremely popular with visitors, most of whom come to visit the numerous perfume factories located in and around the town. From May to September an endless parade of tourist coaches fills the narrow road from Cannes to Grasse, en route for the Parfumerie Fragonard, the Parfumerie Galimard and others. It does not take a rocket scientist to work out that what Grasse really needs is a fast rail connection to the cities on the coast.

Grasse Cathedral

Yet, despite its population of nearly 50,000, its historical attractions and its world importance as the centre of the perfume industry, Grasse somehow managed without a rail passenger service for over 60 years. It was formerly served by two lines: a standard-gauge SNCF branch from Cannes and a long, straggling metre-gauge line linking the city with Vence and Colomars, where it trailed into the beautiful *Chemins de Fer de Provence* line that links Digne and Nice.

When the big transport 'Co-Ordination' policy took effect in 1938, many local train services all over France were withdrawn. Where a minor railway provided a rival service to an SNCF branch, it was usually the former that was closed. In the case of Grasse, however, the narrow-gauge emerged triumphant, and it was the SNCF line that was closed to passengers, remaining open solely for goods traffic. The victory of the metre-gauge, however, was to be short-lived; the line to Colomars was wrecked beyond repair during the Second World War, with many of its viaducts blown up by the retreating German army.

One might have expected the SNCF to reopen their Grasse branch to passengers after the War, but the line remained firmly closed. While main trunk routes were being electrified in the 1950s and 1960s and new French electric locomotives were reaching unheard-of speeds, the only passenger transport to the Cité des Parfums was by road.

By the mid-1970s traffic congestion on the Côte d'Azur had become such a problem that a group of local inhabitants, the Comité Cannes-Grasse, began lobbying the SNCF to reopen the railway. When the Société Nationale showed no interest in improving regional transport facilities (they were more interested in *closing* the nearby Les Arcs - Draguignan line), the locals decided to do things their own way. They acquired an ex-SNCF diesel railcar, repainted it in a bold yellow and blue livery, and from 1978 started running frequent daily services between Cannes and the station of Ranguin, halfway along the line. A weak bridge outside Grasse meant that regular passenger trains could not travel the full length of the branch, but a number of enthusiast specials were operated from time to time. The Comité Cannes-Grasse did not seek out, however, to create a tourist railway: they were more like a real-life *Titfield Thunderbolt*, a group of locals reviving their own branch line.

The Cannes-Ranguin railcar in 1985

I travelled on the Cannes - Ranguin railcar one summer's day in 1985, and enjoyed the sea breezes, the scent of mimosa and the song of the crickets as the small train made its way from the busy summer crowds on the coast to its little temporary terminus. The railcar was well-filled despite an almost total lack of publicity. The SNCF refused to show this private service in their timetables, and through tickets to other stations were not available; the Comité Cannes-Grasse staff issued their passengers with bus-type tickets on board the train. The contrôleurs were friendly and the neat little station at Ranguin was laid out as an information centre for the line, with maps and posters showing the Comité's projects for extensions and expansion of services.

Sadly for the Comité, things did not go their way. The passenger service that had been killed initially by 'co-ordination' in 1938 died again 50 years later as a result of a lack of co-operation by the SNCF. One day the whole French railway network was paralysed by a nationwide strike; the next day, the Cannes - Ranguin train service did not resume.

Things did not end here, however, for the SNCF suddenly decided that they *did* want to re-open the line after all - but on a heavyweight, professional basis. Years of surveys, investigations, costings and planning applications followed. The whole track was lifted and relaid, all stations were rebuilt, and catenary supports were erected for the overhead electrification. Finally, one day in 2005, the first scheduled standard-gauge passenger train for 67 years pulled into Grasse, and the historic city's link with the national network was at last re-established.

I would have loved to have travelled on that inaugural train, especially with my pleasant memories of a return trip to Ranguin two decades earlier, but I did not get the opportunity; in any case, I am sure that the first service would have been reserved for local dignitaries and associated hangers-on. But in October 2007 I took my mother for a week's holiday to the seaside resort of Juan-les-Pins, travelling there by Eurostar and TGV. When I announced to my mother that I was planning to spend an afternoon going to Grasse on the train, she insisted on coming with me.

Train at Juan-les-Pins for Grasse

We walked to Juan-les-Pins station from our hotel. I bought our tickets from an automatic vending machine and stamped them in the *composteur*. The train was a modern double-deck electric multiple-unit, and was reasonably well-filled, passengers ranging from babes-in-arms to couples in their eighties. The first part of the journey along the coastal main line delighted my mother, who looked out for bathers on the beaches as we went by.

Cannes SNCF station is a 1960s ferro-concrete monstrosity, but once out from its gloomy vaults the train picked up speed, headed to the junction and then branched off to the north. There were three or four little halts in quick succession, serving the less-glamorous inland suburbs of Cannes. One of these halts was none other than Ranguin station. Since 1985 the area around the station had become considerably more built-up, and the Provençal-style station building I remembered from my previous voyage had been replaced by a standard modern SNCF house-style halt.

In fact, as we advanced along the railway from Ranguin, it looked as if almost every trace of the past had been obliterated by the SNCF when they had re-opened the line. The occasional disused crossing-keeper's cottage (now in private occupation) and a handful of venerable stone overbridges hinted that this must be an old railway, but the infrastructure was 100% up to date. My mother was very impressed by the quietness of the train and by its smooth running, although she was disappointed not to see any great fields of lavender. We did, however, enjoy glimpses of a large golf course on our right, before entering the station of Mouans-Sartoux.

About two-thirds of the way up the line towards Grasse, Mouans-Sartoux is by far the most important intermediate station. It is a bizarre mix of the traditional and the modern. Whilst the nameboards, fences and passenger shelters are all in the latest SNCF style, the original 19th-century station building still survives, in reasonably good condition. It has been boarded-up but attractive murals adorn the blocked windows on the passenger side; these show imaginary scenes in the life of the station in the *Belle Epoque* (steam trains, elegantly-dressed passengers and smartly-uniformed staff) and in the present day (electric trains, casually-dressed passengers and no staff).

There is some quite attractive rugged scenery between Mouans-Sartoux and Grasse, although the line is never away from housing and roads. We passed a tall chimney and other structures that formed part of a perfume factory, then the train slowed and on our right was a large, disused station building - the old Grasse SNCF station. The tracks have been extended slightly and a brand-new, steel-and-glass station has been built across the end of the line.

Grasse: old station and new train

My mother and I got down from our train and took a few photos before repairing to the Buffet de la Gare, where we sat outside in the warm October sunshine and enjoyed a couple of beers. The drinks at Grasse station buffet were roughly half the price we had been paying in seafront cafés in Juan-les-Pins. We took a few more photos before getting back on the train for the return journey. Grasse is a lovely place and well worth a long stop, but on this occasion we had only come for the train, the photos and the beer!

Our railway adventures were not over, however. On our return journey to England, our TGV train was about an hour late getting into Lille, meaning that my mother and I missed the Eurostar on which we had seats booked to Ashford. There *was* a later train, but it was a direct service to London. When we explained our dilemma to the staff at Lille, they specially arranged for the train to stop at Ashford to let us off! What wonderful service!

8. The Chemins de Fer Corses and a Quartet of Corsican Cats

June 24 - 27, 1991: From Calvi to Île-Rousse, Bastia and Ajaccio

Most guide books on Corsica only give a brief mention of the island's railways. They really deserve to be better-known. Not only do they provide an efficient way of getting around: they are also exceptionally scenic and offer a taste of what some of the vanished metre-gauge systems of mainland France must have been like in their prime.

The island is served by a Y-shaped network of lines, built in the late 1880s. The three termini are at Calvi, Ajaccio and Bastia, and the lines meet up at Ponte-Leccia, yet another example of a junction station in the middle of nowhere. The 158-kilometre Ajaccio - Bastia line is generally regarded as the main trunk route, with Ponte-Leccia to Calvi (74 kilometres) considered a branch. Formerly another line left the Ajaccio - Bastia railway at a place called Casamozza and followed the east coast south to Porto-Vecchio; sadly, this line was badly damaged during the Second World War and was never repaired.

In 1991 I took advantage of a very cheap staff offer - a week in a studio apartment in Corsica! My studio was on the hillside overlooking Calvi beach, with the railway just below. Arriving on June 23, I wasted no time in getting acquainted with the Chemins de Fer Corses. After a swim in the sea, I wandered along to the station and picked up a copy of the timetable. I then had a stroll around the old town, dominated by its Genoese citadel. A heap of ruins that had once been a house was marked by a plaque saying that it was the birthplace of Christopher Columbus! I know that Corsica was once ruled by Genoa but I didn't think the discoverer of America was born in Calvi. "What do *you* think?" I asked a strange grey cat who was sunning himself on a pile of stones. I got an unconvincing "Miaow!" in return.

Corsica has its own very distinctive species of cat, although I have never found the *Chat Corse* listed in any book on pedigree cats. They are quite small and stocky, with huge amber eyes, coarse grey fur and thin, reddish-brown tabby markings. Although they are short-haired, they have remarkably long bushy tails.

The day after I arrived, I got up at 5.30am, dressed and packed a shoulder-bag with food, drink and cameras. At 6.20 I was at the little halt of La Balagne, where I got the morning train to Ponte-Leccia.

The railway from Calvi to Ponte-Leccia is commonly known as the Ligne de la Balagne. As far as Île-Rousse it has a relatively frequent service of stopping trains, providing holidaymakers with access to some of the wonderful beaches along this stretch of coast. I was to sample one of these trains later. Beyond Île-Rousse the line heads inland, and this section had only two return trains a day in 1991. Looking at the remote mountain scenery, I could understand why. Although the comfortable modern autorail was well-filled with passengers travelling the whole length of the line, there was little sign of life at any of the intermediate stations, some of which, such as Palasca, were falling into ruin. The ride gave me some idea of the treats in store on Corsican railways. There were numerous tunnels and plenty of steep gradients, sharp curves and lofty bridges before we reached Ponte-Leccia.

Ponte-Leccia is the only remaining metre-gauge junction in normal public service in France. It must give the traveller an idea of what it would have been like to change trains 50 years ago at Carhaix in Brittany or Le Cheylard in the Vivarais. The station building was well-maintained and the island platform had old-fashioned signs on a lamp-post, giving the destinations of the trains. I looked for 'Ajaccio' and found a new diesel multiple-unit ready to take me on the next stage of my journey. In a blue-and-white livery rather than the red-and-white of the older trains, it was probably the most luxurious metre-gauge vehicle I had travelled on outside Switzerland.

At Ponte-Leccia

As I wanted to do as much sightseeing as possible during my week's holiday, I took this train only as far as Corte. These 25 kilometres were quite exciting, with a succession of tunnels and viaducts, including a wonderful curved stone one with 13 arches. Corte is little more than a village, but is nonetheless a place of great importance, as it was once the island's capital (during Corsica's brief period of independence in 1755-1769) and is still the seat of a University.

Corte's station is below the town centre, and it was quite a stiff walk in the hot sun to the main street, which is long and broad with flights of stone steps leading off it. I walked up one of these side passages to find myself in a delightful shaded square with a fountain. I was about to sit down and have a swig from my bottle of Orangina, when I heard an ear-piercing shriek from somewhere close by. My initial reaction was that two cats were fighting. Knowing the trauma (and vet's bills!) of having a cat with an abscess or torn ear, I looked around for the warring felines to see if I could separate them.

I found them… in the coolest, shadiest part of the square. But they were not fighting. I had come across a male and a female Corsican Cat doing just what comes naturally, and perhaps ensuring a future supply of Corsican kittens. It was, in any event, quite fascinating to watch. The queen was growling fiercely as the tom mounted her, holding the scruff of her neck firmly in his teeth. Afterwards he leaped away and the queen tried to attack him with her teeth and claws, but he was too quick for her.

I did some shopping in Corte, and astonishingly it was still only 10.30am when I was back at the station for the next train to Ajaccio. This was another of the new diesel multiple units, of which the Corsicans seemed to be very proud, as I had found several postcards of them on sale in Corte. The ride out of Corte was splendid enough, with a lofty viaduct and half-a-dozen tunnels, but the real fun started at Vecchio station where there is a wonderful viaduct built by Gustave Eiffel (of the tower fame). This was followed by a series of what I can only describe as hairpin bends as we gained height to reach Vivario, six kilometres further along the line but 142 metres higher! Four tunnels in quick succession followed, then we halted briefly at the prettily-named station of Tattone. The summit of the line came four kilometres further along, at Vizzavona, 905 metres above sea level.

Ajaccio's pleasant station

From Vizzavona to Ajaccio the train somehow had to lose nine hundred metres in a mere 50 kilometres. This was soon forgotten as we plunged into a four-kilometre tunnel, to the delight of the youngsters on board. The majestic Granato viaduct followed, and then we joined the valley of the River Gravone. The descent into Ajaccio was scenic enough but nothing like as spectacular as the middle section of the line.

Ajaccio terminus was nicely-maintained, with a small goods yard that appeared still to be in use. I left the attractive station building and went for a walk around the city, where Napoleon's birthplace is one of the main tourist sights.

I had to do the whole journey all over again in reverse in order to get back to Calvi for 8pm. This involved quite a long stop in Ponte-Leccia, but it had been a wonderful trip.

I spent June 25 on the beach, but decided to 'do' Bastia on the following day. Once again I was at the little beach halt of La Balagne waiting for a train at 6.20am. It consisted of two boxy 1970s railcars, each looking something like a large touring caravan on rails, with a tiny trailer sandwiched in between. The trailer was actually a de-motorised railcar from the 1930s, and appeared to be used mainly for luggage.

As far as Ponte-Leccia I already knew the route. Leaving the sunburnt junction with its obsolete water towers and dusty island platforms, I was treated to a ride along the Golo Valley, with several metal viaducts where the railway decided it would be fun to cross the river. At Casamozza we reached the east coast, and the line now veered to the north to reach the suburbs of Bastia. The station at Bastia was on rather a cramped site and was approached through a longish tunnel, which reminded me of photographs I have seen of the old station at Ventnor on the Isle of Wight.

The main passenger building of Bastia station appeared to have been rebuilt fairly recently in an insipid modern style, so rather than linger here I walked into town. My first impressions were of a dull, workaday place, but when I reached the old port I realised that it had a charm all its own. Beneath an impressive church with twin pepperpot towers I found an outdoor bench and sat down to enjoy my picnic lunch.

There was a polite "Mieu!" and something furry landed on my lap. It was a genuine *Chat Corse*. I stroked his grey fur and fed him most of the chicken from my sandwich. He purred in the self-contented manner of cats everywhere. I felt guilty when eventually I had to leave the bench, but it was time for my next train.

My friend at Bastia

Rather than get the through train back to Calvi, I had decided to break my return journey in two places. First I got a local railcar, known as the 'Metro-Corse', to Biguglia. This must have been the ugliest station on the whole Corsican network, a square concrete structure with GARE DE BIGUGLIA in huge black letters just in case anyone didn't know what it was.

A second railcar took me on to Casamozza, where a large viaduct outside the station still showed evidence of war damage, two of the stone arches having been replaced by a steel span. I had intended to go for a short walk along part of the old trackbed of the lost East Coast line, but unfortunately it appeared to be in private occupation, and a large and unfriendly dog barred my way and snarled at me when I stopped to investigate. Hastily I beat a retreat to Casamozza station and waited in relative safety until the 17.11 to Calvi came.

Casamozza viaduct

On June 27 I used the Corsican railways again. This time I did not venture too far from Calvi. I started with a trip on one of the local 'Tramways de la Balagne' trains to Lumio-Calenzana. This train consisted of a lovely old 1950 Renault railcar towing an even older trailer. They were both painted in the traditional French red and cream autorail livery. The only form of air-conditioning provided on this train was by the crew leaving the doors open!

I had decided to get off at Lumio to visit the historic village church, a fine example of the Pisan Romanesque style, but I was unaware that Lumio village was nearly 10 kilometres from the station whose name it bears, and uphill all the way! I had to ask for directions several times, but the walk was very pretty and the church was quite extraordinary: tall, narrow and dark, with its door guarded by two stone lions.

I felt quite a sense of achievement when eventually I made it back down to the coast, but there was no train due for a while, so I walked along the track to a little halt called Sainte-Restitude, which was right by the sea. I stripped off and enjoyed a swim in the cool, clear water.

I took the next train to Île-Rousse, where the station, flanked by palm trees, is almost on the beach, and one gets the impression that the railway must be fighting a losing battle with the encroaching sand! It was certainly windy and the sand was blowing everywhere, but I went for another swim and tried to have a picnic. Seeing that I had a fair bit of time before the train back to Calvi, I decided to visit the aquarium. This proved to be a remarkable place owned by an eccentric gentleman who pulled giant lobsters, crabs and other sea creatures out of tanks and placed them in his visitors' hands! I had to act as interpreter for an American family, the first American tourists I had met in Corsica.

The Renault railcar that I took back to Calvi that afternoon had some kind of mechanical problem. After making various coughing and spluttering noises, it came to a halt in the sand dunes just off Calvi beach. Perhaps it was a case of 'the wrong sort of sand': I can vouch for the fact that there were no leaves on the line! The motorman and contrôleur dived into the engine compartment and must have sorted it out, for in a few minutes we were off again.

Renault railcar and trailer

Strangely, until now I had not actually been to Calvi station by rail, as the halt of La Balagne was more convenient for my holiday flat, but for the sake of completeness I decided to make my final journey all the way to the pleasant seaside terminus. There were several other railcars here, and the sidings were filled with a motley collection of rolling stock that included an extraordinary home-made square locomotive known as *La Bête de Calvi*. It did indeed look like a bit of a beast, but the wild animals that I most remember from my trip to Corsica were the Lions of Lumio, the Mad Dog of Casamozza, and, of course, the noble and beautiful Corsican Cats!

9. *A Train Ride with a Tibetan, and Trouble with a Tram*

April 2004: I pay a short visit to the Alps

This was actually a work trip: I had to visit two hotels in Chamonix. I will not waste too much time describing what I did while I was there; this is the report of how I got there... and came back!

After a lot of Heathrow flights it was pleasant to fly out of Gatwick, which I always consider my 'local' airport (I have flown out of Lydd a long time ago, which is even closer, but never Manston). As my flight was in the early morning I left the house at 4.30am and took the ridge road from Hythe through Lympne and Aldington to Tenterden, then the A262 to Tunbridge Wells and A264 to East Grinstead. Much more relaxing than the motorway and almost as fast at this time of day. I passed a milk float at Aldington and my first car at Tenterden. There was a lovely full moon and it felt like a drive through medieval Kent. Not much wildlife: one fox, one rabbit and a pure white cat crossed my path! (Now is a pure white cat crossing one's path lucky or unlucky?)

I do prefer country roads to motorways if I have the choice. Sometimes the motorway wins for speed and efficiency, but not this day. (When driving Hythe - Maidstone, one of my most frequent journeys, I always feel a pang of guilt if I forsake the A20 and take the M20 - it seems like betraying an old friend!)

Back to Gatwick airport and my flight to Geneva, which passes uneventfully. I am travelling so light that I have hand baggage only. So at Geneva I am straight out through Customs and down the stairs to the railway station. I notice there's a train to Lausanne - the first leg of my journey - in three minutes. But on my walk to the station I seem to have bypassed the ticket office, which is on a higher level. I know there is usually a surcharge for tickets bought on the train. The conductor is standing by the train waiting to get on. I explain my predicament. He says that I won't have time to go to the ticket office before the train leaves, but he'll sell me a ticket as far as Lausanne without a supplement. Now that's Switzerland for you. The same thing once happened to me in France and I was surcharged!

The train pulls out of the airport station into fresh air between concrete retaining walls defaced by graffiti. Although the permanent way itself is immaculately manicured, it's strange how much graffiti there is beside the tracks in Swiss urban areas. Perhaps it's just the national tradition of freedom and self-expression. But I do notice on this trip that most of it looks quite old and faded and that definite efforts appear to have been made to clean it off or paint over it - the Swiss love of cleanliness and order taking over again. Once out of Geneva, the graffiti disappears altogether and there are lovely views of Lake Geneva. I have ridden this line before, but it's a nice one to do again!

Lausanne station comes up soon, and I hop off and discover I've got a connection to Martigny in ten minutes. There is an endless queue at the ticket office. Luckily I have more than enough loose change in Swiss money to buy my ticket (mostly in the form of 20-centime and half-franc pieces which I bought at a bargain price from an old friend who sorts out foreign coins for a charity!) So I start pumping 20-centime coins into the machine. After accepting about 30 of them, it spits them out again - it obviously can't cope with too many at once! So I try again, this time interspersing the 20-centime coins with half-francs. This tactic works and I get my ticket for Martigny. The machine won't issue me a through ticket to the French border or Chamonix, as the rails beyond Martigny are not owned by the Swiss Federal system.

The journey from Lausanne to Martigny is a delight, with the vineyards on the left, the elegance of Vevey and Montreux on the right and then the Château of Chillon. I enjoy an overpriced but delicious coffee and have a read of the excellent free railway and travel magazine, *Via*, which can be found in all Swiss trains. Luckily it's a French issue. On some long-distance trains they have both French and German copies, but I have occasionally found only a German version if I've been somewhere like Lucerne or Interlaken.

Martigny- Châtelard train

At Martigny I have another 10-minute wait. I put some more change into the ticket machine to get my ticket for the next stage of the journey - to Le Châtelard, on the French border. In many ways I think the best railway journey between two places is the one that involves the most changes! And the little, red and white narrow-gauge electric train to Le Châtelard whisks me uphill on its rack-and-pinion track and before long Martigny looks like a toy town below, with the standard-gauge line I arrived on looking for all the world like a model railway. The little train takes me higher, through pine woods and into the snows above. It is 45 minutes of superb scenery until I get to Le Châtelard. The train looks as if it dates from the 1950s, but is well-maintained and the interior seats have been re-trimmed in very funky colours. The other passengers are mostly elderly peasant types with weather-beaten faces, but a few skiers get on before Le Châtelard.

Nothing at Le Châtelard seems to indicate this is an international frontier. I have 11 minutes to buy a ticket for Chamonix at the wooden chalet station. I am looking forward to this last part of the journey as it is one of the very few narrow-gauge railways left in France. I travelled on the western half of this line - from St-Gervais to Chamonix - 24 years ago when I was a student, but I have never been on the part from Chamonix to the border. So today I am completing a journey started long before.

A contrast to the Swiss train, the French one takes its electricity from a third rail; it is also ultra-modern with very comfortable seats and panoramic windows. It leaves Le Châtelard on a steep gradient and then plunges into a tunnel before finding the bottom of the river valley. The scenery is much the same as

Switzerland, except that it isn't as well-maintained. The neat little stations on the Swiss side have become dilapidated halts with peeling paintwork and graffiti. Most passengers getting on the train are teenagers, who seem to be on their way home from school.

Train at Chamonix

Chamonix station looks just like it did on my last visit - old, grand and rather too big for the purpose it now serves. I leave by the main door and step into the town. A fine sleet is falling. Last time I was here I had great difficulty in finding anywhere open in May that did a cheap snack. Now I see that a branch of McDonalds has opened in the road leading up to the station. But apart from that nothing seems to have changed.

Work completed, the next day I am back at the station at 1pm for my journey home. There has been a fresh snowfall overnight and it is still snowing - Chamonix looks like a Christmas card! But the train is dead on time. I am going back to Geneva by the other route, through France. This is shorter and cheaper, but takes just as long as coming via Switzerland because the French trains don't connect and don't run anything like as frequently as the Swiss ones!

The first section is by the narrow-gauge line to St-Gervais. This bit isn't as pretty as the other half of the line, although it has the world's steepest gradient on an adhesion-only railway (1 in 11). For much of the way the train is dwarfed by the enormous concrete motorway viaduct that is part of the approach to the Mont Blanc tunnel. Mont Blanc itself is invisible behind the mist. At St-Gervais I have a short break before my train to La-Roche-sur-Foron. I walk to the post office near the station. Some new stamps went on sale in France today to commemorate the centenary of the *Entente Cordiale* between France and the UK. I have promised a friend I'd get a set. Unfortunately, the queue at the post office is so long that I give up. Presumably people are busy sending their parcels and cashing their cheques before the Easter break.

The train from St-Gervais to La-Roche-sur-Foron is a real mainline train, with an elderly electric locomotive and carriages from the 1970s. It could well be the same train I rode in last time I went on this line. At that time I would never have believed that I would come back here one day as part of my job!

La-Roche-sur-Foron is quite a small place, and enquiries reveal that the post office is too far from the station for me to be able to get there and back before my next train. So I board the train to Geneva and regret that I could not get the stamps. Then I check the timetable. From the next main station, Annemasse, there is a regular service of trains to Geneva. If I get out at Annemasse, I can have half an hour there before getting the next train to Geneva, and I will still get there in good time for my flight. So this is what I do.

Landscape near Chamonix

The post office in Annemasse is very close to the station, and the queue, though long, moves quite fast. When it is my turn, the counter clerk is quite chatty and asks me if I am from England, and do I know the Queen? I explain that I have seen her once but she was in a car and I didn't get a very good look! He then wants to know what type of car it was. "A Rolls-Royce without a number plate", I say, and immediately regret it as this requires further explanation. Now I understand why there are such long queues at French post offices. Hastily I bid goodbye, sprint back to the station and leap on board the small, grubby two-car electric train to Geneva. It sets off in the direction of La-Roche-sur-Foron, which unsettles me, but then branches off onto a single track curving between derelict-looking warehouses and factories.

There aren't many passengers on the train. But about halfway through the ten-minute journey a young lady of oriental appearance comes up and starts talking to various people on the train, who send her off with a shake of the head. A beggar? When she comes to me she asks if I speak English. When I say yes, she explains that she needs help getting her baby's pushchair off the train and can I help her? I assure her that this will be OK.

Genève-Eaux-Vives is a run-down station in a run-down part of Geneva. I help the oriental lady off the train and carry her shoulder bag while she wheels the pushchair through a small office marked 'Douanes Suisses' and inches deep in dust. We have just left the EC and entered Switzerland. Smugglers and white slave traders, please note!

My companion then asks me how she can get to Zurich. I try to explain that she'll have to get to the mainline railway station in Geneva and then by train to Zurich. I know that there is a tram to the other station, but have to ask a bus driver where it stops. This proves to be a 500-yard walk down the street. I then ask the woman if she has any Swiss money for a ticket. She has - but only in high denomination notes! The ticket machine at the stop takes only coins. I get myself a ticket, but ironically have now disposed of all my small change and don't have enough for a second ticket. Never mind, in most Swiss cities you can also buy them on the tram...

Tram No.16 comes and is held up for about ten minutes when my travelling companion gets the baby's pushchair stuck in the door! Somehow we get it in, with a number of passengers helping. The tram is quite crowded and there is no ticket machine. The oriental woman is worried about not having a ticket. I say the best thing to do is to plead ignorance if the ticket inspector comes! She seems to think the tram will go all the way to Zurich, as she asks me how many stops it will be! Then we get seats, and I ask her where she's from. "Tibet", she says.

Luckily there is no ticket inspection on the tram. I get off at Geneva's main-line station and attempt to help the Tibetan lady off with the pushchair. Again, it gets caught up in the folding doors and we need about ten people to help us get it out. The baby sleeps through all this unperturbed. I look at my watch and see I've only got three minutes before the train to the airport. The Tibetan lady follows me into the station. I find the queue for the ticket counter, push her into it, leave her shoulder bag beside her and tell her "Stay in the queue. When you get to the counter ask for a ticket to Zurich. I'm sure they'll speak English". I hope I'm right. I then do a dash worthy of Roger Bannister to Platform 3 for the airport train.

"Never travel on a tram with a Tibetan with a pram" - there has to be a moral there somewhere!

A tram in Geneva without a Tibetan

10. *The Beautiful Brünigbahn and the Miniscule MIB*

December 28, 1996: A winter ride to Innertkirchen

I am fortunate to have travelled over a fair proportion of the Swiss railway system, both on the State tracks and on the colourful private lines. I have been on the incredible rack-railway up the Jungfrau, I have ridden in the red trains of the Rhaetian Railways, I have taken the rack line up the Gornergrat and the Glacier Express from Zermatt to St Moritz. I have been on a special steam train up the Rigi and ridden on the Panoramic Express from Montreux to Zweissimmen.

Steam train on the Rigi rack-railway

Although other countries may have faster and more modern trains, no other country's railways even approach the kind of service found in Switzerland. Even the smallest Alpine village is never more than a short distance from a railway station - and, usually, one served by frequent, clean electric trains. Line closures have been rare. This is partly for political reasons: railways are effectively protected from bus competition, and most cantons are willing to subsidise local rail services. There is also a very practical reason: many local lines, although not 'profitable', provide the only access to towns or villages in the winter when roads are impassable. Recent years have even seen the construction of a few brand new local railways: the 22-kilometre Vereina line on the metric Rhaetian system was opened in November 1999.

Things *can* go wrong on Swiss Railways, and when they do, it can be spectacular. On June 22, 2005 I was due to escort a group of holidaymakers by rail from Zurich to St Moritz. One of my passengers was delayed, and I sent the others on to St Moritz and waited at Zurich airport. My missing passenger duly arrived and we went down to the station for the train to Zurich Hauptbahnhof. However, when we got to the airport station, they told us that there was a power failure and we would have to get a bus to Zurich-Oerlikon station and then a train from there.

When we arrived at Zurich-Oerlikon, everything was total chaos and we found out that the entire Swiss railway network was paralysed. Realising that there was no way in which we could get to St Moritz that day, I booked rooms at the hotel opposite the station. Services gradually returned to normal and we made our journey the next day. At least we were not among those unfortunate passengers who were trapped for hours in long dark Alpine tunnels! June 22, 2005 has gone down as the darkest day in the history of Swiss Railways.

The Chapel Bridge before the 1993 fire

One of my favourite Swiss journeys starts in the beautiful central Swiss city of Lucerne. The station is by the lakeside, within sight of the famous covered wooden Chapel Bridge. Both the bridge and station have been rebuilt since I first became acquainted with the city in 1981: the bridge was sadly destroyed by fire in August 1993 and subsequently rebuilt exactly as it was before. The station was replaced by a very modern structure in 1991, leaving just a single arch from the old building standing like a Roman monument by the trolleybus terminal. Inside, the new station is functional and elegant, with an underground shopping mall linked to the platform level by lifts and escalators.

City bus outside the old Lucerne station

In the early 1980s Lucerne still had some lovely old bulbous trolleybuses dating from the 1950s, but these have now been withdrawn and replaced by more modern vehicles. The city also has a very useful free bus that links the station with the historic area: this was formerly operated by a bizarre single-deck half-cab conveyance. Whenever I took a group of tourists to Lucerne I would draw their attention to this free bus service; one member of my group once assumed that all buses in the city were free, and spent an entire day travelling around Lucerne without buying a ticket - and without being challenged!

The Swiss Railways' map shows Lucerne at the centre of a dense web of lines, with routes leaving the city in six directions. What is not obvious from the map is that the line running south, through Meiringen to Interlaken, is narrow-gauge. Leaving from the station's furthest platform, this 75-kilometre metre-gauge Brünig Railway not only provides a glorious journey in itself, but has four fascinating tributary lines. Opened from Lucerne to Brienz by the Jura-Berne-Luzern-Bahn in 1889, the line was operated by Swiss Federal Railways from 1903 until 2005, and starts as a fairly conventional suburban railway.

At Hergiswil, by the Alpnacher See, another metre-gauge line veers off to the left: this is the Luzern-Stans-Engelberg, formerly served by its very own red electric trains but now under the same management as the Brünigbahn. I once took a group of British enthusiasts on this line, which includes an exciting rack-and-pinion section with a gradient of 1 in 4. From the terminus we walked to the cable-car station, where we rode the four-section cable-car to the 3,020-metre summit of Mount Titlis, a permanent deep-freeze.

The Brünig Railway, meanwhile, continues to Alpnachstad, where an incredible rack-railway can be seen ascending a sheer cliff on the right. This is the world-famous Pilatus Railway, which climbs to a height of 2,132 metres but is a mere 4.3 kilometres long. The steepest cogwheel line in the world, it was opened in 1889, 29 years too late for Queen Victoria, who had to make the ascent on a pony (specially brought over from England!) when she visited Switzerland in 1860.

Leaving the Alpnacher See, the Brünig train continues through rolling farming country, following the River Sarner Aa to the Cantonal capital of Sarnen. This little town has a ruined castle and sits at the head of a long, thin lake, the Sarnersee, which the train follows as far as Giswil.

The rack section of the Brünig line

Giswil station marks a big change in the railway. Here the train engages the rack and starts climbing up the 1-in-9 gradient to Brünig-Hasliberg. This part of the journey is accompanied by the drumming sound of the locomotive on the rack, and is so slow that in summer one enjoys wonderful views of the wild flowers that grow in profusion beside the track. When I rode the line in December 1996, everything was coated by a mantle of snow.

Brünig-Hasliberg is an isolated station at the top of the pass, serving no apparent centre of population. From here the train creeps downhill, its cogwheels still engaging with the rack. There are dense pine forests on both sides of the line, but these clear to allow spectacular views of the Aare Valley far below.

The train eventually reaches Meiringen station, on the valley floor. Meiringen is not an especially attractive town; it was ravaged by two fires in the late 19th century and thus has few historic buildings, but it makes a very good base for exploring the local area. The town has two main claims to fame: it gave its name to the meringue, and Sir Arthur Conan Doyle chose the nearby Reichenbach Falls as the setting for Sherlock Holmes' epic struggle with Moriarty. One of the most popular tourist sights in Meiringen is the Sherlock Holmes Museum, which occupies the basement of a little chapel and incorporates an 'exact replica' of the interior of 221B Baker Street!

I spent Christmas 1996 with a group of visually-impaired holidaymakers in Meiringen. They were a very happy crowd and it proved to be a memorable Christmas. Each blind passenger had a sighted companion, and we went for rides on buses, local trains and even horse-drawn carriages. On Christmas Eve we attended a dismal Communion service in a local Protestant church with no carols or hymns and a preacher who droned on for hours in Schwyzerdeutsch. Returning to the hotel, our quiet drink in the bar was suddenly disturbed by a mob that swarmed in, ringing cowbells and beating drums. Our host informed us that these folk were seeing out the Old Year, and spent every evening from Christmas to the New Year walking around the town, making as much noise as possible and exhorting free drinks from every hostelry! The Swiss certainly know how to enjoy themselves!

Ringing out the Old Year in Meiringen

In addition to having a major station on the Brünigbahn, Meiringen also has a tiny, metre-gauge branch line to Innertkirchen. I had seen this railway marked as a thin red line on the map, and had read about it in Bryan Morgan's *The End of The Line*, but I had never had the opportunity to travel on it. On Boxing Day 1996 some of my passengers asked if I could organise another excursion for them. "How about a little train ride?" I suggested. The idea was received with enthusiasm and two days later I trooped down to the station in the company of six or seven passengers.

When we reached the station, I was concerned at first that the Innertkirchen Railway might have been closed. There didn't appear to be any indication of its trains on the timetable-board at the station. Then I saw a blue sign marked 'Bahnhof MIB'. This led over a level-crossing to a picturesque little halt with a Swiss chalet building like a large version of the music box that my parents bought me on my first ever visit to Switzerland.

The MIB is one of those typically Swiss 'inter-village' lines that have disappeared from most other developed countries. It is electric and just five kilometres long, and was originally built in 1926 to carry materials and workers for the construction of a new hydro-electric scheme. It was opened as a public railway only in 1946. Although the railway owned one very smart new railcar in 1996, it seemed to be keeping it for best, and our journey was on an old Berne tram, painted bright orange and numbered 7.

Although short, my trip on the MIB was memorable. As the rural tram meandered through wintry orchards by the River Aare and then plunged into a long tunnel, I had the challenge of describing the scenery to fellow-travellers who could not see it. The railway tunnel bypasses the Aareschlucht, a popular tourist attraction that is closed in the winter. The river flows through a deep, narrow, gorge, and pedestrian walkways have been suspended above it to allow visitors to follow its course. The railway has its own station, Sandsteg, at the entrance of the gorge.

Emerging from the tunnel, the river reappears on the right, crossed by a picturesque wooden covered bridge, and the tram-train halts in Innertkirchen-Hof, in the village centre. My small group elected to stay on the train to the terminus, called simply Innertkirchen, where the railway's workshops are located. We then all walked back through the snow to Innertkirchen-Hof to wait for the train back to Meiringen. Once again, it consisted of tram number 7. I spent the return journey discussing *The Archers* with two delightful young women from my group.

The MIB's tram-train in Innertkirchen

The Brünigbahn trains have to reverse at Meiringen station, and it is quite common for carriages to be added or detached here. The journey is now level as the railway follows the valley floor, although there are a number of intriguing-looking electrified spurs leading to locked caves in the mountainsides. I have often wondered what they contain.

The train soon reaches the shore of the Brienzersee, said to be the cleanest lake in Switzerland, and the views on the left side are stunning. I took my party on this stretch of the line to visit a wood carver's workshop in Brienz, the attractive village that for many years was the terminus of the line. Wood carving is the speciality of Brienz, and the carvers will proudly show you wooden animals, musical instruments and the famous cuckoo-clocks.

Opposite Brienz station another railway may be seen climbing the Rothorn Mountain. This is the Brienz Rothorn Bahn, which has somehow escaped electrification. Laid to a gauge of 800mm, it is a rack-and-pinion line and operates in the summer only, so I could not take my passengers there in December 1996. I did once, however, escort another group on this railway. It was a perfect day and the views over Lake Brienz were superb as our steam locomotive pushed its single red carriage to a height of 2,244 metres in one hour. The line is about seven-and-a-half kilometres long and uses a mixture of steam and diesel locomotives; a number of brand-new steamers have been supplied in recent years by SLM Winterthur, using advanced technology that is said to make them cleaner and more economical than diesels. The carriages also have great character: some date from the opening of the line in 1892, while others are more modern and have distinctive curved glass roofs.

The Brienz Rothorn Bahn

From Brienz the Brünigbahn continues along the north shore of Lake Brienz, past attractive villages and chalet-style stations, to Interlaken, at the end of the lake. This section of line was only completed in 1916. Interlaken has two stations: the metre-gauge trains terminate at Interlaken-Ost by Lake Brienz. To travel further west by rail one must join a standard-gauge train; these stop at Interlaken-West, rather more centrally located than the 'Ost' station, and continue along the south bank of Lake Thun towards Spiez.

Interlaken-Ost station has rather charming old wooden buildings and is a fascinating place to watch the trains, for it is served not only by the Brünig line and the standard-gauge BLS line, but also by the chocolate-and-cream trains of the Berner-Oberland-Bahn. These are the trains to take if one wishes to ride to the Jungfrau.

The West station is quite modern and has little character, but at the time of my last visit it boasted a 'penny-squashing machine' that stamped an image of the Mönsch, Jungfrau and Eiger mountains onto an elongated 10-rappen coin. There is also a large model railway nearby, and the steamships on Lake Thun dock just behind the platform.

The pleasant resort of Interlaken is the terminus of the Brünig line, but one day its trains could go further: there have been proposals to lay a third rail along the standard-gauge track from Interlaken through Spiez to Zweisimmen, where the pretty narrow-gauge Montreux-Oberland-Bernois railway begins. This would allow metre-gauge trains to run through from Lucerne to Montreux. They have been talking about it for years, but, this being Switzerland, such a plan may well come to fruition one day.

11. *Saved by the FART: the Glacier Express that wasn't*

October 4, 2000: An interesting journey from Spiez to Lugano

In the first week of October, 2000, I was escorting a group of holidaymakers on a tour called *Switzerland and the Glacier Express*. It was not primarily a tour for railway enthusiasts, but a two-centre holiday spending four nights near Spiez on Lake Thun followed by three nights by the Lake of Lugano. The journey between the two resorts was by train, featuring a ride on the Brig - Andermatt section of the *Glacier Express* route - the highlight of the holiday, according to the brochure. From Andermatt we were due to take the rack-railway down to Göschenen and then the Gotthard main line to Lugano.

On October 3, the day before our *Glacier Express* trip, one member of my party came up to me and said "Have you seen the news? The railway line near Andermatt's been blocked by a landslide!"

I hadn't seen the news, and wondered if there really was any need to worry. The Swiss were normally pretty quick at clearing anything blocking their railways. And in any case, the blockage might be to the east of Andermatt, therefore not affecting our journey. Of course, my informant may have misunderstood the news bulletin entirely. But it was still worth checking, so I immediately got on the 'phone to Spiez railway station, explaining that I had 40 tickets to travel to Lugano tomorrow via the *Glacier Express*. The first man to whom I spoke hadn't heard anything about the incident, but he asked me to hang on while he asked his colleagues. I faintly heard some lively discussion in Swiss German in the background before the railway official came back on the line. Yes, it was true. There had been a serious landslide that had blocked the line between Andermatt and the Furka tunnel, so the Glacier Express would not be running.

I enquired about replacement buses, but was told there was no satisfactory road access to the place where the incident had taken place; indeed, there was no road paralleling that section of line. The only solution would be for my party to travel by a different route. Why didn't we just take the main line north to Berne, then another main-line train to Lucerne, then the Gotthard line down to Lugano?

I thought about it. All my group would already have taken the main line to Berne as part of their journey from Zurich airport four days previously. We had already visited Lucerne on a coach excursion from Spiez, so I didn't want complaints about going to the same place again, even though the railway route was quite different. What I really wanted was a scenic, partly narrow-gauge route that would give my travellers at least something of the flavour of the *Glacier Express*, and would not cover any ground that they had already seen. Then I remembered the international metre-gauge railway that runs from Domodóssola to Locarno, called the 'Centovalli' as it is supposed to cross a hundred valleys. This would offer a beautiful journey, and would be much more direct than the main line, although of course it would be much slower. But speed was not an essential ingredient of this particular railway holiday.

"Would we be able to use our tickets to travel via Domodóssola and Locarno?" I asked. There was more heated discussion in Schwyzerdütsch, as the poor harassed railway official tried to find out if our tickets were valid in Italy. It emerged that they were, and I took the bus to Spiez station to sort everything out.

The railway from Domodóssola to Locarno is generally acknowledged to offer some of the finest scenery in Europe; a photograph of the line was even used by Bryan Morgan as the frontispiece of *The End of the Line*. It is not an especially historic line: it was opened only in 1923, and was seriously damaged by storms in 1978, not re-opening until three years later. The railway and its feeder buses are operated by a company called *Ferrovie Autolinee Regionali Ticenesi,* which appears in initials on the vehicles, causing a few raised eyebrows from English-speaking travellers!

Since re-opening in 1981, the Centovalli's passenger services have been operated largely by modern light-rail tramway-type vehicles, a far cry from the comfort of the *Glacier Express,* on which my passengers had been due to enjoy an included lunch. As far as I was aware, there was no catering of any kind on the FART. I raised this issue with the station-master at Spiez, who made a few important-sounding telephone calls and promised that he would arrange something.

The early morning of October 4 saw me at Spiez station organising the luggage, which was to be sent ahead via the main line. I returned to the hotel for the passengers and then our adventure could begin. Many were obviously disappointed that their Glacier Express journey could not go ahead, but luckily the blame could not be laid on me!

Waiting for the train at Spiez

Spiez station is modern and not particularly attractive, but it is a busy place with plenty of action going on. It is an important through station on the BLS (Bern-Lötschberg-Simplon) route, the only main international line in Europe that has never formed part of a national network. The station has excellent facilities. You can even get a souvenir 'elongated penny' from a machine that squashes 10-rappen coins and stamps them with the image of Spiez Castle on one side and a modern electric locomotive on the other. Apart from this machine and one other at Interlaken West, the only similar machines I have ever seen at railway stations were at George in South Africa and on tourist lines in the USA.

Our train came rolling in, dead on time, with the name of our travel agency on a card in the window. In a few moments we were on board and the train soon plunged into the Hondrich Tunnel. Returning to dazzling sunshine, we passed the pyramid-shaped mountain called the Niesen Kulm as the track entered the valley of the River Kander. The train halted at Frutigen station and passed a couple of castles as it made its tortuous ascent up the north ramp of the Lötschberg to Kandersteg.

A new tunnel has now been pierced through the base of the mountain, but at the time of my journey only the original Lötschberg Tunnel was in service. 14.6 kilometres long, this tunnel took six years to build and was considered an engineering miracle of its day. Once our train entered the north portal, no further sightseeing was possible for ten minutes, so my passengers turned their attention to their books or magazines.

At Goppenstein, the train emerged from the tunnel and entered the south ramp, zig-zagging down a series of gradients that offered tremendous views of Brig and the Rhône Valley below. At each turn, the onion domes of Brig's castle appeared closer and closer. Eventually we reached the station in the valley, where we had to change trains. Normally we would have gone out to the station forecourt and boarded the red metre-gauge carriages of the Glacier Express. But today we stayed on the platform and waited for the Italian State Railways 11h36 train to Domodóssola. It arrived dead on time (a legacy of Mussolini?) and consisted of luxurious, albeit slightly grubby, compartment stock. I warned my passengers not to make themselves too comfortable, as this journey would last only half-an-hour!

Although there was no passport check, there was a ticket inspection during this section of the journey, which was a little inconvenient as my group was split between several compartments, I had the one and only ticket, and the conductor spoke only Italian! The short Brig - Domodóssola trip cannot be described as scenic, as almost half of it is taken up by the Simplon Tunnel, at just under 20 kilometres the longest railway tunnel in Europe until the Channel Tunnel opened in 1994. The border with Italy comes about halfway through the tunnel. As with the Channel Tunnel, motor vehicles can be conveyed through the Simplon on shuttle trains, several of which we passed by the south entrance.

At Domodóssola I was very careful to make sure that everyone had got off, as the train was continuing to Milan and I did not wish to go looking for lost sheep there! Domodóssola station looked a little forlorn, its huge buildings and vast arrays of sidings seemed very under-used, with weeds sprouting between rusting tracks. No doubt the relaxation of border controls across Europe has led to a big decline in the workload at frontier stations such as this.

We were greeted on the platform by a railway employee who called out the name of our travel agency and indicated that we should follow him. He took us down a sloping concrete path into what can only be described as an underground bunker. Here was the light rail vehicle that was to take us to Locarno. We all piled in and the electric sliding doors closed.

Travelling on the FART

Some of my passengers were looking rather disappointed, both with the rather Spartan comfort of the narrow-gauge train and with the inauspicious start to the journey. Bursting out of the bunker, the line crosses two kilometres of untidy industrial scenery. Then, suddenly, the little train starts to climb into the hills, and does a neat loop around a medieval tower-house standing in a beautiful garden. If anyone actually lives there, it must be like having their very own large-scale model railway.

I didn't even try to count the hundred valleys along the line. They are actually side valleys off the main valley of the River Melazza, which the railway follows. It has to cross each valley by a viaduct: these are almost always of steel, unlike the massive stone constructions found on earlier lines.

The first few villages along the railway have a definite Mediterranean appearance, with vineyards, stone buildings and plain churches with tall *campaniles*. The line climbs gradually to Santa Maria Maggiore, one of those little arty towns that so often crop up halfway along beautiful railway lines (think of Romorantin on the Blanc-Argent and Rye on Ashford-Hastings).

At Re, a little further along, there is a large pilgrimage church, and soon afterwards our train reached Camedo, the first station in Switzerland. Quite surprisingly, there was a customs inspection here, and a couple of my group who were non-EC passport holders had their passports taken away and stamped. But, more importantly, a refreshment trolley was wheeled on board - sandwiches, crisps and soft drinks especially for our group! The station-master of Spiez was as good as his word.

The scenery east of Camedo is delightful, with wooded valleys, waterfalls and spectacular viaducts with views down to the river far below. There is more of an Alpine feel to the line here, and the architecture is more typical of central Europe, with timber chalets and Baroque churches. Tucking into their sandwiches, my group were now enjoying their journey.

Camedo's pretty station

The train continued through magnificent scenery, stopping at the stations of Intragna, Cavigliano and Verscio, crossing the River Isorno on a lofty steel bridge. At Ponte Brolla station an interesting selection of old rolling-stock was on display.

The Centovalli line finished almost as it began. On reaching the outskirts of Locarno, the little tram-train dived underground and served a couple of modern underground halts before terminating beneath Locarno's mainline station. Here, once again, we were met off the train by an efficient cicerone and shepherded onto the 14h30 to Bellinzona. We were now on a standard-gauge Swiss Federal Railways train hauled by a typical Swiss slab-sided electric locomotive.

We all had to get off in Bellinzona, a pretty station with views of the town's three castles. Now we were back on the route that we would have taken had the *Glacier Express* been in operation. Once again the station staff ensured that we got on the right platform for our fifth and final train of the day, the 14h57 along the southern part of the Gotthard Line to Lugano.

A station on the Centovalli Line

I had called ahead to make sure that the transfer company were ready at Lugano with their coach. Our luggage had already arrived, so we collected that from the station and loaded it on the coach for the short journey to our lakeside hotel. We had not travelled by the *Glacier Express*, but had achieved an honourable second-best by taking a little-known but very beautiful route.

Big Swiss electric locos at Bellinzona

12. The Train in Spain that stays mainly in the Plain

October 1981: I discover half of the amazing *La Robla* railway; later I finish my journey and take chocolate to Cordoba

In September 1981 I started working in Spain, teaching English at a language school in Santander, roughly halfway along the country's north coast. Although this was certainly not my reason for taking up the appointment, a glance at the *Thomas Cook Rail Map of Europe* showed me that the city was ideally-placed for exploring narrow-gauge railways. Lines ran east to Bilbao and west to Oviedo, whilst a very scenic and pretty electrified branch went south to Lierganes. Further south still, a long non-electrified metre-gauge line left the city of Bilbao, crossed the broad-gauge Santander - Palencia line at a place called Mataporquera, and continued south-west to León. This railway is known as the *Ferrocarril de La Robla*, as it was originally built to link the coal-mining town of La Robla with the port of Bilbao; the diversion of the western terminus to León came later.

Santander's main claim to railway history is that it gave its name to a line that never served it. The *Ferrocarril Santander-Mediterráneo* is a classic example of a lost cause. Originally intended to join the city with Valencia, via Burgos, Soría, Calatayud and Caminreal, this 430-kilometre line was first planned in 1908, but construction did not start until 1924, by which time competition from motor vehicles already posed a threat. By the start of the Civil War, the navvies had reached Cidad-Dosante, on the metre-gauge León - Bilbao line, and they never got any further. A mere 63 kilometres separated Santander from the railhead (as the crow flies), but unfortunately the Picos de Europa mountains were in the way, and the essential tunnel was never bored. My old school atlas, printed in 1968, still shows this line as 'under construction'. A desultory passenger and goods service ran on the remnants of the *Santander-Mediterráneo* until the mid-1980s, when most of the line was abandoned; the local paper in Santander still regularly prints articles demanding the completion of the railway.

I spent several weekends exploring the local transport system, and had already ventured along the Bilbao and Oviedo lines by the end of October. Then a fortuitous saint's day gave me a long weekend and a chance to investigate that intriguing long dotted line on the map. Deciding to visit the historic city of León, I packed a small shoulder-bag and set off for Santander's main-line station, where I boarded an efficient Swiss-built 1950s green-and-silver electric train for Mataporquera.

The main line south from Santander is quite something: it was constructed in the 1850s by an English engineer called George Mould. Only the first few kilometres are level and straight; once the line reaches the Picos de Europa, it has to climb 562 metres in the space of 18 kilometres between the stations of Bárcena and Reinosa. Although it was a fine sunny day, the air outside felt cold when we paused at the mountain halts of Montabliz, Pesquera and Lantueno.

Mataporquera, 108 kilometres and one hour and twenty minutes from Santander, was just a small village, overshadowed by a vast cement works and extremely dusty. It is at approximately the same altitude as the peak of England's highest mountain. Our train pulled into the neat main-line (RENFE) station, and I followed a number of other passengers who crossed the tracks to what I assumed was the narrow-gauge

(FEVE) platform. Sure enough, here were metre-gauge tracks and an unnecessarily large station building that offered no facilities other than a small *cantina* and a ticket office (closed). According to my watch I had about half-an-hour to wait for the train to León. That seemed sufficient time to get to know Mataporquera quite well.

RENFE electric train from Santander

Soon enough, there was a distant rumble and a cloud of dust, and a long train came into the station. It was hauled by a modern yellow diesel locomotive, but most of the carriages looked pretty ancient and it even incorporated a post van, for this was a *Correo*, a mail train running under a contract from the Spanish Post Office.

I rushed up to the train, only to be told that it was going to Bilbao. The León train, which should have arrived first, was running late. Still, I assumed that the two trains would cross at Mataporquera, and thought I would not have to wait too long. I tried the little ticket-office again: it was open, but they were only selling tickets to Bilbao. The train for León would come later.

The Bilbao train sat in the station for a good half-hour before departing in a vast cloud of dust. I decided to risk a walk around the village, confident that I would hear my train long before it came in. Several horse-drawn carts went by; these were a rarity in Santander but seemed common enough here. Beyond the station I found a roofless engine-shed, with a delightful little tank engine named *Begoña*. She seemed to have been abandoned there as if she had just finished work the day before.

It was pleasant enough sitting in the sun for an hour or so, but after two and then three hours had passed, I felt almost that I had been born in Mataporquera. I kept walking back to the ticket-office but the window remained resolutely shut. It was actually nearly 6pm when the León train rolled in, almost four hours late!

The train looked just like the one to Bilbao: a smart yellow diesel loco, a post van and a number of elderly dark green coaches. The ticket-office opened just as the train got in, and at last I purchased my FEVE ticket to León. I boarded one of the more respectable-looking carriages, to find that inside the seats were made of wooden slats. This was to be my home on rails for the next five hours.

A series of hoots from the locomotive and we were off, across the great Spanish plain or Meseta. A flat crossing with the broad-gauge RENFE Barruelo branch provided some interest. The station buildings on the La Robla line, though rather neglected-looking, were delightful; attractive two-storey buildings with their name incised on a plaque. Many of them had ceramic tiles bearing advertisements for services or products that had probably long since been discontinued. A few stunted trees had been planted along the platforms, perhaps to give waiting passengers some shelter from the scorching summer sun.

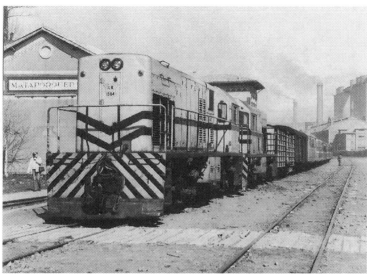
Train for León at Mataporquera

As a stranger and a foreigner, I was an object of some curiosity in my compartment. Unlike British travellers, who board a train and then sit as far away as possible from any other passengers, a Spaniard will probably choose a seat right next to the one other occupant of an empty carriage. Most travellers on the La Robla train seemed to be using it for short hops between stations, which was strange considering how unpunctual it was. Could these peasant women really have been waiting for four hours at a tiny shelterless halt, just to travel ten or fifteen kilometres to a station further along the line? It would have been quicker to walk.

I hadn't brought any food with me, and was feeling quite hungry by the time we reached Santibáñez de la Peña. Here I was joined by a Spanish family who insisted on feeding me lukewarm tortilla, which they had wrapped in aluminium foil, washed down with rough red wine from a leather bottle. It tasted great. Unfortunately my Spanish was fairly rudimentary at that time, and I had not really mastered the difference between saying 'I love' and 'I like', so I think I told them that I was anxious to develop a carnal knowledge of Spanish narrow-gauge railways!

There was a wonderful sunset over the plain, and I half-expected to see Don Quixote and Sancho Panza themselves riding across it. Rocinante would probably have gone from Bilbao to León faster than this train, which was scheduled to take ten hours and 25 minutes to travel 335 kilometres! The Spanish used to tell a lot of jokes about the slowness of their trains, but the La Robla line was legendary.

From Cistierna station, things started looking up. The station buildings were smarter and freshly-painted in the FEVE house colour of blue; the ticket-offices appeared to be open, and there were even a few freight wagons or spare passenger coaches in the yards. For these final 70 kilometres to León actually had a regular service of commuter trains in addition to the daily *Correo*.

It was dark when we rumbled into León's pretty narrow-gauge station, and the handful of working light bulbs on the train gave very little illumination. I was a little worried about where I would spend the night, but I had been in Spain long enough to know that 11pm is not really all that late. When I left the train I looked out for a sign saying 'Hostal' and went in. The man at the reception desk explained that they were full, but, not to worry, he knew a woman who had a flat nearby and she sometimes rented out a spare room. He made a quick phone call and wrote down the directions on the back of an envelope. Looking back now, it seems incredible that this elderly woman was quite happy to let a complete stranger into her flat at such an hour, and that my night's accommodation cost only about £1.50.

León FEVE station

León is a beautiful city, and its Roman city walls, Basilica of San Isidro and magnificent Gothic Cathedral are all well worth a visit. But what impressed me most of all was the Parador San Marcos with its wonderful façade. This incredible building was founded as a monastery in the 12th century to provide lodging for poor pilgrims making their way to the shrine at Santiago. No poor pilgrims stay there now, as it is a luxurious five-star hotel, and in 1981 all I could do was gaze in through the ground-floor windows! Happily, 19 years later I returned to León and this time I really did stay in the Parador!

Parador San Marcos, León

After my weekend in Léon, I longed to explore the other half of the line, from Mataporquera to Bilbao. But I didn't get a chance to do so until the Easter holidays, when I arranged to meet up with some English friends in Cordoba. As I had some time in hand, I decided to start my journey with a ride from Santander to Mataporquera as before, then take the FEVE train to Bilbao and an overnight train to Madrid, from where I would pick up a train to Cordoba. I didn't book the Bilbao - Madrid or the Madrid - Cordoba journeys, just in case my train to Bilbao was as late as the train to León had been!

I need not have worried. This time I only had a short wait at Mataporquera before the 13h40 to Bilbao appeared, dead on time. It looked a lot smarter than it had six months previously; the yellow loco and post van were the same, but the ancient green carriages had been replaced by somewhat younger blue ones. I suspect that the recent electrification of the suburban lines around Santander had allowed FEVE to cascade some more recent stock onto the line. I was relieved to find that now the coaches even boasted upholstered seats!

FEVE Train for Bilbao

The line to the east of Mataporquera was quite different in character to that to the west. The station buildings were similar and the track was equally poorly-maintained, but the scenery was not the same. Whereas from Mataporquera to León the line crosses a high plateau and does not gain or lose much height, from Mataporquera to Bilbao the track must somehow descend to sea level from an altitude of 914 metres. After snaking across the plain for a few kilometres, following the RENFE line to Santander that was just to the left, the metre-gauge rails veered to the right, ducked underneath the N611 trunk road and stopped in a little station called Los Carabeos. None of the stations along this stretch of line seemed well-placed to serve a settlement of any size, yet at most of them one or two passengers got on or off. The conductor, who was quite chatty, pointed out a small stream to me: it was the infant River Ebro, the longest river wholly within Spain.

My train ran alongside the Ebro, then crossed it and entered a scenic valley before emerging on the shore of a vast lake. In fact it was a reservoir, the Embalse del Ebro. It is 20 kilometres long and up to four kilometres wide; we seemed to spend ages riding alongside it. Seven small villages were drowned when the lake was created, and the bell-tower of Villanueva parish church still stands, rising incredibly out of the waters. It can be seen near Rozas railway station. Unfortunately the rough riding of the little train meant that I could not hold my camera steady enough to photograph this landmark.

Leaving the lake, the line lost about 200 metres of height in about 20 kilometres, with lots of sharp curves and quite a few tunnels. The tunnels all seemed rather too large for the train: were they built to fit the tall smokestacks of Victorian locomotives, or were they perhaps made oversize to save costs later if the line was ever converted to broad gauge?

The conductor drew my attention to a small wayside station called Cidad-Dosante. To the left of the metre-gauge track, on a lower level, was the former Cidad-Dosante RENFE station, the terminus of the line that should have reached Santander. It looked forlorn and abandoned, its platforms waiting for trains that would never come.

The narrow-gauge line levelled out and pressed on, through a lengthy tunnel at Sotoscueva, to reach Espinosa de los Monteros, just a large village but by far the biggest place I had seen since leaving Mataporquera. There was a great deal of activity here as sacks were unloaded from the Post Office van behind the locomotive. The conductor advised me that we would be stopping for about ten minutes here, so I had time to get off and take some photos.

Espinosa de los Monteros

The big descent continued after Espinosa, which is at 739 metres above sea level. By the time we reached Anzo, 35 minutes and 27 kilometres later, the altitude was only 469. From then it was a gradual decline all the way to Bilbao.

The line had been following the course of the River Cadagua for some time before we suddenly started passing houses, apartment blocks, cars and some rather scruffy industrial buildings. The little streams crossed by the line became dirtier, and plastic bags and rubbish dangled from the overhanging branches of trees. We passed an old-fashioned locomotive roundhouse with a turntable, and then slowed for the station of Balmaseda. Like Cistierna, this station was the terminus of a suburban service, only this time from Bilbao, and it marked our entrance into the Basque country. From now the train was busier, more and more passengers got on or off at stations, and the stations themselves looked much more purposeful and businesslike. Their names changed too, from the Castilian Mercadillo and Menamayor to the Basque Zalla and Aranguren.

At Zalla I spotted another narrow-gauge train on a railway line over to the left. It was the Santander-Bilbao line. The two lines ran parallel for a while, then joined up at the inelegantly-named station of Sodupe, where it appeared that the former La Robla line had been lifted and all traffic concentrated on the Santander line. A few kilometres further on, the two lines separated again, but were in use as a conventional double-track railway, with trains to Bilbao using one line and trains from Bilbao the other. At the village of Iráuregui, the two tracks were some distance apart, and there were actually separate station buildings for up and down trains! Many of the buildings around here were defaced with graffiti and fly-posting, much of it in support of ETA, the Basque separatist movement. One particularly dramatic mural, protesting against the planned construction of a nuclear power station at Lemoniz (abandoned the following year), showed a plane dropping dollar bills on a pile of skulls, in a parody of the Civil War bombing of Guernica.

View from the train

In 1982 Bilbao was rather a grimy industrial town, well off the tourist track, although the narrow-gauge railway station was an impressive place, far more elaborate than the mainline RENFE terminus. The city has now re-invented itself, notably since the construction of the Guggenheim Museum, and has become somewhere that people visit out of interest, even a short-break destination. It has brought back trams and opened a smart new underground railway.

I did not linger very long in Bilbao on that occasion. I said goodbye to my friend the conductor and walked to the nearby RENFE station, where I bought a ticket to Madrid. I had to change trains in Miranda de Ebro, which despite its beautiful name is actually rather an unexciting place with a big chemical works. The train that took me to Madrid was the overnight service that had started out from Irun, on the French border.

Changing trains in Madrid was very easy. Most trains from the North terminated in the modern station of Chamartín, just to the north of the city. Trains to the south left from the centrally-located Atocha Station, close to Retiro Park and the Prado. An efficient electric underground railway, run by the RENFE and not part of Madrid's metro system, linked the two. I went down the escalator, boarded a bright blue-and-yellow electric multiple-unit to *Atocha apaedero*, and then took another escalator up to the main station with its fine 19th-century train shed. Back in 1982 trains from Madrid to Andalusia were infrequent and slow. I went to the ticket-window to get a ticket for the *rápido* to Cordoba, as my friends had already agreed to meet me off it at the station. Sadly I was told that the train was full. They could only sell me a ticket for the *tren omnibus*, which left three hours later and took almost nine hours!

After a few moments hesitation, I bought the ticket and decided to take a chance. Nobody ever stopped anyone from getting on a Spanish train. If I got on the *rápido* and stood in the corridor, the guard wouldn't be able to throw me off until we reached Alcázar de San Juan, in two hours' time. With any luck I might even get a seat by then. I could even pretend that I didn't speak Spanish and didn't understand that the ticket I'd bought was for a different train!

I left it until the last moment and then slipped on, about halfway along the train. It was indeed full. After walking up and down looking in vain for a seat, I resigned myself to standing up in the corridor at the end of one of the carriages. There were quite a few others standing there, rather dishevelled student types, I guessed. They were laughing and joking and taking about how they would hide in the toilet when the conductor came along. My Spanish had greatly improved since my first trip on the *La Robla* railway, and I decided to strike up a conversation with them as the train set off across the plains of Castille.

Façade of Bilbao FEVE station

They seemed friendly and were quite happy to talk to an English guy who was teaching in Spain. They were indeed students, going home for the Easter holidays. We talked about university life, about Lady Diana and the Falklands crisis, which was the main item on the news. I was asked whether England (they said "Inglaterra" rather than "Gran Bretaña") would send a task force if the Spanish occupied Gibraltar!

During a lull in the conversation, one of the more disreputable-looking of my travelling-companions suddenly nudged me, winked and asked: *"¿Hé, tienes chocolate?"*

'Have you got any chocolate?' seemed a bizarre request. But, as it happened, I had four 150-gram bars of Galaxy in my backpack, having brought them back from a recent trip home. I had taken them to share with my friends in Cordoba, as one of them was a real chocoholic and I knew she hadn't had any English chocolate for months. But the young Spanish students looked as if they needed feeding up, so I unzipped my backpack (which seemed to excite them), pulled out one of the bars and started breaking it carefully into small squares, which I handed out to them.

I was unprepared for the reaction. There was a chorus of guffaws and I wondered whether I had committed some cardinal sin. Perhaps they didn't like English chocolate? Should I have offered the whole bar rather than dividing it into pieces? The students sniggered again and exchanged a few words I didn't understand. I decided they must be making fun of me. Fortunately at that moment the train pulled into Alcázar de San Juan, and I was able to grab a seat. When the conductor came I had to pay a small supplement for upgrading to a faster train.

My friends met me off the train in Cordoba four hours later and we headed off to a bar for a drink. They were with a Spanish friend, and I told him about the incident on the train. He laughed loudly and then asked me:

"Don't you know what *chocolate* means?"

"Yes, of course. Chocolate."

"Yes, but it's also slang for something else!"

"What?"

"Marijuana!"

Spanish railways have changed almost beyond recognition since 1982. Although a Beeching-type axe fell on numerous under-used RENFE lines in 1984, the high-speed network had grown and flourished. And I am happy to say that, after a decade of closure, one can once again travel the length of the metre-gauge line between León and Bilbao. Although, sadly, there is still only one through train a day, it now covers the 335 kilometres in a mere seven-and-a-half hours! If you prefer, you can even travel the line on the luxury *El Transcantabrico* cruise-train.

As for those wishing to travel from Madrid to Cordoba, these cities are now linked by frequent *AVE* high-speed trains that do the journey in just one-and-three-quarter hours. The old 19th-century train shed at Atocha has become a botanical garden, the terminus having been rebuilt to serve the new trains. However you get there, the beautiful city of Cordoba, with its picturesque Jewish Quarter and wonderful Cathedral that was once a mosque, remains a must-see destination. (Galaxy chocolate is an optional accessory).

Atocha station – now a botanical garden

13. Deep-Freeze in Finse and on the Flåmsbana

November 13, 1991: A wintry trip from Bergen to Oslo

When I first started talking to people about great railway journeys, one route that was frequently mentioned as a 'must' was the Norwegian Railways' main line from Oslo to Bergen. Almost everyone agreed that this was a journey not to be missed. The short branch line from Myrdal to Flåm, a tributary of the Oslo-Bergen line, seemed to be equally as famous as the main line. I just had to see for myself.

It would perhaps be more fitting to start the journey in Oslo, but Bergen is a wonderful place to spend a few days either before or after travelling the line. This beautiful Hanseatic city has a great deal to offer with its sensational location, the old timber buildings of the Bryggen quarter, Grieg's house at Trollhaugen and the medieval Rosenkrantz Tower and King Haakon's Hall. Of particular interest to the railway enthusiast is the dramatic, steep, 844-metre funicular up Mount Floien, which acts as part of the city's normal public transport rather than merely as a tourist attraction, and has three intermediate halts, most unusual on a funicular railway.

On this occasion I stayed overnight in the Scandic Hotel in Bergen and took a taxi the next morning to the city's impressive railway station. The first train I boarded was an anonymous red suburban electric unit that I rode as far as Voss. This one-hour journey was splendid enough, when the train was not hiding in a tunnel, and although the landscape was somewhat bleak and windswept there was no snow to be seen.

At Voss I enjoyed coffee and cakes in a café and explored the town, with its ancient, tiny stone church and dramatic mountain vistas. The railway station showed it to be a place of some importance; there was even a branch line leading off from here to Granvin, although this was closed to passengers at the time of my visit and I understand has subsequently been lifted and converted into a cycle path.

Train from Bergen at Myrdal

I returned to Voss station and boarded a second red electric train to Myrdal. The journey from Voss to Myrdal was much more dramatic as the line climbs through the Raundalen Valley and passes through the Gravahalsen tunnel. In places the line was protected by snow-sheds, which, unfortunately, spoiled the view. But before long we were in a driving snowstorm and any further sightseeing was impossible.

On arrival at Myrdal station I stepped off the train into a blizzard! A narrow strip along the edge had been cleared, but the rest of the platform was under a four-foot covering of snow. I made my way gingerly to the waiting-room, which was pleasantly warm. I now had ten minutes to wait before the branch line train to Flåm.

When the Flåm train appeared out of the gloom and the snow, it was a proper locomotive-hauled train rather than a multiple-unit. It consisted merely of an elderly-looking electric loco and two carriages, second class only. But appearances can be deceiving: this modest little branch-line train was apparently equipped with no fewer than five different braking systems. About a score of passengers joined the train with me, and we were soon on our way.

The Flåm train at Myrdal

The journey from Myrdal to Flåm was downhill all the way. The train had to lose no fewer than 863.5 metres in altitude in a journey of only twenty kilometres. For most of the way there was hardly any sign of human habitation, and there were no intermediate stations to speak of, apart from a halt by a frozen waterfall at Kjofossen.

As we lost height, we also left the snow behind. From the permanent deep-freeze that was Myrdal, we came down to a level where there was just a gentle Christmassy sprinkling on the ground and on the foliage alongside the line. When we finally reached the terminus, after 50 long minutes, there was no snow at all - the grass was green and it felt like a normal Autumn day. I left the train, took some photos and inspected an old electric locomotive that was plinthed out of use by the station. Most of my fellow-passengers ran off and boarded a ferry for a cruise along the Sognefjord.

A small exhibition at the station told the history of this remarkable line, which must have been one of the most difficult and expensive of its length to construct anywhere in the world. It took 17 years to build, was completed in 1940, and, incredibly, was operated by steam locomotives for five years before being electrified at the end of the Second World War.

Flåm itself is little more than a hamlet; its railway station owes its existence not to its importance as a centre of population but as a convenient place for onward transport. For most of the year a fair proportion of the travellers on the Flåmsbana are tourists who make the trip as part of a circular tour. Leaving by train from Bergen or Voss, they take the mainline railway to Myrdal, the branch line to Flåm and then the ferry from Flåm to Gudvangen. Here they board a country bus for a journey back along mountain roads to Voss. The whole journey, which can equally well be done in reverse, is marketed by tour operators as *Norway in a Nutshell.*

Flåm Railway Station

Sadly on this occasion I did not have time to do the full trip, as I had a booking on the overnight train from Oslo to Stockholm. So I re-boarded the little electric train that took me back up the mountainside to snowy Myrdal. The weather here had not improved, and, indeed, when I boarded the mainline express to Oslo the snow followed us all the way. At each station stop we lost a few minutes, as we passed over the summit of the line at Finse, 1,222 metres above sea level, and made our way gradually downhill past frozen lakes and icy waterfalls to the Norwegian capital. On our approach to Oslo a conductor passed through our carriage; he apologised profusely about our delay (we were now some 25 minutes late) and checked whether anyone had missed an onward connection. Luckily I had plenty of time before the Stockholm sleeper; in fact, I was rather glad to have spent an extra half-hour on a comfortable warm train rather than in a draughty station waiting-room.

Oslo's main railway station, like its cathedral, is functional but of rather modest dimensions for the city it serves. It is perhaps a slight anticlimax to a magnificent journey, but then perhaps no terminus could possibly match the grandeur of the majestic Bergen - Oslo line.

14. *An overnight ride to Russia*

April 21-22, 1997: Helsinki to Moscow on the *Tolstoi*

There is something quite special about countries that I have only ever travelled to by surface transport. These days most of my longer-distance travelling tends to be by air, but occasionally I have crossed a border and entered a new country overland. Russia is unusual for me as I have only ever travelled there by train.

My first visit to Russia was in 1996, when the company I worked for was arranging a programme of lecture tours in Great Britain and Europe for an American tour operator. On that occasion I flew to Helsinki and then travelled by rail to an icy cold St Petersburg, where I inspected several hotels, met up with suppliers and enjoyed a free tram ride by accident: I had not realised that tickets could not be purchased on board.

Helsinki railway station and tram

The following year I decided to revisit Russia on holiday, but this time I had the country's capital city in my sights. Once again I planned to travel via Helsinki, but now I would be taking the Tolstoi, the once-daily through train, to Moscow. And I would have a travelling companion this time - my good friend Laura. We had previously visited Istanbul and Prague together, and she would come in extremely useful on this trip as she spoke and understood a bit of Russian!

We started our spring odyssey with a flight to Stockholm, where we spent a couple of days exploring the city. We then took the comfortable overnight Silja Line ferry to Helsinki and did a tour of the city on the '3T' tram, which loops around the centre in a figure-of-eight. In the afternoon we made our way to the monumental railway station for our train to Moscow.

Helsinki station, designed by Finnish architect Eliel Saarinen and opened in 1919, is a dramatic granite building with arched windows and a lofty tower, and was obviously designed with care, but there was no shelter of any kind on the platforms. I understand that a glazed overall roof, which was part of the architect's original design, has now at last been provided!

The author by the Tolstoi

Laura and I waited in the booking hall until our train came in. It consisted of a rake of grey-green coaches hauled by a powerful-looking electric locomotive. The latter was Finnish but the carriages were definitely Russian: we had a two-berth sleeping compartment that converted to seating accommodation for day use. The sides were panelled in wood-effect Formica and the upholstery was a deep red with floral patterns. It was not the most comfortable sleeping compartment I have been in, but was one of the more spacious, thanks partly to the broad gauge used by Finnish and Russian railways.

The Tolstoi departed Helsinki at 17.08 and spent two hours covering the 283 kilometres to the border station of Vainikkala. Opened in 1870, this line was very fast considering the roundabout nature of the route: there is no line along the coast east of the Finnish capital, and to reach the Russian border our train had to travel north to Riihimäki, then north-east to Lahti and finally south-east through Kouvola to Vainikkala.

An hour or so into our journey, Laura and I decided to investigate the dining-car. Although we were still in Finland the catering arrangements were rather Soviet-esque. Laura was a vegetarian and there appeared to be no 'veggie' option on the menu; when she explained her dilemma to the catering attendant he returned with a small bowl containing a lettuce leaf, a tomato, a slice of lemon and a small chunk of cucumber.

There appeared to be no reason for long delays at Vainikkala, but our train was scheduled to spend a whole 45 minutes there. There was then a stop in the no-man's land station of Luzhaika before we reached Vyborg. There was another long stop here, and this is where the Russian customs formalities took place. Our passports received a large 'Vyborg' entry stamp with the small outline of a steam locomotive on it. This is where we stepped onto Russian soil - well, concrete - for the first time. Vyborg station was a palatial station with a massive neo-Classical colonnade. I assumed that it dated back to the opening of the line, but I later found out that it was a Stalinist-era construction, the previous building (almost a copy of that at Helsinki) having been destroyed during the Second World War. At Vyborg our modern Finnish electric locomotive was changed for an older Russian one.

Finnish locomotive at Vyborg

On my previous journey to Russia I had seen Vyborg station by daylight, and noticed a steam locomotive parked on a snowy siding. Was it a museum piece or could it possibly still have been in use? On this trip I was unable to confirm this, as it was dark, and once Laura and I were back on the train we settled down for the night.

Russian locomotive at Moscow

Beyond Vyborg we joined the main line from St Petersburg to Moscow. This railway was opened in 1851, the same year as that between Ashford and Hastings, but whereas much of Britain's present-day network had been completed by this date, this was Russia's first trunk line. It has something else in common with the Kent line apart from its date of construction: both had their route decided by a military leader who had no experience of railway engineering. The remarkably straight course of the Russian line can be attributed to Tsar Nicholas I. The story goes that when he was asked to choose the route, he simply sent for a ruler and drew a line on the map between Russia's two major cities. Fortunately the country is flat and there were no major obstacles!

When we awoke and pulled back the curtains, the countryside that greeted us was not especially scenic. It was generally monotonous farming country interspersed with belts of forest. But the towns and cities we passed through were even less attractive. They consisted mainly of featureless concrete apartment blocks, with muddy streets and almost everything a dull khaki colour. I suppose that places like Bologoye and Tver might have beautiful historic districts, but everything visible from the train was hideous in the extreme.

The attendant served us hot drinks from the samovar before we arrived at Moskva Leningradsky station, which still retained its Soviet-era name and its large statue of Lenin outside. The station itself was relatively anonymous, an unremarkable gateway to the city. Laura and I were met by the representative from our travel agency and taken to the Danilovsky Hotel, a relatively modern place built on the premises of a Russian Orthodox monastery.

The Moscow Metro

The outstanding railway feature of Moscow is, of course, its palatial Metro. Its beautiful stations with chandeliers, wall-paintings and elaborate architectural flourishes are well-known from tourist brochures, but in actual fact many of the stations outside the city centre are quite ordinary - though well-maintained and graffiti-free. We had to travel to the city centre to find the underground palaces that are as much part of the city as the Kremlin and the Bolshoi Theatre.

All too soon our holiday was over and we returned by train to Helsinki. Our luggage was checked by the customs officials, who seemed most concerned that we might be illegally exporting works of art. There was something slightly sinister about being stopped and asked awkward questions by a man in a uniform on a Russian train - but I need not have worried: I was not Yuri Zhivago and my companion was not *quite* Lara!

15. Steam trains, a Soaking in Stiege and a Stasi Cat

November 18, 1991: On the wrong side of the former Iron Curtain, I cross the Harz Mountains by steam in appalling weather

I well remember watching the fall of the Berlin Wall on television in 1989. As I had worked in travel for several years by then, I was aware of all the rigmarole of crossing borders. Our tour managers needed things called 'Berolina vouchers' when taking groups to East Germany, and every traveller required a visa and needed to change 25 Deutschemarks a day into Ostmarks. Visas were only obtainable once hotel reservations had been made. All in all, only the most dedicated enthusiasts would actually bother to burrow a hole through all that red tape just to ride on a narrow-gauge railway.

And now, suddenly, it looked as if travel to East Germany was going to become as easy as travel to the West. The psychological barriers were disintegrating as quickly as the physical ones. By November 1991 it was almost as if the East and West Germanies had never existed.

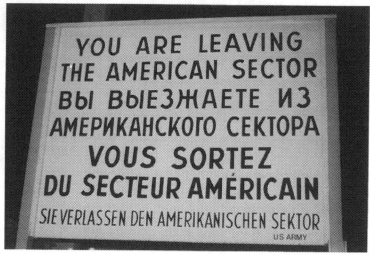

Entering East Germany!

Almost… For whilst the West was as smart and prosperous as ever, the East still retained an air of genteel poverty that was not unattractive. As my standard-gauge diesel-hauled train took me from Berlin to Halberstadt, I sat alone in the top deck of a double-deck second-class carriage and wondered what would await me in the Harz Mountains.

I had 40 minutes in Halberstadt, just enough time for a short wander around the town, where a tiny, twin-axle tram with its destination in Gothic letters was waiting outside the station. I boarded a branch-line train for Wernigerode, which was a very un-Teutonic 20 minutes late. The scenery was rural, with farms, old churches and windmills. Wernigerode was a charming, fairytale town where half-timbered houses clustered around a hill topped by a Gothic castle that looked as if it ought to be home to a beautiful princess.

I had come to Wernigerode to ride on the Harzquerbahn, the steam-worked metre-gauge railway that served the Harz Mountains. Unlike most narrow-gauge steam railways in Europe, this was not a short preserved line but a genuine local transport system operating a main line and branches with a total length of 130 kilometres. Opened in the last few years of the 19th century, the railways of the Harz Mountains had become a living museum, and I was determined to see them before they were either modernised beyond recognition, tidied up for tourists or closed altogether.

Wernigerode Railway Station

My first impression of the railway was slightly disappointing. A passenger train was waiting - yes - and it consisted of exquisite little carriages with open balconies such as I had seen on tourist lines but never before in regular service. But it was hauled by a hideous, oversized diesel locomotive. Could it be that the Harzquerbahn had replaced all their steam engines without telling me?

I went to the ticket-office and consulted the timetable. It was complicated, with few trains travelling the entire length of the 'main' line from Wernigerode to Halberstadt, but it was quite possible to do the trip in three or four stages, and the idea of stopping and changing trains rather appealed to me. In any case, I did not want to travel to Halberstadt today, as I had a hotel room booked for the night in Alexisbad, which was on a branch off the main line.

If I missed the waiting diesel, my next train was not until 14.12. I asked the station staff if it would be a *dampfzug*. I was assured that it would. My mind was now made up. Off I went for an exploration of the town, followed by a pizza for 6DM - the cheapest lunch I had in Germany! The town somehow evoked a sense of the past that was missing in the over-restored touristy villages of the Rhineland and the Moselle Valley that I had visited a few years before.

Around half-past one I was back at the station, watching a real steam locomotive being coaled, watered, coupled and eventually being reversed alongside the platform. Although narrow-gauge, it was quite an impressive size. Its works plate showed that it was relatively young, built in 1954 by the VEB Lokomotivbau Karl Marx at Babelsberg. I wonder what Karl Marx would have thought about giving his name to a locomotive factory?

I took my seat in one of the red-and-cream carriages and waited for our departure. The train was only moderately filled. The railway timetables had not changed since DDR days and seemed to be designed for factories that were no longer working or for shoppers who had now bought cars. A light drizzle started as we headed off, accompanied by wonderful steam-engine sounds, over a busy level-crossing that did not have any gates or barriers. Less than a kilometre later we stopped at out first station, Wernigerode-Westerntor, named after a medieval defensive tower.

Harzquerbahn locomotive

The steam train seemed to be operating a Wernigerode suburban service, as we stopped in two other stations called Wernigerode-something, before going around a horseshoe curve and into the attractively-named halt of Steinerne Renne. The line was now climbing noticeably. We went through Thumkuhlental tunnel, which is a mere 70 metres long but is nonetheless the longest on the system.

A steep climb from the tunnel took us to the junction station of Drei Annen Hohne, where another train was waiting. This was for the steep branch to the Brocken, which at the time of my visit only went as far as a place called Schierke. The 1,125-metre summit of the Brocken, virtually on the border with West Germany, was closed to the public during the Communist era, along with its railway. Happily the line was rebuilt in 1992 and is now by far the most frequented part of the whole network, with ten-coach steam-hauled trains leaving every 45 minutes in high season!

I stayed on the mainline train, which paused at a little woodland station called Elend and climbed through forests to the highest point on the line, just before the station of Sorge. This was the former junction with an east-west running narrow-gauge line, the Südharz-Eisenbahn, which found itself chopped in two with the partition of Germany and was closed in the late 1940s.

My train terminated at Benneckstein, where I had nearly an hour to kill before the 16.40 to Eisfelder Talmühle. Luckily there was a shelter on the platform, but as the drizzle turned to heavy rain I wrapped myself up against the elements. An inspection of the station building revealed one Cold War relic - a wooden East German telephone kiosk, out of use, with a slot for 20-pfennig coins. The 20-pfennig was a uniquely DDR denomination; they never had them in the Federal Republic. I wondered if there had been any protests against the demonetisation of the 20-pfennig coin. Leaving these thoughts aside, I went to the gleaming new yellow Federal-style call-box in the station forecourt, slotted in a few Deutschemarks and made a call home.

The Eisfelder Talmühle train rattled in, dead on time, behind another of those majestic 2-10-2 steam locomotives. It took all of 32 minutes to travel 12 kilometres, with one intermediate stop at Tiefenbachmühle.

Eisdelder Talmühle is one of those strange junction stations in the middle of nowhere, a bit like Mataporquera in Spain or Siquirres in Costa Rica. The station building was quite large, but devoid of any kind of shelter. Luckily I had only five minutes before the connecting train to Stiege, which arrived on time at 17.17, also steam-hauled.

By now it was already almost dark and I couldn't really appreciate the Harz scenery any more. The train reversed out of the station and headed east, up a steeply-graded line with one intermediate station, the surprisingly English-sounding Birkenmoor. The next stop was at Stiege, another junction, where I stepped off, straight into a puddle.

The crew asked me where I was heading. "Alexisbad" I replied.

They indicated that I should have remained on the train, as it was going up to Hasselfelde, terminus of another branch, then back to Stiege and then along the branch to Alexisbad. The prospect of another ten kilometres on a narrow-gauge steam train was certainly much more enticing than the thought of waiting in the rain for half an hour. So I took a seat in the front carriage of the otherwise empty train and enjoyed the sounds of the engine and the warm glow from the firebox. The train reached the terminus at Hasselfelde at 18.16, but I had no time to explore, as ten minutes later we were off again. We made a perfunctory stop at Stiege junction and then started trundling along the line to Alexisbad. This is, strictly speaking, not part of the Harzquerbahn, but a separate railway called the Selketalbahn.

At 19.30 the train reached Alexisbad. I had been riding narrow-gauge steam trains for over five hours! Although my hotel was almost directly opposite the station, I nonetheless got quite wet running there. Getting my key, I went up to my room. The bedroom and bathroom fittings were rather basic in style, but everything worked. I had a soak in the bath, changed and then sat on the bed, thinking about going down for dinner.

It was then that I realised it was now eight o'clock. That meant seven o'clock in the UK. I was then and still am a great fan of *The Archers* and there was a particularly interesting story-line that I didn't want to miss. I dug my little transistor radio from the depths of my backpack and tuned in to 1500 metres Long Wave. There was nothing but crackles and static.

Built-in to the headboard of the bed was an ancient-looking radio, with battered chromium switches and knobs. I turned it on, expecting nothing. The room filled with German pop music. I retuned to Long Wave and found *Barwick Green*, the *Archers'* signature tune, playing loud and clear. I was quite surprised that a hotel radio from the DDR era was able to pick up the capitalist BBC Radio 4 so well.

The next morning the weather had not improved. I was up for a quick breakfast at seven and then crossed the road to the station for the 07.34 train to Eisfelder Talmühle. The scenery was delightful but the conditions were poor for photography. This was my last steam-hauled journey in the Harz Mountains and I enjoyed every minute of it. At 09.07 precisely the train deposited me at Eisfelder Talmühle station.

I now had half-an-hour to wait in the rain at a deserted junction. Pulling up the collar of my raincoat, I sought a platform bench that was sheltered to some extent by the eaves of the station building. Then I had the uneasy feeling that I was not alone. Someone was watching me. Perhaps this was only to be expected in the former DDR, just two years after the Wall came down.

The piercing green eyes that were staring at me belonged to a large, scruffy black tomcat. His battered and scarred ears showed that he had been in a fair number of fights; he was certainly no youngster. Cats are my favourite animals and here I thought was my chance to get a feline perspective on German reunification. This creature must have lived most of its nine lives under Communism. What had it been like? Was cat food any better now? Were the mice any different?

Although I spoke in a mixture of German and cattish, and made all the right noises, Puss just kept staring at me with his huge green eyes. He then hissed, leaped towards me and attempted to scratch me with his razor-sharp claws. I managed to move aside just in time. He then jumped off the bench and dismissed me with a swish of his tail. I am used to that sort of reaction from a woman, but not from a cat.

09.37 came and went, and the scheduled train to Nordhausen did not appear. Since every train I had taken on the Harzquerbahn had been dead on time, I was a little worried, and now I couldn't even ask the station cat whether anything was the matter. The train appeared three minutes late, behind a hideous diesel like the one I had seen the day before in Wernigerode. I found myself sitting next to a group of West German railway enthusiasts, and they told me that the diesel engine was actually a standard-gauge shunting locomotive converted to metre-gauge. No wonder it looked oversized when coupled to those quaint Edwardian carriages - rather like the sort of train a youngster might create from bits picked up at different stands in a model railway exhibition.

On the way to Nordhausen, my travelling companions pointed out a disused spur that once led to the notorious Dora concentration camp, whose unfortunate inmates were employed in making V1 and V2 flying bombs. It all seemed so far away in the reunified Germany of the 1990s.

Nordhausen narrow-gauge station was rather a gloomy affair, not a place to linger. Discovering that the standard-gauge station was next door, and that my train wasn't due for nearly two hours, I decided to explore the town. A little yellow tram was waiting at a stop, its destination showing as 'Marktplatz'. I hopped on and enjoyed my first tram ride in the former DDR. The tram was well-filled as it made its way along the street past the ubiquitous Trabants and Wartburgs. Marktplatz proved not to be very far away at all. I had a look around the shops but found no postcards of the railway.

The ubiquitous Trabant

At Nordhausen main-line station it was almost as if I had entered another era. There at the station platform was a modern blue-and-white diesel multiple-unit of the sort I had seen all over Germany. It whisked me off efficiently along the standard-gauge line towards Northeim, a former cross-border route so recently re-opened that it was not shown on my *Thomas Cook Rail Map of Europe*.

The first few stations along the line were neglected and drab-looking; some of them still had the Gothic style nameboards that I associate with a certain genre of war movie. We then passed a mass of derelict fortifications; watchtowers, razor wire and blockhouses. Shortly after this we pulled into a bright, well-maintained station called Bad Sachsa. We had crossed the erstwhile border and I was back in the West.

Chatting with a German friend and fellow cat-lover in Ulm sometime later, I told her about my feline encounter at Eisfelder Talmühle.

"It must have been a Stasi cat" she said.

NORTH

AMERICAN

JOURNEYS

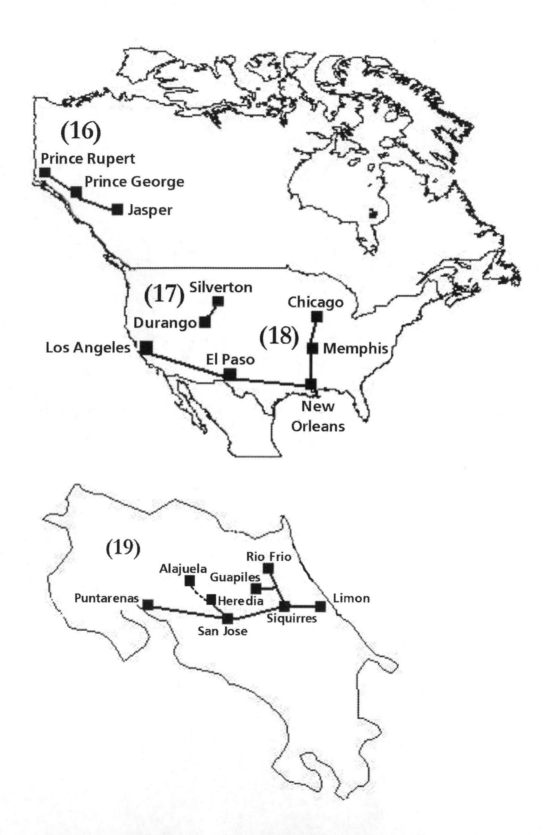

16. Across the roof of Canada

March 24 - 25, 2006: A long, slow and beautiful journey through Alberta and British Columbia

Some years ago in an amateur dramatic production I had to stand up on stage and proclaim "I don't want to go to Canada!" At the time I could not have predicted that one day I would travel right across the country!

Canada is vast, varied and extremely beautiful, with only a fraction of the population of its brasher southern neighbour. Astonishingly, one of Canada's claims to fame is that it has more miles of railway track per inhabitant than any other country on earth.

Whilst the completion of the USA's first transcontinental railroad in 1869 was commemorated with all the panoply of brass bands and the driving-in of a golden spike, the Canadians completed their line in 1885 with little ceremony and a simple iron spike. But whilst the Americans built *their* railroad, it was in many ways the Canadian Pacific Railway that built Canada. The people of British Columbia only agreed to join the union if they could have a railway connection, and its completion transformed a string of separate British colonies into a proud new nation.

Sadly, as in many other countries, passenger rail travel in Canada has declined dramatically since its heyday a century ago. One line closed to passengers in the 1980s was the southern route through the Rocky Mountains, passing through Medicine Hat, Calgary and Banff. Part of this line is now served by *The Rocky Mountaineer*, unashamedly a tourist train, that offers every imaginable comfort to its passengers.

Perhaps the greatest monuments to the Canadian railway companies are the vast hotels that they built for their passengers. The country is studded by them. The Fort Garry in Winnipeg still dominates the city; the Banff Springs Hotel is a 13-storey, 770-room Scottish Baronial castle that would make a perfect set for Warner Brothers - I can well imagine seeing Harry Potter, Ron and Hermione emerge on broomsticks from one of its turret rooms. Perhaps the most famous of all is the Château Lake Louise, at one end of the most perfect lake in the Rockies. At the time of my visit the lake is frozen and the hotel and its grounds look like a picture from a Christmas card.

Driving away from the hotel I can't resist making a short detour when I see a sign pointing to the Historic Railway Station. About two miles from the hotel, it is a delightful log-cabin type building festooned with icicles. The station and hotel were opened at the same time by the Canadian Pacific railway company, but now no passenger trains stop at Lake Louise. A huge freight train rumbles through the station and I get some photos before driving off, for one of the most beautiful roads in North America beckons - the Icefields Parkway. More prosaically called Highway 93, it leaves the Trans-Canada near Lake Louise and heads north through an Arctic wilderness to Jasper. The carriageway is perfectly clear, but there are huge mounds of snow by the sides and most of the rest areas and side roads are closed. The scenery is stunning and I keep stopping for photos.

The old railway station at Lake Louise

Roughly halfway along there is a motel and gas station where I stretch my legs and get a bottle of mineral water. The dry cold air of the Rockies seems to have made me thirsty.

Up to now I have seen no wildlife at all. Just on the approach to Jasper, however, I see something move by the road and pull off for a closer look. Two quadrupeds are grazing. Deer of some sort? No antlers though. Can they be elk or even moose? I take a photo and later have them identified as white-tailed deer.

Jasper was a surprise - a kind of lumpy New Romney. The streets are lined with 1930s English-seaside-looking bungalows with neat front and rear gardens. There are a few shops in the main drag by the railway line, but the town is much smaller than I expected. One very un-New Romneyish feature are the little brown balls that are on the ground everywhere - elk droppings. It seems that every elk in Alberta uses Jasper as a toilet.

I stay overnight at the Jasper Inn. There is a lovely clear starry night.

After breakfast the next morning I walk into town to see if I can find the Thrifty car rental office so that I will know where to return my car. The free map I picked up at a gas station yesterday shows it as somewhere near the railway station. When I get there, I find that the office is actually INSIDE the railway station, which is ideal, as I am leaving at 12.45 on the *Skeena* train to Prince Rupert. Jasper has quite an impressive station building, with a huge totem pole and a stuffed-and-mounted steam locomotive. The station nameboard gives the distances to Montreal as 2,408.8 miles and to Vancouver as 534.9 miles, but there is no mileage shown for Prince Rupert, the destination of the *Skeena*.

I return to my hotel, check out and drive my now filthy rental car to the station.

The *Skeena* leaves dead on time at 12.45, which is the only time it will be on time in 2 days. In summer this train is long and elegant and boasts luxurious observation cars, but in winter it is reduced to a diesel locomotive, an ordinary carriage and a wonderful 1950s dome car that has a tiny buffet underneath, an art-deco curved lounge at the rear and an observation saloon on top. These dome cars were built by the Budd Company for the Canadian Pacific Railway in 1954, and the one on my train is called *Strathcona Park*.

There are only about ten passengers on the train and most of us soon forsake our reserved seats and move up to the dome car. Apart from myself and two women from Belfast, the passengers are either tourists from the USA or weather-beaten locals who stay for only a few stops and then hop off at tiny halts in the middle of nowhere. Our conductor is straight-talking Louise from Quebec, who asks if anyone on the train speaks French. I chat to her in French, but once she's established that nobody doesn't understand English, she leaves the work to her colleague Rick, a born comedian. On discovering the two Irish women he tells them he once boxed Barry McGuigan. He also claims to have driven the Royal Train that took the Queen across Canada in 1959, but since he also gives his age as 52 (which seems about right) this would have made him rather young at the time!

The journey on the Skeena is an endless parade of mountains, frozen rivers, forests and occasional small, rather down-at-heel towns. At a tiny village called Penny, Louise gets off to retrieve the mailbox and to deliver the incoming mail to the post office. This shows that the train is not just put on for the tourists. At McBride, which is about the largest place we see all day, a huntsman gets on with lots of boxes and crates that take Rick ages to load. We drop him off in the middle of a forest about 20 miles further on.

The Skeena stops at McBride

The journey is almost monotonously beautiful, but it has to be broken at Prince George, where the *Skeena* stops for the night and I walk to the Ramada Hotel, where a room has been reserved for me. Prince George is a modern industrial city of the most unbelievable dreariness, although the countryside either side of it is stunning.

My train journey continues with Rick and Louise on Saturday through the pristine and unspoilt wilderness of British Columbia. There are a few more station stops today and the villages look prettier, often with totem poles by the wayside. We go through a blizzard which reduces the visibility from the dome car somewhat. We see deer and bald eagles. I spot what looks like a large German shepherd dog walking across a frozen river - and then realise it's a wolf. There is also some serious engineering here, with tunnels and spindly trestle bridges, making one feel very vulnerable on this small train on a single-track line carving its way through the mountains without any trace of human habitation in view.

I love travelling by train but after two days on the Skeena, having heard most of Rick's jokes twice, listened to Neil Young's latest CD at least four times on my personal stereo and got to know the life histories of several elderly American couples, I am not sorry when we finally pull in to Prince Rupert. Now, if it was the summer train with the proper dining-car and luxury observation coach, and longer daylight hours to look for the wildlife, that would be another matter...

View from the rear of the Skeena

There has been a tragedy in Prince Rupert. A ferry taking passengers to Vancouver Island hit a rock and sank. Nearly all the passengers were saved but two are unaccounted for. The town - population 17,000 - is full with reporters and TV vans. Fortunately the Crest Hotel has held my room. From the station I hail a taxi, which is driven by a Chinaman. The taxi looks as if it will barely make it to the hotel. He informs me proudly that it's a 1980 Chevrolet. I lower myself into the ripped, sagging passenger seat and hope for the best. The hotel is only two kilometres away but seems further. The fare is eight dollars. I give a ten-dollar note and tell him to keep the change. I don't want to over-tip but I reckon the driver should start saving for a new cab.

The lounge on the Skeena

The Crest Hotel is swarming with hard-drinking journalists. I can't resist trying the open-air hot jacuzzi with a sea view. The restaurant is full, and the bar is crowded but I get served eventually - a nice burger and fries.

Another good night's sleep and it must be Sunday. I have already found out that the bus to Prince Rupert airport leaves from the Howard Johnson Highliner Hotel. My Chinese friend had offered to take me there, but I can see that it's only just up the road from my hotel, and I want to explore the town anyway. There's not much to see, but it's far prettier than Prince George, with some brightly-painted weatherboarded houses. On reaching the Howard Johnson, I board a wonderful 1960s or 70s stainless steel bus marked AIRPORT and sink back into a leather seat. It fills up rapidly. Just before it leaves a delightful young woman comes and sits beside me. She has big blue eyes and curly chestnut hair. Her name is Whitney (as in Houston) and she's a tourist guide, working on whale-watching cruises. At present these aren't running, so she's off to Vancouver for a few days. She talks about the ferry disaster. All Prince Rupert is talking about the ferry disaster.

I ask Whitney how long it takes to get to the airport, and she tells me the airport is on an island and we have to go there by ferry. Not the one that sunk, luckily. The coach drives onto a landing-craft type ferry and we have a very scenic mini-cruise across the bay to the airport, which is basically a log-cabin type structure and a runway. They DO check all the luggage very thoroughly, though. The plane to Vancouver is a tiny little thing with two propellers - a Dash-something-or-other, but unfortunately it's too cloudy to see anything, and Whitney is sitting several rows in front. Meanwhile Rick and Louise on the *Skeena* will already have left the station, and the train will be creeping back towards Jasper.

Cigarette break on the Skeena

17. *After a night with Marty, I ride the Rails from Durango to Silverton*

June 7, 2003: I travel on 'America's Railroad'

In the early summer of 2003 I had the chance to drive around the Wild West to research a new touring holiday for my employers. My route took me into Colorado, Arizona, Wyoming and Utah. It was in Colorado that I got the chance to travel on one of the world's most wonderful narrow-gauge railways.

The Durango & Silverton line was once part of the Denver & Rio Grande Railway, and was built to a gauge of three feet. It was constructed during the general optimism and euphoria that followed the ending of the American Civil War. Silverton was a classic boom town of the 1870s, and gained its name from the fact that silver was found here by the ton. The 45-mile railway from Durango was constructed in an incredible 11 months, by about 500 men. The adoption of a narrow gauge made construction quicker and easier, but even so it seems unbelievable to us that a railway could have been built in so short a time.

Silverton locomotive 480

I phoned the Durango & Silverton Railroad to explain that I was researching a new tour, and they offered me a complimentary journey on the line. To get myself in the mood, I spend the night before my trip in the wonderful 19th-century Strater Hotel, which backs onto the railroad tracks. Although it was a warm night, I didn't sleep particularly well: I felt unusually cold, and had the impression that somebody else was in the room with me, although I never saw them. At breakfast the next morning I was told by the staff that my room (Number 244) was haunted by a ghost called 'Marty'.

After breakfast I walked to the station to collect my ticket. The station staff treated me like royalty and issued me a pass for the rear coach of the train, a comfortable parlour car with a rear balcony offering a superb view of the track. My travelling companions were either railfans or travel agents or both, and came from all over the world. The balcony proved to be extremely popular and most of us spent some time out there, waving to the public like an old-time US Presidential candidate!

The Durango & Silverton train consists of delightful old yellow-painted carriages, with open balconies and clerestory roofs, hauled by incredible steam locomotives festooned with pipes, cylinders, bells and cow-catchers. They are of the 'Mikado' 2-8-2 wheel arrangement, and look remarkably ancient although they actually date from the 1920s. They were the last narrow-gauge steam locomotives to be built for passenger services in the USA, and must be incredibly powerful, since they are capable of hauling a ten-coach train effortlessly up a gradient of 1 in 25.

The departure was announced by a series of blasts from the engine's five-chime whistle. The first part of the journey took us through downtown Durango, past the back of the Strater Hotel and a number of old bank buildings - Durango evidently had plenty of money in the 1880s! Leaving the town, we crossed a long girder bridge and passed a large trout hatchery. The next few miles were green and tranquil as we passed along the broad Animas Valley. To remind us that we really were in the twenty-first century, there were a few level-crossings with modern flashing lights and automatic barriers.

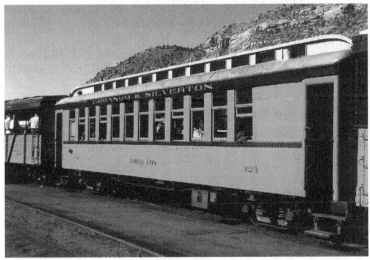

Durango & Silverton carriage

About eleven miles out of Durango, we made a brief stop at a small settlement called Hermosa. From here the landscape would change, as we followed the Animas River up into the mountains. The deciduous woodland gave way to ponderosa pine and aspens, and there were fewer and fewer houses or other signs of civilisation. A guide would occasionally pop into our car and tell us about the history of the line, about a crash that had occurred in such-and-such a place, or a Hollywood movie scene that had been filmed at a particular bridge or cutting. The Durango & Silverton Railroad is quite a star of the silver screen: perhaps the best-known film sequences shot on the line were those in *Butch Cassidy and the Sundance Kid*.

Seven miles beyond Hermosa, the train starts to climb a rock ledge some 400 feet above the Animas River. If you are travelling near the rear of the train, and you are quick, there is a chance to photograph the locomotive and the front few coaches on this ledge, which is known as the 'High Line'. The railway twists and turns so much, and there is such a lot of lineside vegetation, that it is actually quite hard to get good photos 'along the train', and if you miss a good opportunity you may not get another one!

The next point of interest is the 'High Bridge', where traditionally the fireman and engineer open the locomotive's 'blowdown valve', ostensibly to clear sludge from the boiler, but really to create a dramatic show of steam and mist for the photographers! Just beyond the bridge is a hydro-electricity plant whose employees use their own railcar for access.

Along the Animas River

There are a few luxury resorts in the woods alongside the railway, and a large station building at Cascade Canyon that marks the limit of winter operations. From here to Silverton the grey peaks of the Colorado Rockies dominate the scene, as the line forces its way up the increasingly narrow Animas Canyon.

My fellow passengers were quite excited by the journey, as was the pretty barmaid in the buffet-car when I handed her a Kennedy half-dollar in part payment for a coffee. I can never understand why these sensible and user-friendly coins are not seen more often in change. Every time I go to the USA, I obtain about ten dollars' worth from a bank and put them back into circulation.

It was noticeably colder beyond Cascade Canyon, and there was even snow on some of the higher peaks. At Needleton we stopped by a quaint Victorian water-tower to take on water; beyond here is a spur to a still-operational uranium mine. Passing a mountain called Mount Garfield, which in profile resembles a gorilla rather than a fat ginger cat, the train comes out into a wider valley and crosses the Animas for the last time before running into Silverton.

We passed through Silverton's old station, or 'depot', without stopping, coming to a halt in the downtown area where we were greeted by cowboys and cowgirls on horses. The town is at a height of 9,300 feet above sea level and is frequently cut off by snow in the winter. Yet, despite all appearances, ir still has a year-round population and is the administrative centre of San Juan County.

I was met off the train at Silverton by my colleague Judy, who had driven my hire car up from Durango. I got some 'squashed pennies' showing the train for souvenirs from a machine, and we had lunch in a former brothel, now called the 'Shady Lady Saloon', before heading off along the US550 Highway to Colorado Springs. The next day I drove to Denver airport for my flight home.

Beyond Cascade Canyon

The USA have closed many of their railways, but it is to their credit that the Durango - Silverton line has been protected as a National Historic Landmark. Marketed as *America's Railroad*, it runs daily services, its rolling-stock is beautifully-maintained, and it manages to strike just the right balance between sheer entertainment and 100% accurate historical reconstruction. What more could one ask for?

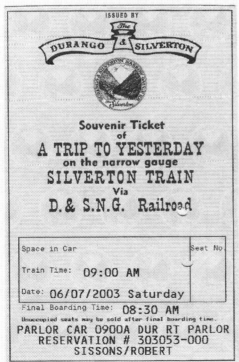

Ticket for the train from Durango to Silverton

18. *Across America by Song Title*

October 28 - 31, 2000: I travel by Amtrak from the City of Angels to the Windy City via the House of the Rising Sun

The United States of America has a vast railway network, but only a fraction of it is actually open to passenger trains. Most long-distance passenger services have been run since 1971 by the quasi-government Amtrak organisation, but even when a railway line is shown on the Amtrak map, there is no guarantee that it enjoys a frequent service. Many trains run only once daily, and others only three times a week. There are honourable exceptions, such as the North-East Corridor (Boston - New York - Washington) and the San Diegans (the Los Angeles - San Diego route). But between these two extremes are many, many miles of track with few, if any, passenger trains. In Europe it would be almost unbelievable for a city with a population of 250,000 to have no railway station: in the USA it is quite commonplace.

My longest-ever trip on Amtrak began just after I had completed a 2,400-mile drive along Historic Route 66 with a friend - a fascinating journey, although not a railway one. Once my friend had flown home from LA, I still had a few days' holiday left, plus the return half of an air ticket from Heathrow to Chicago O'Hare. I dropped off my rather dusty hire car, booked a room in a small hotel near Los Angeles Union Station, and planned my journey.

Los Angeles Union Station

Union Station in Los Angeles is a wondrous Spanish Mission-style cathedral of a station. It has an immense vaulted waiting room with long polished wooden benches, and an overwhelming air of under-use. This great monument to the age of the train was not completed until automobiles and airplanes had already started to make inroads into the railroads' monopoly. One can imagine Hollywood stars of the 1930s and 1940s being met off luxurious Southern Pacific express trains and whisked off to the movie studios in Cadillacs or Duesenbergs. Today one feels a bit shabby sitting under that magnificent vault drinking Starbucks coffee from a Styrofoam cup.

I could have gone directly by train from LA to Chicago via Flagstaff, Arizona on Amtrak's *Southwest Chief*. However, I had already travelled on that train, and I had plenty of time in hand, so I decided to travel via New Orleans and Memphis, spending one night in each of these cities. So the train I took from LA, the *Sunset Limited*, followed the more southerly route out of the city, passing the Sonora Desert and Palm Springs.

Amtrak's Sunset Limited

I was quite surprised that I appeared to be the only foreign tourist on this train. Most of the passengers were black. Quite a lot of them were travelling together, and belonged to a Gospel Choir; they were on their way to a concert in Louisiana. Several of them gave a delightful impromptu recital in the bar car for the benefit of myself and other passengers, who included the Vargases. Mr and Mrs Vargas were millionaires who were scared of flying. They owned a house and a yacht in both California and Florida, and regularly used the train to travel between the two.

The bar car was unstaffed except when a rather bored Amtrak attendant materialised to serve coffee. This came in a large polystyrene cup and cost a very reasonable 85 cents. Most passengers would give a dollar bill and tell the barman to keep the change. I followed suit although I would never dream of tipping the man who comes down the corridor with a trolley of overpriced drinks on the London - Dover train back home.

Apart from the barman, the other Amtrak employee we saw quite frequently was the conductor. He checked our tickets, and then tore about three-quarters of them off to leave us with a miserable little stub. He pointed out various points of interest along the way, and also, most importantly, advised the smokers when we would be stopping at a station for long enough for them to get off and enjoy a 'quick drag'.

I was talking to two particularly attractive ladies from the Gospel Choir when we were joined by a young, smartly-dressed black man, who said his name was Duke and started chatting up the younger and more nubile of the two women. She wasn't taken-in by his sweet-talking, and seemed quite horrified at his suggestion that we should all play cards together. After half-an-hour or so, he got bored when our two companions started a rendition of *Shall We Gather At The River?* and moved along the carriage.

A little later, the conductor passed by, and asked us whether we had seen a man called Duke. We told him that we had, but didn't know where he had gone. Shortly after that, I went back upstairs to my reclining seat and fell asleep.

Passengers on the Sunset Limited

The next morning the conductor pointed out some aircraft that just seemed to be parked in the middle of the desert. From the number of them and their different markings, it looked as though this must be a major international airport, but it was nothing of the sort. The conductor explained that these planes had been withdrawn from service and were awaiting buyers; the airlines stored them here because they would not decay in the dry desert air. He also told us that Duke had been thrown off the train during the night because he had been playing poker with other passengers and taking all their money!

For some distance, the railway followed the Rio Grande. Despite its impressive name, it was little more than a muddy ditch. The conductor pointed out the high border fence that separated the USA and Mexico, and announced that we would have a 15-minute stop in El Paso, just perfect news for all the smokers.

El Paso is a city under siege: the Mexican border seems to run right through the town, and even the railway station looks like a fortress. High, barren red hills loom over the city. I was reminded of the Marty Robbins song *El Paso*, where the hero returns on horseback to see his beloved Felina and sings:

'And at last here I am on the hill overlooking El Paso; I can see Rosie's Cantina below'.

Places in the USA often do not live up to their song descriptions; Amarillo is not a 'pretty city'; San José in California is not the idyllic small town that one might believe Dionne Warwick is asking the way to - and many of the places given a name-check on Bobby Troup's *Get Your Kicks on Route 66* are little more that signposts on the I-40 pointing to a few shacks and a gas station. But El Paso was just as I imagined it, and a lonesome cowboy on his way from the Badlands of New Mexico could easily look down from those red stone hills onto Rosie's Cantina, if it really exists.

The Amtrak train took me and my companions slowly but safely across the desert, past hi-tech Houston and into the State of Louisiana. We were due to arrive in New Orleans at 8.30pm and the conductor was most anxious to check that everyone getting off there had accommodation arranged for the night. At one of the station stops I was able to book myself a room in a modest Canal Street hotel recommended by the *Lonely Planet* Guide.

My friend and mentor from the Gospel Choir was keen to give me advice on what to do in New Orleans. "You watch out in the French Quarter" she said; "You'll have chicks approaching you, saying they love you, saying they want to marry you! Now don't you be believing it!"

Taking her words seriously, I decided not to go to the French Quarter alone, but in the company of another young woman I had met on the train. I assume that the hustlers of Bourbon Street left me alone as they thought we were a couple. We walked past the *House of the Rising Sun* (Animals, 1964) and tried some *Jambalaya* (Carpenters, 1974). The French Quarter was lively and throbbing to the beat of classic jazz.

The next morning I explored a bit more of the city, walking around the French Quarter in daylight and visiting the historic cathedral. I also took the Riverfront Streetcar for a ride along the shore of the mighty *Mississippi* (Pussycat, 1976). The Riverfront Streetcar is a modern reproduction of an old-time American 'trolley' or tram, in a bright red livery. (Confusingly, Americans use the word 'tram' to describe a Swiss-style mountain cable-car, whereas 'trolley' these days tends to mean the tourist sightseeing buses, designed to resemble old streetcars, which can be seen operating tours of many cities in the USA).

New Orleans, however, has the real thing - and I was not going to leave the city without at least riding on a portion of it. The St Charles Line is a genuine old streetcar line, using authentic green-liveried 1920s vehicles. It passes along St Charles Avenue, a broad thoroughfare lined with charming antebellum wooden houses, but the streetcar itself is no museum piece - it still performs a necessary public transport function. It was a New Orleans streetcar like this (but on the now-defunct Desire route) that gave its name to Tennessee Williams' famous play. I hopped off at Lee Circle, one of the few traffic roundabouts I have ever encountered in the USA, and, with the aid of the free city map I had picked up from my hotel, I made my way back on foot to New Orleans' exceptionally unprepossessing Amtrak station. I was now going to travel on an American legend (and another song title) - the train they call *The City of New Orleans*.

Streetcar in New Orleans

The City of New Orleans runs daily between New Orleans and Chicago. The train's main claim to fame is that it was the subject of a song written by Steve Goodman, immortalising a journey from Chicago to New Orleans in the early 1970s when passenger services were being steadily run-down. The train is described as having '15 cars and 15 restless riders, three conductors and 25 sacks of mail'. On October 30, 2000, the train was quite crowded. We were not allowed onto the station concourse until it was time to board. Photography was impossible. Once onboard, the train staff made it clear that they knew they were part of an American legend - the conductor announced "Welcome aboard The Train They Call The City Of New Orleans!" as we set off north through rural Louisiana. The leisurely pace of the train matches perfectly the rhythm of the Arlo Guthrie recording of the song.

The scenery from *The City of New Orleans* is pleasant and varied without being truly spectacular. Some of the stations on the Louisiana stretch have French names and the vernacular architecture even has a vaguely French style. The passengers were a mixture of nationalities - mostly Americans, but quite a few tourists. I was sitting opposite a couple from Australia and their teenage daughter. Like me, they were getting off in *Memphis, Tennessee* (Chuck Berry, 1959).

Memphis is a large city on the Mississippi, but its one and only inter-city train service arrives and departs at most inconvenient times. I had reserved a room in a downtown motel, and the conductor was most concerned about me attempting to make my way there on foot at dead of night (although the journey looked quite feasible on the map in my *Lonely Planet* guide). Luckily an American couple, who had been sitting close to me on the train, told me that they had left their car in the station car park and would willingly drop me off at my motel.

I had precisely 24 hours to explore Memphis. My first place of pilgrimage the next morning was Sun Studio, where Elvis recorded his first single. I'm afraid that my recording of the Everly Brothers' *All I have to do is dream* was not in the same league, but it made a nice souvenir. It was at Sun Studio that I made the acquaintance of another North American icon. I arrived a little too early for the guided visit, and the girl at the ticket counter told me "Go and wait for ten minutes in the soda fountain!" I had heard of soda fountains in American literature, but had never been quite sure what they were - I had always had a mental picture of an ornate piece of street furniture with statues and jets spraying soda water everywhere. The reality turned out to be more prosaic: a bar serving Coke, fizzy lemonade and 7-Up.

Like New Orleans, Memphis is served by streetcars, but these are a relatively recent re-introduction, and originated from Melbourne and Oporto. They do, nonetheless, provide a cheap and frequent means of transport, and look very much at home as they make their way up Main Street.

Walking in Memphis (Mark Cohn, 1991) was certainly a bizarre experience. The city still seems to be divided into distinct racial zones. On one street I would see only white people and prosperous-looking shops and homes; two blocks away the faces were all black and the flats and stores were shabby and dilapidated. I visited the Smithsonian Rock n'Soul Museum for a taste of the city's musical history, before getting a free shuttle bus to Graceland, the former home of Elvis Presley. I had seen and read so much about this place that I knew roughly what to expect, but I was still surprised that one of the richest and most successful men in America had chosen to live in a house so close to a busy main road, offering very little privacy. The attractive female guide gave a suitably airbrushed account of Elvis's life and career, and I got a few 'squashed pennies' for souvenirs from a machine across the road before heading off to Beale Street, the throbbing heart of Memphis.

Everyone who was anyone was on Beale Street. It was the night before Halloween, and young children were dressed up ready to go 'trick-or-treating'. I bumped into my Australian friends from the train, and we went off for a burger and fries in a restaurant where the TV was showing endless repeats of *Bewitched*. After dinner it was simply pleasant to stroll along Beale, enjoying the jazz, folk, rock and indie music that emanated from the various bars. A parade of floats passed by, all festooned with spooks and skeletons, as Memphis got ready to celebrate Halloween.

I had to be at the station at 10.40pm for the train to Chicago. If I had missed this train, it would have been a 24-hour wait for the next one. As in New Orleans, I travelled to the station by streetcar, passing along the way the Lorraine Motel, where Martin Luther King was assassinated in 1968. Finding my way to the right platform was far from straightforward, as about half of the station seemed to be closed off for repairs. I was concerned that *The City of New Orleans* might be late, as I had heard nightmare stories of Amtrak trains running several hours behind schedule, and this was the first time I had ever caught a long-distance train in the USA from an intermediate station. But the locomotive's powerful headlight appeared right on time, and I found my carriage without difficulty. I was finishing my holiday in style, travelling overnight to Chicago in a sleeping-car.

The carriage was decorated appropriately for October 31, with pumpkins, cut-out paper witches on broomsticks and dangling fluorescent skeletons. The beautiful raven-haired attendant handed me an envelope containing a card that wished me a Happy Halloween and assured me that Jesus was with me. With this strange mixture of the Pagan and the Christian, I climbed into my bunk and fell asleep, as the train covered the very track where Casey Jones had perished in his fatal crash a century earlier.

I woke up just in time to see the train pull up at a wayside station. I strained my eyes to read the inconspicuous signboard - 'Kankakee'. Of course, this was one of the stops mentioned in Steve Goodman's song. I attempted to photograph the station building from the train window as we pulled out. One hour and forty-seven minutes later *The City of New Orleans* arrived in *Chicago* (Frank Sinatra, 1957).

The Loop in Chicago

I had a full day and night in Chicago before my flight home, and in addition to taking a lift to the top of America's tallest skyscraper, the Sears Tower, I managed a trip on the 'Loop', the famous elevated line that not only runs around but actually gives its name to the city's central business district. Unlike other American cities that have put their urban railways underground, Chicago has retained its elevated lines and they are well on their way to becoming a tourist attraction. The steel viaducts are an eyesore at street level, but the views from the trains are as spectacular as any urban line can be, and the trains themselves are mercifully clean and free of graffiti. It was on board one of the *Chicago Transit Authority's* trains (sorry - a band, not a song title!) that I travelled to O'Hare airport the next day for my flight home.

The USA that I visited in October 2000 was full of confidence and optimism, and travel was relatively carefree. Less than a year later, hijacked planes struck the Twin Towers and the Pentagon, and America was never the same again.

December 1984: I explore Costa Rica's wonderful railway system

The tiny Central American country of Costa Rica has become quite a fashionable destination for eco-tourism in recent years. Back in 1984, when I went on holiday there, British tourists were a rarity. Even then, the country's glossy tourist brochures seldom mentioned train travel, and nowadays I imagine that most visitors enter and leave the country quite unaware that it ever possessed a rail network.

Looking back, I realise now that I visited Costa Rica at a time when its railways had reached the peak of their development. The system had been as efficiently modernised as limited resources would allow. Passenger services were being improved and there were ambitious plans for full electrification, revamped suburban services around San José and the construction of new lines north to Guanacaste and south to the Panamanian border. It looked as if the country nicknamed 'the Latin American Switzerland' would soon have a railway worthy of Switzerland itself.

Smart new electric loco in 1984

Sadly it all went wrong. Economic problems, changes of management and of government played their part, as did the inevitable increase in private car ownership and the unfettered development of competing bus services. But Mother Nature delivered the greatest blow: a massive earthquake on April 22, 1991 wrecked the line from San José to the Atlantic Coast. Bereft of its main trunk, the rest of the system gradually withered, and today there are just a few local commuter trains in San José and a *diesel-hauled* weekends-only tourist train along part of the 'Pacific' line. It is a great shame that a country that promotes itself as a 'green' destination, with 26 designated National Parks covering over a quarter of its territory, should have lost the ecological benefits of a pollution-free electrified railway.

But let us step back to 1984 when the system was at its peak. Costa Rica is a small country at almost the thinnest point in the Americas. The capital, San José, is situated in the centre, roughly midway between the Atlantic and Pacific coasts. It was an Englishman named Richard Farrer who first introduced railways to Costa Rica: he laid the first 14 kilometres of what was to become the Pacific line in 1857. American Henry M Keith started work on the Atlantic line in the 1870s. The difficulty of building railways across the mountainous centre of Costa Rica meant that both projects were constantly being shelved, abandoned and then re-started. The Atlantic line, from San José to Limón, was finished in 1891 and the Pacific line, from San José to Puntarenas, in 1910. Long branches were soon grafted onto the Limón line, principally to serve the United Fruit Company's banana plantations. The Atlantic and Pacific railways ran as separate companies until 1977, and each had its own station in the capital, although an electric tramway-type line linked the two stations, permitting the transfer of freight and stock between the two systems. As the lines were built by an Englishman and an American, the gauge chosen was a very un-metric 3 feet 6 inches!

I decided that my first Costa Rican rail journey should be on the Puntarenas line. Not wishing to get up at an unearthly hour, however, I made the outward journey by bus and returned by rail. This meant that I had a reasonable lie-in but also had plenty of time to soak up the sun on Puntarenas beach, and enjoy some snorkelling in the clear waters.

The morning train to Puntarenas

The railway station at Puntarenas was right by the beach, so I would have had no excuse if I had missed my train. It was quite a modern station, as were the majority of the locomotives, although a handful of wonderful 1930s German engines were in evidence, dating from the electrification of the line. The first part of the journey followed the Pacific coast, serving the port of Caldera and a number of small beach resorts before heading inland.

One of the most incredible things about any Costa Rican railway journey was the ticket. I believe that there were only two types of tickets printed: one covering the Atlantic line and its branches, and the other the Pacific line. The travelling conductors on the trains had a stock of these, about two inches across and about nine inches long, listing all of the stations in order along the line. If you travelled along the whole line, you received a complete ticket; if you boarded at an intermediate stop, the ticket would be carefully torn so that you just got the part showing the stations from your boarding-point to the terminus. A ticket from somewhere like Cartago to San José, therefore, was about as long as it was broad.

A ticket for the whole journey from Limón to San José, showing the names of all the stations along the Atlantic Railway.

As my train headed inland from the coast into Costa Rica's central Meseta, I remembered that night always comes early when you are near the Equator. The daylight was visibly failing at 4.30pm as we stopped at a station called Jesús María. By the time we reached the imaginatively-named halt of Kilómetre 81, it was almost dark. But I could tell already that Costa Rica had no great gems of station architecture. Most major passenger stations consisted of a corrugated-iron shed, whilst some quite sizeable settlements had no facilities other than a rusting nameboard pushed into the grass beside the track.

Though there was little to see now when looking out, the inside of the train was much more interesting. There was no official in-train catering, but at almost every station we were joined by women and young boys who would walk from carriage to carriage selling soft drinks, tortillas, homemade crisps, roast peanuts and assorted tropical fruits.

My journey finished at San José Pacific Station, a grand but rather gloomy Art-Deco building with lots of chrome and marble. Passing through the waiting room on the way out, I saw models of steam and electric locomotives in glass cases, and a huge Christmas crib, decorated with fairy lights. It looked quite a professional piece of work, but a notice said that all the tiny figures of the Holy Family and animals had been carved by railway employees in their spare time.

Preserved steam locomotive 59 in San José

A few days later I was at the Atlantic station, ready to take the 11am train to Puerto Limón. At first I had the impression that the train would be hauled by steam - surely that was the unmistakeable silhouette of a steam locomotive just beyond the station, pointing towards Limón? As the ticket-office was not yet open and I had a few minutes in hand, I walked over to investigate. Indeed it *was* a steam loco, 2-6-0 No.

59 of the Costa Rica Northern Railway to be precise. However, it was obviously a preserved museum piece. My train was hauled by a neat modern General Electric diesel, hauling rather nice old carriages with end balconies identical to those used on the Pacific line. I should state here that all the Costa Rican trains I rode were outstandingly clean and well-maintained.

The Limón train left San José about half-an-hour late, and the first part of the journey was quite a thrill, with the horn sounding continuously as we crossed numerous busy roads and passed right by San José University campus. The first stop was at Cartago, where some kind of impromptu market was taking place in the station yard. Founded by Spaniard Juan Vásquez de Coronado in the 16th century, Cartago is one of the oldest cities in Costa Rica, but little is left of the original settlement as it was destroyed by an eruption of the nearby volcano, Mount Irazú. The volcanic soil is ideal for crops, and vast acreages of coffee plantations were visible from the train.

The next stop was at Paraiso. Although the station was little more than a halt with overgrown platforms, we made quite a long stop here, and I couldn't resist the opportunity to get off and have a stroll. My companions on the train informed me that the name, meaning 'Paradise', was given to the valley by the early colonists, who, having suffered earthquakes and diseases in their old settlement of Ujarras - where the ruins of the Mission Church can still be seen - moved across the mountains of the Cordillera Central until they found a place which seemed so perfect that they named it 'Paradise'.

The route from San José to Limón was a scenic delight, as we traversed the mountains of the Continental Divide, crossing bubbling streams and passing the peaks of extinct and active volcanoes. The train crept around spirals, popped through tunnels and clung to the sides of steep hills. A spectacular steel girder bridge took us across the Reventazón, the country's longest river.

Our progress was leisurely to say the least. Although officially a passenger train, it was really a mixed one: there were two or three goods wagons behind the engine, and occasionally there would be a lengthy stop at a station where the locomotive would disappear to perform various shunting manoeuvres, leaving all the passengers stranded for fifteen or twenty minutes. There would be other delays when we waited in loops for trains to go by in the opposite direction: freight trains, conveying oil and bananas, took precedence over passengers!

The daily train to Limón

Sitting opposite me in the train was a beautiful *tica* called Estrella. She had long wavy dark hair, big brown eyes and a mischievous smile. She and her mother were travelling up to Limón to visit relatives.

They ran a small hotel, the Managua, in San José, and I asked for their business card as I was looking for somewhere to stay, not wishing to trespass on the hospitality of my friends in San José for too long.

Ticas, as Costa Rican women are called, are known for their beauty, but there is no dominant physical type. Many people are of pure European descent, but *ticos* and *ticas* range from the blue-eyed, blonde-haired and pale-skinned to the Afro-Caribbean blacks who are the descendants of the Jamaicans who came over in the late 19th century to help build the railway. As my train neared Limón more and more black passengers got on, many of them speaking the sing-song English that they use in preference to Spanish.

The last third of the journey towards Limón was a mixture of banana plantations and dense tropical jungle. As the light faded I saw an incredible sight: a billiard-room in the middle of nowhere, with bamboo walls and a tin roof, where players were chalking their cues and playing their shots on an immaculate green baize table. Strangely, the railway station where we halted, just after passing the billiard-room, was called Liverpool!

Limón is a lazy, hot, tropical town, where the sloths swing between the trees in the central park. It has that slightly down-at-heel and disreputable air of ports everywhere, but I did not feel in the least threatened. The only people approaching me at the station and asking for money were offering me money in return: Costa Rica had recently introduced new coins, and public telephones had just been modified to take the small new stainless-steel 2-colon coins, which seemed to be in short supply. "Tiene una moneda de dos colones - una *nueva*?" was the familiar question.

I spent a night in a small hotel in Limón that had been recommended to me by friends in San José. "It's very good - it's air-conditioned!" they had said. Air-conditioning is quite a status symbol in Costa Rica, even though in much of the country it is hardly necessary. Sadly, the hotel proved to be grubby and noisy; the bedclothes definitely looked as if someone had already slept in them, and the drone of the much-vaunted air-conditioning unit, which didn't appear to have an 'off' switch, kept me awake for half the night.

The train stops in the town centre

From Limón it was time to head for the next Costa Rican passenger line. I took the train back from Limón, through Liverpool, Buffalo, Boston and Madre de Dios, to a place called Siquirres. Meaning 'If you like', this was the junction between the Atlantic line and its major branch that meandered north through the banana plantations to Rio Frio ('Cold River').

Both this branch and the Siquirres - Limón section of the main line had recently been electrified, and there was a monument with a plaque commemorating this on the station platform.

The Siquirres - Rio Frio train was much like that from Limón, but had fewer carriages and a few more goods wagons. The first station out had rather a sinister name, La Junta, but soon we were off to the more poetical halts of Cairo, Williamsburg and Africa. I indulged myself on the usual delicacies that passed along the train, until we got to Guácimo, where the train split. The electric locomotive took several wagons and some coaches on to Rio Frio, while a diesel was hooked onto the remaining coaches for my ride up the tributary line to Guápiles.

Guácimo to Guápiles was the most rural branch in Costa Rica, cutting across pleasant farming country and ending in true 'Wild West' style, running straight through the main street of Guápiles, a tiny place with wooden-balconied hotels and American-type boardwalks. Here I found a traditional, non-air-conditioned hotel for about half the price I had paid in Limon: it was delectably quiet and perfectly comfortable. The few shops in town were still open and I had a look around before turning in. I found an establishment with a window full of assorted bric-a-brac and old clocks. I went in and asked the shopkeeper if he had any old coins: I had hoped to purchase a few old Costa Rican coins as a souvenir, but had not yet found any on sale except in smart expensive shops in San José. The dealer in Guápiles apologised and said he had no old coins, but he did let me sort through an enormous bowl of still-current Costa Rican coins - some of which dated back to the 1930s, and help myself to any I wanted.

The next morning I left Guápiles on a slow cross-country bus to Rio Frio, intending to spend the night there and get the train back to San José the next day. Although it looked only a short distance on the map, the journey took the best part of a day, with the usual unscheduled stops for refreshments. The bus ride was spectacular after a fashion, as the dirt road wound and climbed among a forest of bananas.

Changing trains in Costa Rica

There didn't appear to be very much to Rio Frio. A small, deserted railway station, some farm buildings, a little café/bar - that was about all. I approached two young women, who were sitting on an outdoor bench, and asked them if there was a hotel nearby. They told me to go down the road, across the bridge, and then after a few hundred metres I would come to the 'Onda'. "What was the Onda?" I asked, being unfamiliar with this word in Spanish. The explanation was that the small hotel was above a motor garage servicing Honda cars and motorcycles. The letter 'H' having fallen off the garage sign, the place was known locally as the 'Onda'.

The accommodation at the 'Onda' was basic but perfectly adequate. After leaving my backpack I walked back into Rio Frio and met again the two young ladies who had showed me the way to my hotel. I found out their names were Olga and Xínia, and bought them drinks; for no apparent reason, they bought me a plastic comb. I enjoyed the standard Costa Rican basic supper of black beans and rice, and returned to the 'Onda'. Before going to bed I sat on the terrace for half-an-hour or so reading a Cold War thriller about a submarine chase in the icy North Atlantic, which seemed the most wonderfully incongruous book I could have chosen in such surroundings.

I was at the station at 5.30am the next morning. It was still quite dark and I remember little of the scenery, although I am sure that bananas were growing in abundance on both sides of the track. This line was relatively new and noticeably smoother-riding than the Guápiles branch. At Guácimo some carriages from Guápiles were connected, and a young man came along the train with a small urn on a trolley, dispensing piping hot coffee for the equivalent of 8p a cup. It was about the best coffee I have ever tasted. When I told him this, the vendor explained in English that he was from the USA and was with the Peace Corps! I cannot think why supplying Costa Rican train passengers with refreshments was considered a suitable task for a Peace Corps volunteer, but it was much appreciated by one English traveller!

The train from Rio Frio terminated at Siquirres station, and here I changed for San José. I spent most of the journey sitting out on the open balcony of the coach, eating roast peanuts as I enjoyed the magnificent scenery.

There remained only one passenger line in Costa Rica that I had not travelled on: the short suburban spur from San José to Heredia. At the time of my visit, this line had but one return passenger train daily, taking commuters from Heredia into San José in the morning and back home in the evening. The 12-year-old son of one of the families I had met in San José agreed to come on the train with me, and we walked to the Atlantic station together one evening. It was quite a fun journey, with the blue carriages full of happy people on their way home from work. Heredia is a lovely old colonial city, only six miles from San José, with a beautiful 18th-century Spanish church. We had a quick exploration in the twilight before catching one of the frequent minibuses back to San José.

Heredia's lonely station

Heredia station was a typical corrugated-iron shed, but it had rather an elegant roof with an incredible semaphore signal mounted on top. Beyond the station the rails continued, for freight only, to Alajuela. Shortly before I left Costa Rica I took a bus to Alajuela and had the opportunity to investigate its station.

It was similar in construction to that at Heredia, and displayed a yellowing 1963 timetable showing passenger trains to San José! Two open vans of over-ripe bananas occupied a siding, but there was no sign of any life, human or animal. Feeling hungry, I grabbed a couple of bananas and ran back up the street to catch my bus.

Heredia parish church

Recent reports from colleagues who have visited Costa Rica show that the inhabitants are as friendly as ever, and I would love to go back and try one of those amazing 'zip-line' tours across the canopy of the rainforest. They now even have a Rainforest Aerial Tram, although this is a 'tram' in the American sense - a suspended cable-car - rather than an urban vehicle running on rails! Perhaps the best hope for any future rail revival in the country lies with the tourist industry. Apart from the tourist trains between San José and Caldera, operated by America Travel, there has also been some activity on the 'Atlantic' line recently: on March 15, 2009, passengers from the cruise liner *Spirit of Adventure* were treated to a ride on the 'Banana Train' along some rehabilitated track near Siquirres.

SOUTH

AMERICAN

JOURNEYS

Machu Picchu

Cuzco

Puno

(20)

Asuncion

(21)

Encarnacion

Buenos Aires

San Isidro

(22)

(22)

Ushuaia

20. Rails Through Deepest, Darkest Peru

December 5-7, 1990: From Lake Titicaca to Machu Picchu

My old schoolfriend Ian and I had listened to all sorts of horror stories about the Puno - Cuzco railway as we backpacked our way across South America. "It's very dangerous!" we were told. "They lock foreign tourists in so that nobody can get at them!" someone said. "The locals will get on board the train and rifle through all the luggage".

It did not sound encouraging. But before we could embark on this life-threatening journey we first had to get to Puno. And from La Paz in Bolivia that did not seem to be easy. My travel agent back home was unable to make any suggestions for this stage of our journey, being confident that something would turn up. One of my old railway books mentioned a narrow-gauge railcar from La Paz down to Lake Titicaca, which connected with an ancient paddle-steamer across the lake to Puno. However, both railcar and steamer were long since out of use, and the impressive colonial-style station at La Paz was eerily deserted when we went there. Public buses seemed non-existent. It was a chance meeting with two Australians, Graham and Margaret, in the lift of our hotel that provided the solution. They were also heading to Puno in order to take the train to Cuzco, and had hired a minibus for the first part of their trip. There would be plenty of room, so we would be most welcome to join them.

Stuck on the main road to Puno!

We set off with the Australians and their two young daughters on what proved an epic ride to Puno. There were stops for lunch and sightseeing along the way, but it soon became clear why no scheduled buses ran on this apparently major international highway, as it degenerated into a dirt track. At one point the minibus got stuck up to its axles in mud, and all the passengers had to get out and push. A little later on, the road crossed a village football pitch. A game was in progress, and the players all moved across to the sides to let us through, resuming play as soon as we had crossed.

It comes as no surprise that our opinion of Peruvian transport was not exactly high even before we had boarded our first train. With experience we learned that the most remarkable thing about travel in Peru was that in most cases you actually made it to your destination. Roads were in an appalling condition: cars were battered wrecks on which any form of lighting after dark was optional. Almost any private motorist seemed to put a sign reading 'TAXI' in his or her windscreen, so there was little difference between hailing a taxi and hitch-hiking. I was amazed at how Volkswagen Beetles could remain on the road despite numerous major components being absent - God forbid if Disney should ever send Herbie to Peru!

Domestic air travel in Peru was equally adventurous. The natives' habits of crossing themselves before boarding the plane and applauding the pilot on landing made one wonder about the airlines' safety record, while the most amazing sight was a *live* turkey tied up in a plastic bag, going round and round on the carousel in the baggage reclaim area with a dazed expression on its face.

But to return to the railways… It would be inaccurate to state that Peru has a railway network, since the lofty mountains and the dense Amazonian jungle that make up much of the country effectively hampered railroad construction. The country instead has three small, separate, unconnected systems, on both the standard and the narrow gauge. What makes it all worthwhile to the traveller is that this relatively small mileage includes some of the highest and most dramatic railways on the planet.

Ian and I were quite lucky, as our travel agent had obtained our rail tickets in advance, avoiding any risk of an undignified free-for-all at Puno station. We travelled to the station with Graham and Margaret, and were left waiting on the platform as the timetabled departure time came and went. A rake of red-and-yellow carriages was waiting at the platform but there seemed little hurry to make them into a train. When eventually a grimy diesel locomotive appeared and reversed onto the coaches, there was a hideous crashing sound and it was announced that there had been a derailment. This would have been a major catastrophe at Clapham Junction during rush hour, but at 8.30am at Puno it was probably an everyday occurrence.

Tourist carriage at Puno station

Eventually our train was ready for us to board, and we left approximately one hour late. My friend and I were in one of the special 'tourist' carriages, which, though not particularly deluxe, were marshalled at the rear of the train near the kitchen-car. We were sharing our compartment with Graham and Margaret and their daughters, plus a Japanese backpacker, an Italian student and two Irish nurses, Ann and Hilary. A truly international crowd!

The first part of the journey follows Lake Titicaca and then crosses the Peruvian Altiplano, past salt lakes where pink flamingos stand looking rather bored, and past occasional llamas, guanacos (the tall skinny ones) and alpacas (the thick-set shaggy ones). A moment of excitement came when Hilary went to use the wc. She returned in hysterics. I went in to investigate. It was far better than many train loos I have used; it had paper, a functioning washbasin and a normal sit-down lavatory. Although the sleepers and ballast were clearly visible through the hole for personal ablutions, this was not the cause for concern. The main problem with the loo was, quite simply, that the exterior window was filled with clear rather than frosted glass, so that the occupant would be perfectly visible to anyone outside. This did not matter so much when crossing the Altiplano, but, once we were proceeding at a snail's pace through the streets of Juliaca, where a market was being held alongside the tracks, it was not such a good idea to want to spend a penny.

Spending a penny - or rather a few hundred thousand *intis* - was very much the order of the day during the station stop at Juliaca. Some market traders would leap on board the train, walk through the carriage with a quantity of sweaters, leather goods, imitation Inca jewellery and other items, and then attempt to sell them before the train set off. Others would remain outside but would simply push their goods through the train windows and hope for a sale. The best chance of a bargain was just before the train left, when the trader was getting everything together in a desperate attempt to leap off. I bought a lovely 'baby alpaca' woollen sweater for about the equivalent of five US dollars, and it is still almost as good as new nearly 18 years later.

More carriages were joined onto our train at Juliaca; they had originated in Arequipa. The train left Juliaca with plenty of blasts on the horn, leaving numerous limbless market traders in its wake, and set off for the next station.

Ian and I talked with the two Irish nurses and the Japanese backpacker, and a simple lunch was served, consisting of rice, sauce and an unidentifiable meat of some sort. The train continued its leisurely progress, stopping at countless villages where trackside traders would offer their wares. Each station seemed to have its own speciality; at one stop, Pucará, we were offered strange pottery bulls that were apparently unique to that village. At La Raya, we reached the highest point on the line, 4,321 metres above sea level, although the track would remain at well over 3,000 metres all the way to Cuzco.

Passing a train going the other way

At a station called Aguas Calientes ('Warm Waters') we passed a train going in the opposite direction. The warm waters in question were hot springs, just across the track from the station building. We could see locals splashing around in them, but sadly we had no time to enjoy them, as our train paused but five minutes and then headed off for Cuzco.

There are two railway stations in Cuzco - the standard-gauge (Wanchac) station for Puno and the narrow-gauge (San Pedro) station for Machu Picchu. I have absolutely no idea what the standard-gauge station looks like, since we arrived late at night, and after running the gauntlet of the touts offering us cheap accommodation, taxis and restaurants, we spotted a man holding up a clipboard with our names. We were then led out to a car that took us to the Hotel Royal Inca II. Sitting in our hotel room later, my friend and I reflected that we had survived the journey and that it hadn't been nearly as bad as everybody had said. The constant hassling of the market traders could get on your nerves after a bit, but we certainly hadn't felt in any danger at all.

Cuzco is one of the most historic and beautiful cities in Latin America. Much of its street layout goes back to the time of the Incas, and the incredible Inca walls, built of huge pieces of stone that fit together perfectly without mortar, were used by the Spanish to support many later buildings. The Plaza de Armas, where we strolled after dinner and met up again with the Japanese man and the Irish nurses, is wonderful, with its Renaissance-style Bishop's Palace and the magnificent cathedral. In the painting of the *Last Supper* inside Cuzco Cathedral, Jesus and the apostles are seen tucking into a guinea pig, a local delicacy here.

Cuzco's Colonial-style cathedral

A stop of at least one night in Cuzco is essential when travelling by train from Puno to Machu Picchu. The narrow-gauge railway that runs from Cuzco to Machu Picchu was built in 1920, some nine years after the ruins of the Inca citadel had been discovered by Hiram Bingham. It is by far the best-served railway in Peru, with locomotive-hauled trains for local residents and a frequent service of *autovagónes* (diesel railcars) for the tourists, charging a premium fare. The railway is always busy as it provides the only surface transport to the ruins: there is no road from Cuzco to Machu Picchu, and only the really keen walker would attempt the Inca Trail.

Ian and I presented ourselves at the narrow-gauge station early in the morning, together with Graham and Margaret and their children. The station was right next to a beautiful colonial church, and an old steam locomotive was on display. We took our seats in a relatively modern and comfortable diesel railcar, and were soon up a steep gradient, looking down over the red-tiled roofs of Cuzco. In the foreground we could see guinea-pigs in wire pens in the back gardens of a row of terraced cottages.

"Oh look, there's a branch-line going off!" said Graham. In fact, our train had crossed a set of points and there, to the left, were two shiny rails heading off uphill. "I wonder where that's going?" asked Margaret. She did not have to wonder long. Our railcar ground to a halt and the driver then left his cab at the front and walked to another at the rear. We then set off in the opposite direction, taking the 'branch line' for a few hundred yards until we came to another 'junction', where the railcar reversed again. What we were actually doing was climbing a mountain on a series of switchbacks.

Over the years, railway engineers have employed different methods of conquering mountains. The best way is simply to burrow straight through - but that is also slow and very expensive. Some railways use a rack-and-pinion or a central Fell rail, but these systems both require specialised equipment. The easiest and cheapest way is simply to zigzag up the mountain in a series of switchbacks, allowing the train to gain a little bit of height at a time. This system was frequently used in cash-strapped Latin America. The disadvantages are that travel is very slow and trains have to be quite short!

Eventually we were over the mountain and into the 'Sacred Valley' of the Urubamba river, which we were to follow all the way to Machu Picchu. At first the valley was broad and green, and we passed through several small stations without stopping. They were served by the all-stations local trains and we were on the express railcar. The inevitable trackside traders could only look on in frustration as we sped by.

We were between stations, in the middle of nowhere, when suddenly the *autovagón* ground to a halt. We heard a sound like someone attempting to start a car, but nothing happened. A small cloud of black smoke came from the exhaust and the engine spluttered and died. The driver and guard got off and started gesticulating and talking furiously in rapid Spanish, but this had no effect on our progress. Eventually most of the passengers got off too; it was pleasantly warm, and we were able to take photos of the scenery, something that had not been possible from the fast-moving railcar as it had bumped over the roughly-laid rails. There were the usual voices of complaint, especially from the North American passengers: Machu Picchu was the highlight of their holiday - how could they possibly miss it? What on earth were they going to do?

Train to Machu Picchu, broken down

We had been stuck by the track for about 45 minutes when we heard the two-tone horn of another railcar, which had been following us. It came to a halt behind ours, and there followed considerable debate from the motormen while we waited and wondered. Someone had the clever idea of coupling the railcars together, but the good car didn't seem to have enough power to push the failed one all the way to Machu Picchu. It could, however, *pull* it. We were asked to remove all our possessions from our railcar, and the second car towed it back along the line to a siding at the last station. The new *autovagón* then returned to pick up all the passengers. Since it had already been full on leaving Cuzco, and all seats on ours had also been occupied, it was a case of standing room only for the displaced passengers, although one or two people gave up their seats for the most elderly of the standees.

The train was now so full that looking out of the windows was difficult, but I was aware of the valley gradually closing in until we were running through a narrow gorge alongside the fast-flowing river. At last we came to Puente Ruinas station, where we left the train and joined a bus to the ruins of Machu Picchu.

In my ignorance I had expected the train to take us right to Machu Picchu. In fact, on a map the station is right next to the ruins. But it is four hundred metres *below* them. Linking the station and the famous archaeological site is an incredible mountain road with numerous hairpin bends: it takes about fifteen minutes for a bus to get to the top. It must count as one of the world's most amazing bus journeys, but it is not for the faint-hearted, and I think we were all feeling slightly sick and giddy when at last we arrived at the great Inca citadel.

Nothing can quite prepare one for one's first glimpse of Machu Picchu, and the traumas of the journey were soon forgotten as we followed our guide, who had the unlikely name of Benny, on a tour of the city, passing houses, storerooms, aqueducts and the enigmatic Temple of the Sun. Like all visitors to the site, we wondered what purpose this remarkable site had really served: there was no archaeological evidence of it ever having been a final defensive position against the Spanish, and very few human remains had been found there. Perhaps it had a religious rather than a military function, but, whatever the case, one cannot but admire the way its builders had shaped and fitted these vast boulders without using any metal tools.

Our guide, Benny

After lunch in the on-site restaurant, and a close encounter with the on-site alpaca, we boarded our bus for the return journey to the station. As we left the site, a little boy ran in front of the bus, shouting "Bye-bye! Bye-bye!" We waved at him and went on our way, rounding the first hairpin bend. At the next bend he was there again. "Bye-bye! Bye-bye!" he shouted as he ran across the road.

This continued for the rest of the way down the hill. The little boy was running down the sheer mountainside. Occasionally he just missed us, crossing the road just after the bus had gone by. But usually he was there ahead of us, shouting "Bye-bye" before running down to greet us at the next hairpin bend.

When the bus finally pulled up in front of the station, we thought we had lost him. But as the first passengers started getting off and walking towards the train, he came running out of the woods. "Bye-bye! Bye-Bye!" he shouted. He held out his hand for tips, and I am sure that most of the passengers gave him something. I have no doubt that he rode back up to the ruins on the bus so he could show his trick to the next group of tourists.

Machu Picchu

Our train ride back to Cuzco was less adventurous than the morning's journey, as the *autovagón* behaved itself impeccably. The crew did save one last surprise for us. As we reached the hillside and were about to take the first of the switchbacks down towards Cuzco, they turned off all the lights and put on a tape of *El Condor Pasa,* played on the pan-pipes. To this tune we descended towards Cuzco, the lights of the city gleaming in the valley below and gradually becoming brighter as we zigzagged down to the terminus. It was an unforgettable experience.

I was lucky enough to do the Puno - Cuzco - Machu Picchu journey again by train five years later, escorting a group of British tourists on a two-week trip around Peru. Nothing had changed, although fortunately the railcar did not break down *en route* to Machu Picchu. Since then, Peru's railways have been taken over by the Orient Express company, and I believe that the Puno - Cuzco trains now offer all kinds of undreamed-of luxuries, including a proper dining car and an open observation platform. I only hope that they have done something about the lavatory windows!

21. The Great Paraguayan Train Robbery

November 28, 1990: I lose my bag on the night train to Asunción

In 1990 I planned a holiday across South America with my friend Ian. The itinerary was deliberately planned so as to include a ride on the Paraguayan Railway from Encarnación to Asunción, which then ran on Wednesdays only.

The Paraguayan railway network was something of a legend among enthusiasts, and although it most definitely did not run for tourists, it did not offer reliable or efficient transport for locals either. It was probably the world's most decrepit public railway, with infrequent services, overgrown tracks and all trains hauled by a fleet of almost-centenarian wood-burning steam locomotives, many of which had been built by the North British Locomotive Works at Glasgow.

El Gran Capitán at F Lacroze station

We started our holiday in Buenos Aires, and after an interesting tour of the city, the local agents took us to Federico Lacroze railway station, where we got the night sleeper train to Posadas. This station was the terminus of the General Urquiza Railway, which, unusually for Argentina, was a standard-gauge line. Our train went by the impressive name of *El Gran Capitán*, and was long and relatively modern, with blue-and-white coaches that included sleepers and a buffet car. The journey took us across the flat and almost featureless pampas - the Andes were hundreds of miles to our west. We passed huge farms, twirling windpumps and English-looking stations with dog-toothed canopies over the platforms. Ian and I kept ourselves amused by playing Scrabble and listening to a transistor radio, where we heard the BBC World

Service announce the appointment of John Major as Prime Minister.

Our sleeping compartment was clean and comfortable, although unfortunately the window was badly cracked; it looked as if someone had fired a gun at it! We had a reasonable sleep and arrived at Posadas, on the Paraguayan border, at about 11.30 a.m. The station here was a hive of activity with lots of passengers getting on and off.

Dining-car on El Gran Capitán

Although my Thomas Cook Overseas Timetable showed that there were through coaches from Posadas to Encarnación, nobody on the train seemed to know about them, so we got off here and looked around for a taxi of some sort. A battered red pick-up truck stopped and we negotiated the fare with the driver and his wife. The journey took us to the Customs post where we had our passports stamped, and then across the mighty new suspension bridge over the River Paraná to Paraguay.

Our transport across the border

Paraguay's border town, Encarnación, was quite a lively place. The road surfaces were largely of beaten red earth, most buildings were single-storey affairs and a huge street market seemed to be in progress. Ian and I had lunch before setting off to the station, where the train to Asunción was scheduled to depart at 15.30. A few people were milling about, but there was no sign of any train, although a number of unkempt steam locomotives were in evidence.

We were able to purchase tickets to Asunción, although the stationmaster could give us no idea of when the train would leave. Encarnación station was a low, sprawling, red-brick building, with a battered nameboard giving the distances to Asunción and Buenos Aires. The station 'loos' were in a separate small detached building and must have been about the most disgusting I have seen (or smelled!) anywhere. The most interesting features of the station were the large corrugated-iron engine shed and the huge stacks of timber that formed the fuel for the locomotives.

Nameboard at Encarnación station

After waiting for a couple of hours, with no sign of any obvious activity, I managed to ascertain from the stationmaster that our train would not be leaving until at least 8pm. So Ian and I went off and explored the pleasant and colourful town. We changed some money into *guaranis* and bought a couple of cokes in an unbelievably dilapidated café. We also explored the street market, which seemed to sell mostly after-shave, deodorant, shampoo and assorted cosmetics.

Returning to the station, we witnessed a display of shunting that could have come out of a Laurel and Hardy film. A steam locomotive was marshalling some rolling-stock in an effort to make up a train, with the crew gesticulating and talking loudly in Spanish. Somehow one carriage got derailed on a set of points, which caused the crew and station staff to come and stare at it. Although the derailed carriage was fouling the main line, no-one seemed in a hurry to clear it out of the way. Our train was now five hours late.

Encarnación station may have been somewhat lacking in passenger comforts, but it was a great place to look at the night sky. The stars and the Milky Way were amazing. The only light pollution was the occasional shower of sparks from the chimney of the steam engine. All Paraguayan steam engines, incidentally, bore the date '21-X-1961' on the firebox door. This was not the date the locomotives were built, but the date the railway, known officially as the *Ferrocarril Presidente Carlos Antonío López*, was taken over by the Paraguayan State. The other extraordinary feature of the engines was their odour: a lovely wood-smoke smell like an autumn bonfire, quite unlike the classic oily-coal smell of a typical steam train.

At about 10pm we were exhorted to take seats in a rake of carriages, but someone then came along and told us that those coaches were going to Buenos Aires, so we got out and waited on what passed for the platform. Finally, locomotive number 54 (a 2-6-0 built by North British in 1911) reversed onto a second rake of coaches, and at 11pm we were off on our way to Asunción.

Two notable features about Paraguayan train travel: it was not very fast (14mph or so) and there was a constant rocking movement owing to the appalling state of the track. Most railway travellers are used to the 'clickety-clack' of the wheels on the rail joints, and the occasional clatter as the train crosses a set of points, but the up-and-down motion of this train had to be experienced to be believed. Still, it did manage to lull me to sleep…

I was woken up by a fellow passenger asking me in Spanish whether I had lost my bag. I looked up at the luggage rack and saw that it was indeed missing. Another passenger said he had seen a young man running down the carriage with the bag, which had been almost new and quite distinctive. After a few moments of panic, I called the guard and reported the loss. He brought the train to a halt in the small hours of the morning, at an apparently deserted station where a single light bulb burned. The stationmaster asked me to describe my bag. The guard was able to establish that the thief had got off the train at a particular station, and the stationmaster made a phone call. I was beginning to feel worried about the trouble I was causing, not to mention adding to the already long delay, when the phone rang and the stationmaster picked it up. He told me that the bag had been found lying beside the track apparently untouched! I had to put my trust in his assurance that they would get it back to me tomorrow in Asunción.

For the rest of the journey I kept a very close eye on my remaining shoulder bag. The guard had asked me if he could do anything to help, and I told him I would like to have a cab ride on the locomotive. He said that he would arrange this, and that he would let me know when.

Steam train across Paraguay

After sunrise, the guard came and tapped me on the shoulder. The train had stopped in the middle of nowhere, and this was my opportunity to ride in the cab. I got a couple of bottles of beer from the quaint old buffet car and walked up to the locomotive. The crew seemed to be quite prepared to welcome an enthusiast: I was allowed to take the controls (after they had showed me what to do!) and I also helped shift some of the big logs from the tender into the firebox. It was very hot on the footplate, and I think the driver and fireman were grateful for their cold beer! The up-and-down motion of the train was much more obvious when riding on the locomotive, and looking ahead it was sometimes hard to believe that there were any rails under the grass!

Locomotive No. 54 seemed to be losing steam, and I slipped off the footplate when the crew brought it to another unscheduled stop. We did not get going again for some time, so I went back to find Ian. At

6.30 am we limped into a station called San Salvador, where we should have arrived at 11.35pm! Here there were more delays as No. 54 was detached from our train and replaced with No. 152, a youngster dating from 1953 and built in Sheffield by the Yorkshire Engine Company.

We had breakfast and lunch on board, and even picked up a little time. We stopped at small, tumbledown stations where horse-drawn carts waited and the occasional passenger would get on or off. We passed numerous small villages, consisting of a handful of white cottages with corrugated-iron roofs. At Sapucay we passed the main locomotive workshops, where several steam engines could be seen, in various states of repair. From Ypacarai the railway took on almost a suburban character, and at 3pm we trundled into Asunción's grand colonial-style station, about eight hours late.

Train arriving at Asunción station

The agents had promised to meet us at the station, but I think they had given up and gone home long ago! We got a taxi to the Hotel Guarani, which was superb, with excellent rooms and facilities including a swimming pool , shops, lavish public rooms and a stunning receptionist!

On top of the fridge in our room was a small packet of sweets that looked rather like Smarties. Assuming this to be complimentary, we opened it and shared the contents. The following day, on checking out, I discovered that they counted as part of the mini-bar, and the price I paid for the sweets (about £2) was approximately the same as we had paid for our overnight train journey!

This luxury hotel contrasted vividly with the very run-down and old-fashioned impression we had gained of Paraguay. Asuncion proved to be an attractive city with neat parks, smartly-dressed inhabitants and lovely old colonial buildings. There were even trams running along the main street - I discovered later that these had been purchased second-hand from Brussels!

On the Friday morning, after a wonderful night's sleep, I got up early and headed for the station. I arrived just in time to watch the suburban train from Ypacarai enter the station, and I took a photo of it. I then went to the lost property office to see if they really had found my bag. Amazingly, there it was! I opened it and found that only a few minor items such as toiletries were missing; my clothes, a zoom lens from my camera and my guide books were untouched. I wonder if my shampoo, deodorant and after-shave appeared later on one of those stalls in the street market at Encarnación?

Later that day Ian and I were taken to the airport for a Lloyd Aero Boliviano flight to La Paz. This was a stopping flight calling at two provincial Bolivian airports, and the atmosphere was more akin to a country bus than an international flight.

We saw no trains in operation during our short stay in Bolivia, although we explored that city's imposing railway station with its clock-tower and its remarkable selection of antiquated rolling-stock.

Street scene in Asunción

The Paraguayan railway was obviously on its last legs in 1990, having surprisingly outlived several more sophisticated Latin American systems. In 1995 work started on the Yacyretá Dam Project, which raised the level of the Paraná River and flooded part of the line. A steam hauled suburban service continued to run out of Asunción, latterly at weekends only, until July 2000, when a train derailed, killing two passengers. The beautiful old station with its grand overall roof is now a museum, and, as for the trams, they stopped running in 1997. In 2004 there was a revival of sorts. A tourist train, using steam locomotive No 54(!) and a few restored coaches, began operating between Jardín Botánico (a new station on the outskirts of Asunción) and Areguá, a distance of about 7 kilometres, but this service was suspended in December 2006. The Sapucay workshops are reportedly still intact and there are long-term plans to rehabilitate the track between there and Asunción, but at present the only trains running in Paraguay are in the far south, taking agricultural produce to the freight terminal in Encarnación. Incredibly, they are still hauled by wood-burning steam locomotives, but there is now a big gap in the tracks and they can no longer run north to the capital.

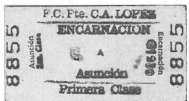

Ticket from Encarnación to Asunción

22. The Railway at the End of the World

October 2004: I travel on trains old and new in Argentina

The Argentineans never seem to know what to do with their railways. Once upon a time they had by far the best network in South America, if it could be called a network, since the main lines had been built by different foreign companies, all of whom used different gauges, rather like in Australia. In the 1990s the government shut down much of the system and withdrew almost all passenger trains overnight, but the opening years of the new millennium have seen a change of heart, with hundreds of kilometres of track refurbished and reopened.

Accompanying a group of British holidaymakers on a tour of Argentina, I was delighted to find that our sightseeing tour of Buenos Aires included a trip to the picturesque Tigre Delta, where we went on a boat cruise on the Rio de la Plata followed by a ride on a very scenic coastal suburban railway that is marketed as *El Tren de la Costa*. We joined the train at San Isidro, a lovely old colonial town with a beautiful church.

Street in San Isidro

None of us quite knew what sort of train would be coming, and it was quite a surprise when it turned out to be a modern two-car light rail unit. But the line itself dates from the 1890s and its origins were clearly British: most of the eleven stations along the 15-kilometre route retain their Victorian canopies and brick platform buildings. The station buildings have generally been converted to other uses: several are cafés or restaurants, and others are used for art exhibitions. Barrancas station is home to a vast flea market that occupies both platforms. Tickets are sold from a conductor on board the train; there are no longer any ticket offices at the stations.

The Tren de la Costa

The Tren de la Costa is fast, clean and smooth-riding, but seems to be more popular with foreign tourists than with local travellers. Perhaps the residents of these upmarket suburbs all have their own cars (or boats!) to travel into Buenos Aires, or perhaps the locals just aren't used to the line being open again for passengers after a long period of closure.

The train terminates at Maipú station, where there is little more than a set of buffer-stops: the site of the original station has been obliterated by a vast new shopping mall, although many of the shops were still empty at the time of my visit. But it was an enjoyable trip, and this venture to get passengers back onto Argentina's railways deserves to succeed.

From Buenos Aires we flew to Ushuaia, arriving late in the evening and transferring by coach from the airport to our hotel high above the town. It was a very comfortable place with quite luxurious rooms, although the TV in mine didn't work. Never mind, BBC World Service on short wave radio was clear, thanks to the relay in the Falklands - sorry, Las Malvinas! It wouldn't do to 'mention the war' here, as I saw a recent newspaper article saying that Malvinas veterans are to have an increase in their pensions, and very prominent on the seafront in Ushuaia is the Malvinas Memorial, with the names of the dead and the legend *Volveremos* (We shall return)! Even the airport is called Aeropuerto Malvinas Argentinas!

Strangely enough, there is a half-page report in today's Buenos Aires paper about the withdrawal of London's Routemaster buses! And the brand name on the pack of toilet paper in my hotel room is... Sussex! Funny how things over here can remind one of home.

The next mornng I awake to a light dusting of snow outside and soft flakes of snow are falling. I half expect to hear Johnny Mathis singing *Winter Wonderland* as I go in to breakfast! At 9 o'clock we are off to the Swiss-chalet-style 'End of the World' railway station to take the *Tren del Fin del Mundo*. This little narrow-gauge steam train takes us into the heart of the Tierra del Fuego National Park. It was originally built so that convicts from the prison in Ushuaia could bring timber from the forest to the city for use as building material and firewood. Ironically the little railway that was formerly responsible for damaging the environment now provides an environmentally-friendly way for tourists to visit the National Park!

Our train is hauled by a little tank locomotive called 'Camila', which looks genuinely Victorian but was in fact built only a few years ago by Winson Engineering of Daventry. The carriages are in a smart green livery, and a guard locks the doors on the *outside* before the train leaves. This causes one female passenger in our compartment to panic, as she was once involved in an accident on the Romney, Hythe and

Dymchurch Railway when her train hit a car at a level-crossing and overturned! She didn't fancy being trapped inside if we hit another car. But there are no cars and no roads where we are going.

Ushuaia Railway Station

The journey is pleasant and the scenery is quite spectacular. We cross the River Pipo and stop at an intermediate station called Cascada de la Macarena, where we are let off by the guard so we can view a nearby waterfall and a reconstructed native homestead. All around are tree stumps, relics of the old days when the convicts cut down the trees for timber.

Tren del Fin del Mundo at terminus

Reaching our terminus, at Parque Nacional station, we join a coach for a guided tour of the park. The scenery is excitingly wild. We are shown beaver dams and whole areas where trees have been brought down by beavers. 25 pairs of beavers were brought over from Canada and released here about 50 years ago by someone who thought it would be a good idea and that they would give the natives something to eat and make fur coats with! Sadly the Canadian beavers didn't grow the same thick furry pelts they did back home, and the meat wasn't much good either! So now there are 60,000 beavers in the Tierra del Fuego and they have no natural predators - a huge ecological mistake! But despite their numbers, we never saw one!

It was back to Ushuaia for free time and lunch. I must confess I was disappointed in Ushuaia. The name conjures up an end-of-the-world remoteness and loneliness, but, though the location *is* stunning, the city itself is rather unattractive. It reminds me of the shanty towns I've seen outside Cape Town, Port Elizabeth and other South African cities: hundreds of tiny, ramshackle wooden houses, put up with no regard to appearance or the neighbours. Some resemble giant dog kennels! In fact, perhaps they *are* dog kennels, because large, fierce looking dogs seem to be everywhere, not obviously belonging to anybody. Discarded plastic carrier bags and other litter blows around, and ancient Fiats rust at the roadsides. The centre has one street with fairly cosmopolitan shops, but beyond that the dirt roads lead away from the harbour and up to the mountains, lined with shabby wooden shacks.

"This is one of the most desirable areas of the town: a house here costs 30,000 pesos" says our guide. We look out and see the usual wooden dog kennels, mangy dogs and dismantled pick-up trucks. There are also derelict factories, built by Grundig and other European companies in the 1970s but closed and abandoned when the economic bubble burst.

It's time for our cruise along the Beagle Channel, and the catamaran really is immaculate. We sail past islands where seals and cormorants bask in the afternoon sun (yes, the weather *has* changed), and circle around the little island with the red-and-white *Eclaireurs* lighthouse. They put *Orinoco Flow* on the PA system (why is Enya ALWAYS playing wherever you go in Patagonia?) and we cruise back to Ushuaia. In the twilight it actually does look quite romantic.

Next day we are off to Lago Escondido - a hidden lake that nestles in the mountains. On the way, we stop to see some husky dogs, who have their own miniature Ushuaia to live in! We stop at a restaurant that has daffodils in bloom outside (the first I have ever seen in October!) and we have some delicious roast lamb for lunch. Now who forgot to pack the mint sauce?

Ticket for the Tren del Fin del Mundo

ASIAN AND

AFRICAN

JOURNEYS

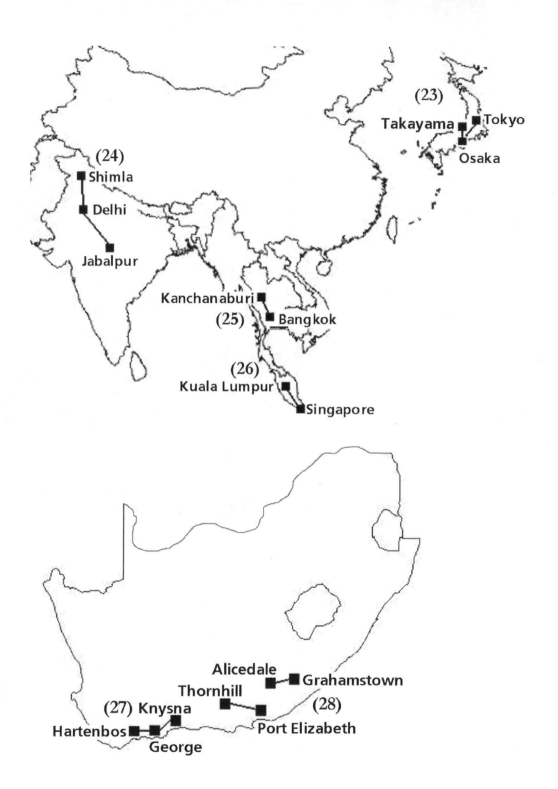

23. Going Japanese: Fast and Slow Lines in Japan

November 15 - 23, 2003: I enjoy seaweed, great coffee and excellent service on Japanese Railways

It was like a dream come true when my employers asked me to fly to Japan in 2003 to check out the route and hotels for a planned new tour. An added bonus was that much of the travelling was by train.

And so I found myself in the Land of the Rising Sun (if you see what they charge for English newspapers in Tokyo, then you understand how it got that name). What an amazing country! The mountains, lakes and thermal springs are straight out of New Zealand, the cleanliness, order and punctuality are straight out of Switzerland, but there's also a very distinct Japaneseness - the hundreds of salarymen in their identical dark suits, the Buddhist temples that crop up in the most unlikely places, the charming little gardens and the identical drab blocks of flats without a single piece of litter or graffiti.

I arrived at Tokyo and was greeted off the plane by Nori, my guide for the first few days. (Her name means seaweed in Japanese). She was a charming lady but she didn't stop talking. I was taken around the Asakusa Kannon Temple, the Meiji Shrine and the Imperial Palace Plaza, and given a whole potted history of the Japanese Meiji Emperors. By 3pm I was ready to collapse, and had already fallen asleep in the car a couple of times. Luckily we then got to the hotel, and I was able to crash out on my bed at 3.30pm, having been up for about 36 hours.

I woke up and saw the clock said 6.00. Not sure if it was AM or PM. By 6.30 it definitely hadn't got any lighter, so I decided it must still be PM. Thinking it would be a shame to waste the rest of the day, I spent an hour and a half doing my reports and then walked to the local railway station. I had been reading my *Great Railway Journeys of the World* book before leaving home, and it recommended a ride on the Yamanote Line. This line does a loop all around the city of Tokyo in 1 hour 15 minutes, and all you need to do is buy one ticket for 130 Yen - less than £1. It proved to be quite simple to use, the directions at the station are all in English and Japanese, and it was quite fun watching the locals getting on and off the train. Even at this time on a Saturday night, the train was crowded. On return to my starting point, I wandered around the various restaurants at the station, but decided to play safe and get a takeaway from McDonalds, which I consumed in my hotel room before going to bed again!

Sunday 8am and it's down in the lobby with Nori. We head off in a car past a number of hideous industrial suburbs and surprisingly beautiful beaches, full of surfers in wetsuits. Our goal is the Giant Buddha at Kamakura. I remember a picture of this in a 'Wonders of the World' book I had as a child. In the book, the picture was a most artificial blue-green, and the statue is actually of pure copper which has weathered to a green colour. It was wonderful to see it in real life.

After last night's cop-out, I allowed Nori to take me to a Japanese restaurant for lunch. For about £7 I get a small bowl of watery noodles with some green stuff and a large, dead-looking prawn floating in it. It tastes better than it looks. I ask Nori what the green stuff is, and she says "Nori".

143

We leave Kamakura and join a rather featureless motorway through flat farming country. Suddenly Nori gets the driver to stop the car, and points excitedly to the right. I can't see anything but clouds. "It's Mount Fuji!" she exclaims. I look again, and sure enough part of the cloud is actually snow. But it wouldn't come out on a photo so I don't attempt to take one.

Our programme was to have included a ride on a cable-car that afternoon, but it was so windy that they had closed it down. So instead Nori took me to Lake Ashi where we went for a mini-cruise on a large and comfortable boat. The lake and landscape strongly reminded me of Queenstown in New Zealand.

At 4.30pm we arrived at the hotel. Nori says I must try the spa. This meant that I had to put on a pair of slippers and a bathrobe called a *yukata*, and walk along a corridor to a bathroom, where I left my clothes, washed in a shower and then walked through stark naked into a hot bath filled with sulphurous water at 40 degrees Celsius and lots of Japanese businessmen. The bath was about the size of a small swimming pool, but less than a metre deep. I haven't a clue what the Japanese businessmen were talking about, and I'm not sure if I wanted to know!

After a day in the Hakone area, getting a much closer view of Mount Fuji, I said goodbye to Nori (lovely lady but her incessant talking was a bit of a burden!) and was taken to the station for my first-ever Japanese Shinkansen train ride. The bullet train was fast, smooth and perfectly on time. In its white livery it looked quite plain from the outside, even lightweight, but was very comfortable inside.

Japanese station nameboard

When we got to Nagoya, after an hour and a half, I accidentally let my suitcase fall on a Japanese businessman's head as I got it off the rack. Were I to do that in the UK I'd be sworn at (at least), in the USA I'd probably be sued. The poor Japanese man just wasn't bothered. I suppose the country is so crowded and public transport so tightly packed that most people over here just expect this sort of thing to happen. I don't know if the Japanese have a word for "Excuse Me" or "Sorry", but in the street people just barge in or push by without saying anything.

At Nagoya station I was met by Sato, younger, prettier and much less talkative than Nori! She took me to another platform for the local train to Takayama. This was a narrow-gauge diesel train, much slower than the Shinkansen, but still modern and comfortable. I was by now developing quite a taste for Japanese Railways coffee, though at nearly £2 for a small cup, it ought to be good! And the railway packed lunch, known as *ekiben*, that I bought at Nagoya to eat on the train, was delicious. The scenery along this line is fantastic, as it follows a river gorge for most of the way, and we passed tea plantations and an old castle. It's definitely the smoothest ride I can remember on a railway of less than standard gauge. I even wrote several postcards quite legibly, something which I could not have done on a train in New Zealand, South

Africa or the Montreux-Oberland-Bernois line in Switzerland, if travelling at the same speed as this one. Unfortunately, photography was difficult, as railways in Japan still have telegraph poles along them, and the lines were on my side of the train for this journey!

Sato meets me at the station

Takayama is really quite delightful, a low-rise city with lots of old traditional wooden houses, and Sato took me to the Festival Floats Museum. Here we saw some of the huge decorated floats (200 - 300 years old) that are paraded around the city twice a year at festivals. Now, why hasn't Hythe got a Venetian Fete Museum? They could build one next to the RH&DR station.

In the morning I was off to the station again for the train, this time heading for Kyoto. The journey was beautiful until we reached the outskirts of the large city. Kyoto Station is a vast teeming anthill that incorporates a large food court and shopping centre.

My hotel room in Kyoto overlooked a very British-looking car park, full of Nissans, Toyotas, Mazdas and Daihatsus. Luckily the place listed in the Lonely Planet Guide as having Internet Access came up trumps, so I could check my e-mail. The city looks rather dull and modern from the station, but has some of the oldest temples in Japan, and an amazing moated castle that looks nothing like those in Europe.

Takayama branch line train

I had a magnificent but exhausting two days with my very enthusiastic local guide Kaz. One of the highlights of Kyoto had to be the Three Springs. This is a temple with three streams running down, where you walk underneath and have to catch the water in a long handled ladle and drink from each spring. One is supposed to make you have a long life, another is supposed to make you rich and the third is supposed to make you better looking. I tried all three.

Kyoto temple gateway

Then there were the two stones about 40 feet apart. You are supposed to close your eyes and walk between the stones. If you can reach the second stone with your eyes closed, then it means you will be lucky in love. The result for me was a foregone conclusion - I set off from the first stone and collided with a wall about the right distance away but at completely the wrong angle!

From Kyoto I was taken by car we drove to the temple city of Nara, which looks much like any small Japanese city apart from the huge parks and the deer, which are everywhere! They sell little bundles of biscuits for 150 Yen for you to feed them with. The deer follow you about and are very friendly.

The temples I saw in 48 hours have all long since dissolved into a haze. I suppose if I took an average Japanese Buddhist over to England and gave him guided tours of Rochester, Canterbury, Salisbury, Winchester and Exeter cathedrals in two days, he would feel the same way. The temples are very historic and beautiful - it's just trying to remember what went where! The Todaji Temple is supposed to be the largest wooden building in the world - although I thought that was the old Government Buildings in Wellington, New Zealand! And the Horyuji Temple main building and pagoda date from shortly after 700AD and are supposed to be the oldest wooden buildings in the world... So I saw the oldest and the largest in the same day, and fed some deer into the bargain.

My final rail journey was via the delightfully-named Kinki Nippon Railway, run by the Kintetsu Corporation, from Nara to Osaka. This narrow-gauge line starts from an underground station in Nara's main street, but soon emerges into the open air to pass through some neat suburban stations before diving underground again as it approaches Osaka. The best thing about this railway is the ornate livery of its trains, which show deer, geisha, temples and other icons of the area. No 'tags' to be seen here, and they all look immaculately clean.

Geisha portrait on Kintetsu train

After a guided tour of Osaka Castle and some free time in the Dotonbori district, I go for a ride on the Osaka subway, but am a little disappointed that a line shown on the map as the 'new tram' turns out to be some kind of guided trolleybus. However, the 'Modern Transportation Museum' proves to be much more interesting than it sounds, with a collection of steam, diesel and electric locomotives, a very early Bullet train, motor vehicles and even a San Francisco cable car!

Preserved locomotive at Osaka museum

24. Jabalpur to Shimla: Monkey business in India

May 2005: Across India by broad and narrow gauge

My first experience of travelling in India was by car across Kerala. As a front-seat passenger it was a terrifying experience, as my driver repeatedly overtook on blind bends, nearly colliding with tuk-tuks, overloaded trucks, dilapidated buses and Hindustan Ambassador taxis. Although the Highway Code is technically much the same as in the UK, most Indians seem to drive in the centre of the road, unless something comes along in the opposite direction. The most important component of any car in India is the horn, and each driver must test his at least once every two minutes, to make sure that it still works. And, of course, cows *always* have priority.

After the roads, the Indian railway system is remarkably organised and efficient, once you have forced your way through the teeming anthills of its stations. My first Indian rail journey was an overnight train ride from Agra Fort Station to Jabalpur.

A busy Indian station

I normally enjoy train travel and this was no exception. India looks a lot different from the train as there is less litter, you don't see the ugly roadside stalls and highway detritus, so the villages look prettier. All along the line I could see tall chimneys indicating brickworks, surrounded by huge piles of bricks drying in the sun. You even get to see cows *in fields*. I had previously considered them a purely urban phenomenon in India.

The only thing I dislike about India, apart from manned urinals, is the litter. Along every road, and, to a lesser extent, railway track is an endless parade of carrier bags, plastic bottles, crisp packets, broken glass jars, cardboard and paper. When my guide finishes his plastic water bottle I am absolutely horrified to see him pull down the window and throw it out. I see other railway passengers drink their glass bottles of fruit juice and deliberately throw them out to try to smash them against an embankment wall. The only areas that seem to be immune from this menace are National Parks and historic monuments like the Taj Mahal, where there are big signs saying DON'T LITTER and amusing animal-shaped litter bins with PLEASE USE ME written on them. Railway stations are also quite clean, cleaner than in the UK. You often see young boys with broomsticks sweeping up any rubbish that has accumulated on the tracks, although I suppose they could be Harry Potter fans looking for the entrance to Platform Nine and Three Quarters. And railway stations and trains are blissfully free from graffiti, vandalism and scratches on windows, although perhaps there are so many staff around that the vandals don't get a chance.

At every railway station people get off to have a cigarette or stretch their legs. When the train pulls out they jump on, often after it has started moving. Each station is a mass of colour and it seems all India is travelling at the same time.

Unfortunately I get practically no sleep on this train. This was partly due to the noisy but ineffective fan revolving a few inches above my head, and also due to my Indian guide, who has accompanied me throughout my journey, snoring a few inches below.

Jabalpur is a busy, noisy, ugly, hot and dusty city with an immense railway station. Built by the British, the city is full of deliciously decayed Victorian buildings. The ruins of a Gothic Revival church or school somewhere in the centre look like Tintern Abbey. I am forcibly reminded of Maree in Australia, although Jabalpur has a population about 100,000 times greater!

There is also a narrow-gauge line at Jabalpur, but I do not get a chance to sample it, as my guide ushers me into a modern four-wheel-drive car to the Kanha National Park, passing through rural villages and narrowly missing oxcarts and hideously overloaded trucks. The main means of personal transport here appears to be the bicycle. They must make very good bike tyres over here.

At Kanha we are taken on an evening safari. The jeep stops and the guide says "Look! A tiger". I cannot see anything. He says "It's over by that green bush". This is not very helpful as there are green bushes everywhere. He then says "Look it's by the termite mound!" Then it is clear. A large ginger cat stalking through the grass with its tail held high just like my Rammy does when he is pleased with himself. I am amazed at how the stripes almost manage to conceal it. If it were still it would be very hard to make out. We also see monkeys, wild boar, Samba deer, spotted deer and plenty of birds, but nobody seems interested after the tiger.

Despite this, the real highlight of my stay in Kanha was when I was sitting by the hotel swimming pool when I saw a tree some distance away suddenly bend, heard a thump and then saw something walking along the ridge of the hotel roof. It leaped onto the wall around the hotel and then stood looking at me from under a bush. It was a grey langur monkey. Once it had discovered that I posed no threat, it walked to the pool, got on its hands and knees and started drinking from the pool. It must then have called to its family as seven or eight others came down and did exactly the same thing. One was a mother with a baby hanging from her stomach. The baby was almost hairless with bat ears and a very human appearance.

Almost before it seemed possible we were back at Jabalpur station. My guide looked worried. He says that he is extremely sorry but he has only been able to book us berths in separate compartments. But not to worry because he will swap with someone else when we get on the train. I tell him it is not necessary but he is determined. I say a little prayer.

My prayer is answered. In our compartment are a married couple and a Sikh soldier. My guide has a long argument with the latter but he has his ticket and reservation and seat number and there is no way he will move. He threatens to call the conductor. My guide slinks off to another compartment and I enjoy a glorious sleep from 9pm to 6am the next morning. I even discover how to switch off the noisy ventilation fan!

The travelling vendor sells me a delicious coffee for seven rupees in the morning, and we get off in Delhi, where I enjoy a sightseeing tour with a local guide, Parul. She shows me the beautiful Jama Masjid Mosque, and the Raj Ghat where Gandhi was cremated. She even organises a cycle-rickshaw ride through the warren of streets that make up Old Delhi. I find the Government area of New Delhi rather frigid and unappealing, like Canberra, the other planned capital I have visited. But the Lutyens area around Connaught Place has more character. Very British-looking neo-Classical buildings with great colonnades and pillars stand in testimony to the British Raj. Most of them however are in a terrible state, subdivided into tiny shops, with extra storeys added halfway up the columns and much of the exterior concealed by advertising hoardings. Elegant sash windows are broken or mended with cardboard, and there is lethal-looking electric wiring hanging off the walls like spaghetti. Wherever there is a gap between the buildings a whole row of little shacks has appeared. Since 1947 it looks as if the Indians are determined to make New Delhi into another Old Delhi.

From Delhi my guide arranged for me to go by train to the hill station of Shimla, the summer seat of Government during the period of the Raj. It has lots of Victorian buildings, a Colonial-style theatre and an impressive Gothic church. It is packed at this time of year but most of the visitors are Indians, which means that the market stalls cater for locals and the stallholders do not hassle you. The weather is a pleasant English summer climate. And looking out of the window of the hotel where I am staying, across the immaculate lawn, I could be in England. My hotel is a delightful Edwardian mansion that retains its original plumbing and electrical fittings. The furniture is solid and old, and the walls are lined with faded sepia photographs. Even the staff look like Colonial servants.

The narrow-gauge train to Shimla

Getting to Shimla was half the fun. A mainline train to Kalka and then a five-hour, 60-mile journey on a narrow-gauge train. I have been on the Ffestiniog Railway in Wales, and this is similar but three times the length. The scenery is stunning as long as you ignore the inevitable rubbish by the track. There are plenty of colonial relics along the way including an overgrown cemetery just outside Kalka where long-forgotten Victorians sleep their last sleep.

Some services on the Shimla branch are operated by amazing old railcars that look like Model T Ford trucks on rails, but I travelled in a proper locomotive-hauled train, which was well-filled, although there was nobody on the roof! Most of my fellow passengers were Indians and seemed to be going on holiday. Many of them were looking out of the windows at the scenery and kept leaping off to get photos of the train - and themselves - at the numerous en-route stops.

Refreshment stop en route to Shimla

At Solan the train - bizarrely - went right through a brewery. At Kandaghat station, we stopped to let another train pass, and here I bought an inexpensive and delicious cup of railway tea, served in a small disposable earthenware cup like a little flowerpot. Many other passengers finished their teas and simply threw the cups on the ground to smash them. At least this is more ecologically sound than throwing away polystyrene cups. Several monkeys looked on from the trackside during our stop here, and I chatted to two young Irish women who were on their first trip to India.

The famous Tunnel 33

The railway is noted for steep gradients, sharp curves and, of course, the tunnels, greatly appreciated by the children on my train. There are no fewer than 102 of them, each one of which is numbered. None are particularly long; the longest, Barog Tunnel (Number 33), is only about three-quarters of a mile. There are also some spectacular bridges. Unusually for a railway opened as recently as 1903, these are mostly built of superimposed rows of masonry arches, and remind me of the *Pont du Gard* Roman aqueduct in southern

France.

About two miles before Shimla, there are wonderful views of the hill station from a halt called Summer Hill. But whilst the wayside halts on the Shimla line are picturesque and well-maintained, the terminus is large, modern and devoid of any character. It does however enjoy magnificent mountain vistas, and there are a number of sidings full of interesting old stock and a shed containing a diminutive steam locomotive.

When I returned to Delhi, the last stop on my itinerary also had a railway connection. I was taken by my guide to New Delhi's Hazrat Nizauddin Station, where I saw the headquarters of the organisation called PRAYAS, who run a shelter, in a former goods warehouse, where children can receive food, clothing and emotional support. Delhi has an estimated 500,000 street children, and many of them congregate at the railway stations, where they are joined by others who have travelled from all parts of India. My guide has been working as a volunteer with PRAYAS, and hands out pens, pencils and exercise books to the eager youngsters. Some boys start an impromptu game of football on a piece of rough ground by a disused siding. I am shown around the shelter, which has a dormitory with bunk beds, and a schoolroom with computers, where children can practise their literacy and IT skills. I am assured that they have access to health care and counselling, and that, where appropriate, they will be reunited with their families or settled into residential care.

Each of these youngsters must have a tragedy of some kind in their past, but for now they are smiling, and, when I announce I am going to take a photograph, they eagerly pose for the camera. They are so keen to see the result on the little screen on the back of my digital camera that it gets passed around until the battery expires. I send them a print when I get home, together with more stationery. They are doing a wonderful job and deserve every success.

Viaduct like the Pont du Gard

25. The Living Portion of the Death Railway

February 16, 1999: Bangkok to the River Kwai Bridge

How many train passengers ever pause to consider the people who built the railway they are travelling on? Enthusiasts may think of the great engineers who planned it, whether it was Isambard Kingdom Brunel on the Great Western or Holman Fred Stephens on the Kent & East Sussex. But the thousands of navvies who laboured to build the embankments, dig the cuttings and lay the rails are generally forgotten.

Yet the Victorian navvies who constructed most of Britain's railways, despite their often appalling working conditions, had it easy compared with the unwilling builders of what is now the Thai State Railways branch line from Ban Pong to Nam Tok.

During the Second World War, Japanese forces invaded and occupied Burma. Any supplies to their troops in Burma had to come by sea, so they were very vulnerable to attacks by Allied submarines. In June 1942 the Japanese therefore started work on a railway to connect Ban Pong in Thailand with Thanbyuzayat in Burma, through the Three Pagodas Pass. Most of the rails came from lines that the Japanese dismantled in occupied Malaysia. But what has shocked the world ever since is the way forced labour was used in its construction. About 60,000 Allied prisoners-of-war and 200,000 Asian civilians worked on the railway. The living and working conditions on the railway were horrific. About a quarter of the prisoners-of-war died of overwork, malnutrition, and tropical diseases. The death rate of the Asian civilian workers was even higher. The dead POWs included over six thousand Britons and nearly 3,000 Australians.

The Death Railway was brought to the attention of the world by French author Pierre Boulle's book *The Bridge on the River Kwai* in 1954 and by David Lean's famous film three years later. Whilst loosely based on real events, the actual bridge was built in eight months (rather than two months as in the film) and was not sabotaged just as a train was crossing it. The original wooden trestle bridge erected by the POWs remained in use until it was replaced by a more permanent structure of concrete and steel in April 1943. Neither of the wartime bridges resembled that seen in the movie, which was actually built especially for the film - in Sri Lanka!

Some people may find the idea of travelling on the Death Railway distasteful. But surely the greatest tribute to its builders is that the south-eastern section of the line, reconditioned by the State Railways of Thailand after the War, is today providing a useful transport service for local people?

I spent three days in Bangkok on my way to New Zealand, and booked a number of sightseeing trips through the hospitality desk at the Royal River Hotel, where I was staying. For my last day, I had planned to book a trip to the Bridge on the River Kwai, which would include a short train ride and the chance to walk across the bridge. Unfortunately the courier refused to book me, as he was concerned that I would not get back to Bangkok in time for my flight.

Disappointed, I had a look at the *Thomas Cook Overseas Timetable*. It was not encouraging. There was a train from Bangkok to Nam Tok at 7.40am, but it would be impossible to get back in time for my flight. Then I saw a note in the timetable advising that there were 'frequent buses' from Kanchanaburi, five kilometres from the River Kwai Bridge, to Bangkok. Making my mind up, I booked an early morning call and a taxi from the hotel.

I had already inspected Bangkok's main Hualampong railway station on a walk around the city. It is a magnificent place, clean and smart with a great arched roof and efficient-looking modern trains. It was probably the grandest metre-gauge station I had ever seen. The Nam Tok train, however, left from Thon Buri station, which was across the Royal River, some distance from the city centre. Thon Buri looked much more like a South-East Asian station in a cheap movie - run-down, dilapidated and with some kind of impromptu market taking place in its concourse. I paid a ridiculous 29 Bahts (about 50p) for my third-class ticket to the River Kwai Bridge, a distance of 138 kilometres.

The train for Nam Tok

The train, consisting of a biggish diesel locomotive and a rake of old-fashioned carriages, filled gradually and left on time. The first part of the journey, rather like any suburban line, took us past the backs of other peoples' houses. Unlike the passengers on the Eastern and Oriental Express, almost all my fellow-travellers were locals, most of them only travelling short distances. The Thais are among the most courteous people in the world and they don't tend to speak to strangers unless spoken to. This means that the overseas tourist is not continually pestered by vendors or beggars, but also that it is not so easy to strike up a conversation.

There was one other obvious Westerner in my carriage: a pretty, plump girl of about eighteen, with pale skin and long fair hair. She told me she was from the USA, and, like me, her main reason for taking this train was so she could visit the River Kwai Bridge. But she seemed more interested in listening to her Sony Discman than in pursuing a conversation.

At Ban Pong the train left the Bangkok - Butterworth - Kuala Lumpur international line and headed north onto the branch. We were now out in the country, and the scenery became more attractive as we entered the jungle. The little stations were well-maintained with flower-beds and potted palms on the platforms. At one of them we stopped in a passing loop to let a long, magnificent train go by: the *Eastern and Oriental Express*, which does a side-trip to the River Kwai on its luxurious journey between Singapore, Kuala Lumpur, Butterworth and Bangkok.

The largest town served by the erstwhile Death Railway is Kanchanaburi, 133 kilometres from Bangkok. Here many thousands of allied POWs sleep their last sleep in a huge cemetery maintained by the Commonwealth War Graves Commission.

River Kwai Bridge Station

My train made an extended stop at Kanchanaburi station, and suddenly lots of British people got on! My carriage was filled with white faces. Someone said "Hi! Fancy seeing you here!" and I looked around to see the courier from the Royal River Hotel. He had brought his group to Kanchanaburi by coach and was now taking them on the train as far as the River Kwai Bridge. He was quite amazed that I had got there under my own steam, and very concerned that I was not going to get back to Bangkok in time for my flight!

The diesel locomotive hooted cheerfully, the last passengers took their seats and the metre-gauge train left Kanchanaburi. Seven minutes later we pulled into the flower-decked River Kwai Bridge station. Here nearly everyone got off: the plump American girl, the courier from the Royal River and his party, and myself. We watched our train leave the station, head across the famous bridge and disappear into the distance. Then we all started walking across the bridge in the wake of the train, looking down at the waters of the River Kwai. The steel bridge, the second to be built by the allied prisoners-of-war, was bombed towards the end of the war, and some of the spans have subsequently been rebuilt in a different style. A number of small, colourful boats were taking tourists on short pleasure-cruises below the bridge, while a couple of elephants and their mahouts waited for business. One of the original steam locomotives used on the line was on display near the bridge.

Train crossing the River Kwai

I didn't stay very long as I knew I had to get back to Bangkok airport. I hailed a *tuk-tuk* - the ubiquitous three-wheeled auto-rickshaw found all over Thailand - and asked the driver to take me to Kanchanaburi bus station. Here I was in luck, as a bus was just about to leave, and the next one was not for two hours. I bought my ticket from the driver, loaded my luggage and climbed aboard. Although it was a comfortable modern vehicle, it had neither air-conditioning nor opening windows. The long ride back to Bangkok was something of an endurance test, as the road surface was appalling and the heat stifling.

When the bus deposited me in a coach station somewhere in Bangkok, I had no idea where I was; only that I was supposed to check-in for my flight in half-an-hour. A *tuk-tuk* was waiting on the street corner. Could the driver take me to Bangkok International Airport? He could. I hauled my back-pack onto the tiny vehicle and we set off.

Almost at once I regretted my choice of transport. Bangkok is one of the most polluted cities on the planet and the *tuk-tuk* passenger is exposed to the exhaust fumes of all the other road-users. What was worse was that this particular driver seemed to have a death wish. We weaved dangerously in and out of traffic, mounted kerbs, crossed central reservations and took short-cuts along leafy back streets that ran alongside stinking canals. I had been feeling bad enough when I had got off the bus; after fifteen minutes in the *tuk-tuk* I was feeling quite sick and giddy.

A walk across the bridge

It was the most terrifying taxi ride I have taken outside Santiago in Chile. But, amazingly, we did it. The driver pulled up outside the international terminal precisely two hours before my flight was due to leave. I gave him a generous tip, but resolved to get a proper taxi next time - or to allow a bit more time and take the airport train!

26. The Art of Travelling Graciously: Singapore to Kuala Lumpur

December 2003: I explore the Malay Peninsula by rail

In December 2003 I went on holiday to Australia and New Zealand. I tried to book a flight via Kuala Lumpur, as some friends from the UK were working there. However, the only flight available was via Singapore. A glance at the *Thomas Cook Overseas Timetable* showed that it ought to be possible to do a side trip to Kuala Lumpur during my short break in Singapore…

I didn't get much sleep during the flight from Heathrow to Singapore. No turbulence or hijackers, but I was in the middle of three seats right next to the galley. A nervous woman of unidentified middle-European nationality was in the aisle seat, and a fat Australian guy with a weak bladder in the window seat. The plane was completely full, so they ran out of choices for food. But I *did* get to see the film *Pirates of the Caribbean*.

So when I got to Singapore my first thought was to get settled into a comfortable hotel. Fortunately I had made a provisional booking with the New Otani, and had an e-mail from Richard Tan at the hotel to prove it. So I hopped on Singapore's very smart and immaculate light rapid transit system, and after changing twice and passing smart and immaculate houses, flats and office blocks, I came out of Clarke Quay station and there was the New Otani just across the river. Once in, I produced the letter from Mr Tan, and the reception staff sent me up to the 7th floor where, it seemed, the lobby was located. (Why be boring and have a lobby on the ground floor?)

Mr Tan was charming and gave me a room straightaway, and booked me onto a 'trolley tour' and a river boat ride. The bedroom was fantastic. I had to pull a bit of paper saying SANITIZED from the loo before using it. Actually, the same word could be applied to the whole of Singapore!

I relaxed for a couple of hours and enjoyed the view from my room, before going downstairs to join the Trolley. My complimentary ticket, on closer inspection, was inscribed *Valid until December 31, 2000*, but the trolley driver didn't seem bothered by this, and ushered me on. The trolley is basically a bus designed to look like a 19th-century electric tram or streetcar, identical to the sightseeing trolleys in Boston and some other American cities. The commentary was not very clear, but you can't really complain about a free trip! I managed to stay awake for the whole circuit. Afterwards, I walked into Chinatown and had a look at the food stalls. Many were somewhat unappealing - Chili Crab and Fish Head Curry, for instance, but I found a stall selling vegetarian curry and got a well-filled plate for $2 (about 80p).

My next task was to contact my friends in Kuala Lumpur and see if we could meet up. A phone call proved positive, so I walked to Singapore railway station to buy a ticket for the next morning's train to Kuala Lumpur.

Singapore station is in a time-warp. Whereas everything else in the city is either brand new or heavily refurbished, the station is an Art-Deco gem in a backstreet location, overshadowed by a huge modern concrete motorway viaduct and with only a handful of cars in its car park. It's as if the city has forgotten it had a mainline rail station. The modern light rail system ignores it totally: you can only get there on foot or by bus. Inside, it is just about the only building in Singapore that is not air-conditioned! A handful of brass electric fans, straight out of *Casablanca*, whirl ineffectively on the walls. Even the travel posters showing various places in Malaysia have a 1930s look to them.

Façade of Singapore Railway Station

After getting my ticket, I had quite a good walk around the city before returning to the hotel and having a short snooze. I then went downstairs to join what is euphemistically described as a 'bum boat' for a cruise up and down the Singapore River. Bateau-mouche it ain't, but the commentary was clear and we got a wonderful view of the *Merlion* - the half lion, half fish statue/fountain that is the symbol of Singapore. Also saw some lovely Victorian colonial architecture and realised that this place really has STYLE.

After returning from the cruise, I got another cheap meal from a smart-looking food stall in Clarke Quay, then walked back to the hotel. I couldn't resist the thought of the swimming pool, so had a swim before collapsing into bed around 9pm.

Friday morning 7am and I had a splendid 'American' breakfast before leaving for the station. I took just a small shoulder bag, having left my backpack at the New Otani. The station was full of a heaving multitude, but there was no way of getting on the wrong train as there are only two platforms: #1 for departures and #2 for arrivals!

The train was very long and made up of fairly modern stainless steel coaches hauled by a diesel loco. I travelled in 'Air-conditioned Second Class' which was more than adequate for a daytime journey. The railway was built 100 years ago by the British, and this must be the reason why the trains have the alarming habit of suddenly coming to a halt in the middle of nowhere, although here it's in the wilderness, not opposite the *Great Mills DIY Superstore* just outside Bickley! The railway corridor through Singapore is like a tentacle of untamed jungle running into a well-manicured garden. It is so obviously a Malaysian enterprise.

After crossing the causeway into Malaysia proper, we all had to get out at a huge modern 'station' in the middle of nowhere - the rather sinister 'Train Control Point', and go through Passport Control and Customs before re-boarding the train. It reminded me of Port-Bou or Hendaye circa 1981!

I would be a liar to describe this as one of the greatest scenic railway journeys I have ever undertaken. The line is relatively straight and level, and most of the way all you see is dense jungle, with occasional very un-Singaporeish settlements and little wayside stations. At times the vegetation (comprising mainly of things that look like giant rhubarb) seems to be pressing in on the train and threatening to engulf the track: this narrow-gauge, single-track link seems quite fragile. Long-abandoned telegraph poles alongside the track have been colonized by creepers and look like strange exotic trees.

Train for Kuala Lumpur at Singapore

You realise you are coming into KL when the railway suddenly becomes electrified, the shabby country stations change into neat concrete halts and you start passing suburban commuter trains. These are mostly blue with a yellow front end, and I think they look very smart - then I realise that it is almost identical to the old pre-privatisation British Rail livery! You do also get good views of the lofty Petronas Towers.

I will not dwell much upon my time in Kuala Lumpur as it consisted largely of catching up with a couple of friends I had known for years and who had recently moved to Malaysia to teach English for two years. They knew the city well enough to take me around by car, but we also took taxis and the most incredible monorail to explore parts of the centre.

To summarise KL - it's vast, it's very cheap and very modern. In one street a quaint old building bears the date 1962 on its façade. And the National History Museum, opened in 1963, is officially listed as a historic structure! Of course, there are the occasional Colonial wonders, such as the amazing neo-Moorish railway station, sadly no longer served by the trains from Singapore, which stop at a characterless modern shopping-mall-type place called Kuala Lumpur Central (which it isn't). A highlight of my stay in KL was watching monkeys cross the road!

I had tried to book a sleeper for my overnight journey back to Singapore, but sadly none were available. This seems to be a popular train and gets fully booked. I had to settle for Air-conditioned Second Class again, but this was not as much fun by night as by day, For one thing, the lights were left on all the time in the carriage! And I was near the front, so I could not fail to be aware of the video screen on which an extremely loud and violent American war movie was playing. Then a very fat man came and sat next to me! I tried to curl up, and put my Walkman headphones on, plus one of those eyepatch things you get on planes. It succeeded and I soon fell asleep, only to be rudely awakened by the guard inspecting my ticket!

The worst thing about the journey was not so much the light and the noise from the film, but the bumpy condition of the track and the constant squealing of the wheel flanges against the rails! The sort of things which add character to a daytime journey are less appealing when you want a good night's sleep!

Taking Kuala Lumpur's monorail

Of course, I had got to sleep again when it was time to be woken up as we were ushered off the train so they could do the passport check, and we had to go through Customs just in case anyone was trying to smuggle any chewing gum or other illegal substances into Singapore. And I think someone must have been, as we waited about an hour after Customs before they would let us back on the train. It then carried on at a snail's pace to Singapore, arriving a little over an hour late.

Light rain greeted me on my arrival in Singapore. I returned to the New Otani Hotel, showered and changed and dumped some luggage, and spent an interesting day sightseeing and shopping. In the afternoon I walked to the elegant, colonial Raffles Hotel, entered the Long Bar, sat down and ordered a Singapore Sling. It was a vivid pink colour and was delicious. I could easily have had more than one, had I not been a bit pushed for time.

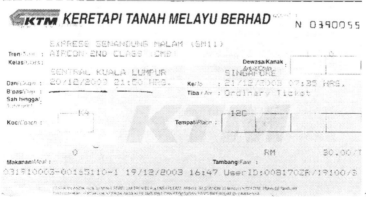

Ticket from Kuala Lumpur to Singapore

During my stay in Singapore, the three quite substantial meals I purchased cost $2, $2 and $3.50 respectively. The Singapore Sling cost $18.45! But it came with a bowl of roasted peanuts, and, when you shell them, you are actively encouraged to throw the shells on the floor. So you are paying for a permit to litter in this otherwise litter-free city! And the atmosphere is fantastic - you can just imagine Noel Coward or Joseph Conrad stepping in!

And all too soon it was back on the immaculate MRT light rail system to the immaculate Changi Airport for my flight to Sydney. My final sight of Singapore's transit system was of a poster stating 'Graciousness is caring for others by giving up your seat to those who need it more'. How much more poetical than the similar exhortations on London Underground!

Singapore Transit poster

April 16, 2002 and March 21, 2007: The Glorious Garden Route

In the mid-1980s, when taking groups on coach tours around Europe, I occasionally had South Africans among my customers. Once they realised I was a railway enthusiast, they would do their utmost to persuade me to go there: lots of steam trains, wonderful scenery and a great way of life. At the time, any idea of going to South Africa was totally anathema to me. I remember once being in Lisbon and a South African woman in my group refusing to go in the lift at our hotel because there were a couple of black gentlemen in it.

My first visit to South Africa was in 2002, eight years after the collapse of the apartheid regime. By this time steam had disappeared altogether from the main lines, and the country had changed completely. The South African agent who took me from Durban to Kimberley reminisced about the 'good old days', and, once he found out I was a railway enthusiast, took me to a dump outside Kimberley station, where we saw row upon row of derelict steam locomotives.

South African railway graveyard

It was on a second trip to the country later that same year that I was to make my first journey on a South African train. I was staying in Port Elizabeth and decided to spend a day driving along the 'Garden Route' to take a trip on the 'Outeniqua Choo-Tjoe', billed as South Africa's last scheduled steam train. I phoned ahead to book my seat, and left early in the morning in my hire car. I decided to do the round trip from Knysna, a beautiful town set on a lagoon that is apparently noted for its oysters. Knysna was founded by a man called George Rex, who is said to have been an illegitimate son of King George III of England; George Rex's grave is reached by a rough track from the main road.

I drove to Knysna on the N2 from Port Elizabeth, parked in a quiet-looking side street, and walked to the railway station on the quayside, where an immense steam locomotive was waiting at the head of a train of red-and-cream coaches.

Although South African railways are laid to a gauge of only 3 feet 6 inches, their steam engines look huge when you see one at close quarters, and their passenger compartments are remarkably spacious. The only time you realise that you are on a line of less than standard gauge is when you occasionally feel a bit of rough riding on the track.

The Outeniqua Choo-Tjoe at Knysna

I collected my ticket from Knysna station office and boarded the train. Some of the six carriages were booked 'en bloc' for tour groups, but seating within others was unreserved. I found a window seat by the buffet car. The coach was a delightful period piece with varnished wood and polished brass handles, and the sort of windows you raise or lower by means of a leather strap. There was a long 'toot' from the steam whistle and we were off.

The train was almost full: a high proportion of the travellers were from coach parties, most of whom were taking the train in one direction only as part of a tour of the Garden Route. A small selection of drinks was available from the period buffet-car.

Leaving Knysna, the train crossed the lagoon on a long trestle bridge that was so low it gave the impression that we were steaming along the water. Beyond the lagoon we passed the suburb of Belvedere. This is a very English-looking spot, where large, old houses set in leafy gardens surround a perfect reproduction of a Norman village church. The train descended in a series of curves to Goukamma, crossed the Zwartvlei River and then came to a halt in Sedgefield station, where we passed another steam train going in the opposite direction: a rare sight on South African railways.

Leaving Sedgefield we entered a wild region of tidal lakes where we saw vast numbers of wild ducks. There were several little halts here, but the next proper station was called Wilderness. Despite its name, this is actually rather a civilised seaside resort with neat bungalows and a lovely long sandy beach. After Wilderness, our train passed through a short tunnel and then crossed the most remarkable feat of engineering on the line: the curved Kaaimans River Bridge. Seen in numerous South African holiday brochures, this bridge took two years to build and was one of the reasons why this branch line was said to be the most expensive stretch of railway in the world at the time of its opening in 1928.

Crossing Knysna Lagoon

Many passengers were leaning out of the windows trying to get photographs, but the movement of the train made this difficult. After the bridge, our train shot through two more tunnels and then emerged on a high cliff face above the sea. The final part of the journey towards George was chiefly through scented bluegum forests and was on a steep gradient. We passed by the old railway station and locomotive workshops of George (named after King George III and the sixth-oldest town in South Africa) before coming to a halt at a new platform adjacent to the Outeniqua Railway Museum.

The museum was a real treat, with steam locomotives, old carriages (including one once used on a Royal Train), other items of rolling-stock and a number of historic road vehicles. The range of souvenirs and books on sale was rather disappointing, but I was delighted to find a 'squashed penny' machine, dispensing elongated coins with a fine portrayal of a steam locomotive for a very reasonable five rands.

The brochure I picked up in 2002 described the 67-kilometre George - Knysna railway as the most beautiful train journey in the world, and emphasised how it was being preserved as a cultural treasure for generations who never knew the excitement of the steam age. The line also still saw occasional freight trains, including a 'binliner' train that took out all Knysna's waste. It seemed as if this beautiful line and its immaculate locomotives (mostly SAR Class 24 2-8-4s dating from 1948) would go on forever.

Alas, in August 2006 the Garden Route was hit by a series of storms and heavy rainfall. Landslides washed away much of the track in the Wilderness area, and also caused serious damage to the parallel N2 main road. At first the Outeniqua Choo-Tjoe's website announced that services would be restored as soon as the line could be repaired, but it then became clear that the cost of repairs would be astronomical. At the time of writing the railway is still closed and there is no rail access to Knysna; no steam whistles can be heard on the Lagoon and no 2-8-4s thunder across the Kaaimans Bridge.

But they had to do *something*. Fortunately the locomotives and rolling stock, shedded at George, were still intact, and the management of the Choo-Tjoe reached an arrangement with South African Railways to run their train along a section of the main line between George and Hartenbos.

In March 2007 I returned to South Africa and decided to sample the 'new' Outeniqua Choo-Tjoe. I drove to George, paid another visit to the railway museum and enquired about a seat on the train. Although I should have booked 24 hours in advance, there was no problem in obtaining one. The train consisted of only five coaches and was barely half full. It was hauled by a heritage diesel locomotive (built by General Electric in 1960); owing to the dry weather there was a risk of veld fires and steam engines were temporarily banned.

The tour parties who made up the majority of the passengers were doubly disappointed. Many of them had been expecting to ride to Knysna; all of them had been expecting to ride behind steam. Our brave little engine made a valiant attempt at jollity with a few sharp blasts on the horn as we left the museum platform, passed through the empty George station and then continued straight ahead on the line towards Cape Town; the disused Knysna branch curved off to the left.

Scenically, this centenarian line was a very good second-best to the Knysna route. The first few kilometres were rather scruffy, as we passed farms and some of the sprawling townships outlying George. After crossing the Gwaiing River, the train started a long, slow climb into the Maalgaten Valley. The highlight of the journey was crossing the Maalgaten River on a very high steel bridge. Beyond the river the line descended gradually towards the sea, with superb views of the Indian Ocean on the left. These views were temporarily interrupted by the only tunnel on the line.

Diesel-hauled 'Choo-Tjoe' at Hartenbos

There was another large bridge, across Great Brak River, before we reached Hartenbos station. This was quite nicely maintained, with some lovely flowering shrubs on the platforms and a restaurant in the station building. Just before entering the station, the train passed a line of rondavels - traditional circular thatched huts.

I stepped down from the train and walked down towards the beach. On the way I passed the rondavels, and discovered that they were in fact accommodation units in an upmarket hotel. There had been no buffet car on the train, so I went into a supermarket for something to eat and drink. Everyone there was white and they were all speaking Afrikaans. Two or three 1960s cars were parked outside, adding to the impression that I had stepped back into another era. The beach was sandy and the sea looked inviting; I asked two golden-skinned Afrikaans-speaking women if they would keep an eye on my clothes while I went for a swim. I had to step very carefully into the water as there were a few jagged rocks, but by following the locals I was able to avoid them. Once I was safely past the rocks, the water was fantastic.

I later found out that Hartenbos had been founded in 1936 as a holiday resort for white railway workers by the Afrikaans Language and Cultural Society. It therefore made quite an appropriate terminus for the Choo-Tjoe, but services have now been extended along the coast to the historic port of Mossel Bay.

28. South African Contrasts: The Game Train and the Apple Express

March 28-31, 2007: After a false start I ride from Grahamstown to Alicedale; then I join the tourists on board the *Apple Express*

Most South African passenger trains fall into one of two categories. There are crowded suburban services on which virtually all the passengers are black, and luxurious long-distance trains on which most of the passengers are white - or foreign tourists. The main lines were generally built to open up the country and to link the cities and harbours that had been built by the colonial powers: they would have been totally alien to the native population. The suburban lines were built later, to bring the black workers from the townships into the white cities. To many black Africans the railway must have been a symbol of oppression. During the Apartheid era, train driving was an occupation reserved exclusively for whites, whilst passenger trains had separate carriages for whites and non-whites: the 'white' coaches were always marshalled at the rear of the train. Even small stations had separate footbridges for black and white passengers; large stations such as Cape Town had concourses in duplicate.

Nowadays most mainline passenger services are run by an organisation called *Shosholoza Meyl*. The rural branch line is practically extinct in South Africa, at least as far as passenger trains are concerned. One of the last survivors is the 57-kilometre route between Alicedale and Grahamstown.

Grahamstown city centre

166

Grahamstown is a charming university city in miniature that is one of the oldest and most beautiful towns in South Africa. It was founded in 1812 and by the start of Queen Victoria's reign was probably the second-largest city in sub-Saharan Africa after Cape Town. A military base, a centre for learning and the seat of a bishop, it was naturally expected that the main railway north from Port Elizabeth would pass through here. But the discovery of diamonds in Kimberley changed all that, and Grahamstown was bypassed. It was eventually served by a branch line from Alicedale, opened in 1879.

On my first visit to Grahamstown, as part of an organised sightseeing tour from Port Elizabeth, I was taken to the fascinating Victorian *Camera Obscura* at the top of the Observatory. Here I had a remarkable view of the whole town, including the railway station. When I had a bit of free time before rejoining the bus, I decided to walk to the station to have a look around. Outside was an old Garratt steam engine that had obviously not turned a wheel for many years. But an inspection of the station showed that *it* was still active. I heard a train approach and soon a blue diesel locomotive came into view, hauling two carriages. Twenty or thirty passengers got out and walked through the booking office and up to the High Street. Then all was silent again. A glance at my Thomas Cook Overseas Timetable showed that this train ran once daily, and was scheduled to leave Grahamstown at 2.30pm. Sadly that day I had no means of getting back to Port Elizabeth from Alicedale, so I had to let the little blue train leave without me.

Train at Grahamstown in 2004

Three years later I found myself back in Grahamstown. I hitched a ride there on another excursion bus from Port Elizabeth, and presented myself at the station at about a quarter past two. All was quiet. I saw someone who looked like a member of *Shosholoza Meyl* staff locking up the ticket office, and asked him when the next train was to Alicedale. "Tomorrow!" he said. "But the timetable says 14.30!" I said. "Yes", he replied, "but it leaves at 13.00 on Tuesdays!" So I had to get a lift back to my hotel.

I was determined not to leave South Africa this time without travelling on that train. I discovered that Peter, a very knowledgeable gentleman who takes groups on trips from Port Elizabeth, was driving his daughter to Cradock at 6am the following morning, and that he could drop me off in Grahamstown. What was even better was that he was scheduled to pick up a tour group at Bushman Sands Game Reserve, near Alicedale, that afternoon and transfer them back to Port Elizabeth. He said "Just ask the train driver to stop to let you off at Bushman Sands. You'll know you're there when the train crosses the golf course!"

I had plenty of time to kill in Grahamstown the next day, but it's a very interesting city to kill time in, and I saw relics of the early settlers in the History Museum, came face-to-face with a preserved coelacanth in the Institute of Ichthyology and walked to the corner of Worcester Street to post some cards in South Africa's oldest pillar-box, a fluted red 'VR' specimen dating from 1860. I then pretended to be a student and had a picnic in the grounds of Rhodes University. A final walk along the broad High Street took me past the fine Gothic cathedral (designed by Sir George Gilbert Scott) to Birch's clothing store, where an overhead wire system taking cash and bills from the various departments to a central cash desk remains in working order. I can remember as a child being mesmerised by a similar 'cash railway' in an old department store in Maidstone, Kent.

View from the Grahamstown train

I reached the station early and purchased my ticket. I found the train driver and asked him to drop me at Bushman Sands. He said something in Afrikaans which I hoped was in the affirmative. A handful of passengers boarded the train and we set off. Apart from the driver, I was the only white person on board. The carriages had evidently been refurbished recently, and were clean and comfortable, but the colour scheme, both inside and outside, was a little garish.

It was assuredly a most scenic journey. The line loops around the city, with good views of the cathedral and some of the grand Victorian school buildings. Then we started climbing along a steep embankment and passed the remains of a large brickworks, which had once obviously had its own private siding. A single tall chimney remained, with a ceramic lavatory bowl incongruously perched on the top of it: the highest public lavatory in South Africa!

The train climbed steadily to a station called 'Goodwinskloof', where we did not stop, and also passed through quite a lengthy tunnel. Most of my fellow-passengers looked like university students and were more interested in their studies than in the scenery. The line does see occasional tourists, some of whom ride it as part of a package marketed as 'The Game Train', for reasons that will soon become obvious.

I kept shifting from the left to the right to get the best views, as the line turned and twisted along a high escarpment to reach Atherstone station. Now rather run-down, the station is named after the man who identified the first diamond found in South Africa. The nameboard outside the corrugated-iron waiting-room showed the distance to Alicedale in miles. A little boy was playing on the platform, pushing an old bicycle wheel up and down. He waved at us while the train made a perfunctory halt.

Beyond Atherstone, the line started to lose height quite dramatically. There was parched red countryside on both sides, and tall fences. I have been in South Africa enough times to know what that means: game reserves. It is apparently quite common to see rhinos and elephants along this part of the line, but I didn't, although I did see zebra, blue wildebeest, several antelopes and a warthog - the latter was right beside the track. The train continued through this very African landscape, then reached the broad New Year's River. We passed a large dam that had been built to supply water for the steam engines that formerly worked the line. After a short curved tunnel, the landscape suddenly changed to manicured grass and immaculate parkland. We were crossing a golf course! The train slowed and I stepped off. I saw Peter and his group waving to me from a verandah across the fairway. I had arrived at Bushman Sands.

Train crossing the Golf Course

The train carried on to Alicedale station, a little further along, where it connected with the main-line sleeper from Port Elizabeth to Johannesburg. The present station is an unlovely concrete structure, but in the days of steam Alicedale was a major depot and included a railway training centre. This was the very building where I was now sipping a glass of Castle lager five minutes after getting off my train - the old railway structures have been refurbished and now form the Bushman Sands Hotel. The hotel's 18-hole golf course not only incorporates an active stretch of railway track, but also a small cemetery where a number of victims of an early train crash are buried.

Peter's group had ridden on the train two days previously, and we swapped game-viewing stories. "Was the boy with the wheel still there?" one of them asked.

I returned to Port Elizabeth by road, but I made another railway journey three days later, and this time the train left from Humewood station in the 'Friendly City' itself. Port Elizabeth, affectionately known as 'P.E.', somehow succeeds in being a busy port, a cultural and historical centre and a beach resort at the same time, but the best beaches are to be found to the west of the city, in the slightly genteel English-looking suburb of Humewood. I am fortunate in having some very good friends living there.

I was staying in the charming Humewood Hotel, a 1920s gem across the road from the beach, and I walked to the station with Heather and Lindsay, a Scottish couple who were spending their holiday in the same hotel. The line that we were about to explore is built to a gauge of only 2 feet. It is remarkable because of its length: most 2-foot gauge railways are short feeder lines, but this one is 285 kilometres long!

It also features the 77-metre Van Stadens Bridge, the highest narrow-gauge railway viaduct in the world. The line goes from Humewood Road station to Avontuur, but most of it has been closed to regular passenger trains for many years. A tourist train, the *Apple Express*, runs two or three times a month as far as a station called Thornhill, and this was to be our destination that day.

The Apple Express is normally steam-hauled, but we were disappointed to see a modern orange diesel locomotive being coupled onto our train: steam traction was not permitted owing to the dry weather and the high fire risk. The station ticket office was shut, so we assumed we would have to buy our tickets on the train. Heather, Lindsay and I took seats in an empty compartment and waited for the conductor. He came along and asked for our tickets. We explained that we didn't have any, and he told us that we couldn't sit there, as we had to buy our tickets first from another man on the platform, who would allocate us our seats. We found the ticket queue and at last handed over our money. When we received the tickets, we had been allocated seats in the very compartment where we had just been sitting!

Apple Express at Humewood Road

With a blast from the two-tone diesel horn, the Apple Express left the platform, passed the old depot where a couple of forlorn steam locomotives were rusting on a siding, and then crossed the main coastal road on a modern bridge. We saw King's Beach in the distance to our left as we travelled up a green valley, passing the modern locomotive works where the operational steam engines are kept. The train then began to climb steadily. We passed some of Port Elizabeth's townships, where the children gathered by the track to wave at us, and then went right past Port Elizabeth Airport. I have driven from Humewood to the airport on several occasions, and it is no great distance, but how much more fun it would be if they re-opened the line for a regular passenger shuttle service to the airport, especially if it were steam-hauled?

Leaving the city behind, we crossed fertile farmland as we headed west. We passed several derelict halts and stations, but our first actual stop was in a station called Chelsea. A rusting siding on the right here was once an industrial branch line, but it now seemed to be used only for storing condemned wagons. The station building was little more than a shell, but a stop was made here for photos.

Back on the train, we continued our steady climb, passing through a disused station called St Albans that looked little like the one in Hertfordshire, although the trees and fields around here *do* have a rather English look. We also stopped at Witteklip, where a large number of modern goods wagons could be seen, loaded with timber. This is the principal freight now carried on the line, although, as one might expect from the name of the train, it was originally built to carry fruit and other agricultural produce.

The highlight of the journey was 43 kilometres out from Port Elizabeth. Here we stopped in front of the great chasm that is the Van Stadens River. The conductor walked along the train inviting passengers to get off and walk across the famous viaduct, and wait on the opposite side of the river to take pictures as the train came across.

The forlorn Chelsea railway station

Walking on the bridge was quite an experience. Through the sleepers you could see the river 77 metres below, and downstream in the distance was the graceful N2 road bridge that I had driven across on several occasions. Most of the railway passengers took advantage of the chance to walk across, and I became aware that this was the most racially-mixed train journey I had yet taken in South Africa!

Walking across the Van Stadens Bridge

Heather, Lindsay and I took photos of the train as it crossed the viaduct, and the locomotive then sounded its horn several times to make sure that everyone knew it was time to re-board. The countryside was green and lush, with the Elandsberge mountains on the horizon to our right. The celebrated Garden Coast was only a few kilometres to the left, but this was not evident. The line does in fact pass close to the seaside resort of Jeffrey's Bay on the freight-only section beyond Thornhill.

The train's arrival at Thornhill was celebrated by the sight of children waving from the trackside and then running alongside the moving train as it slowed for the station. The corrugated-iron station buildings here were well-preserved. The locomotive was uncoupled and 'ran around' the train, and I adjourned with Lindsay, Heather and the majority of the train's passengers to the Thornhill Hotel, where I sat in the garden with a cool glass of Castle lager and enjoyed the packed lunch I had brought with me from Humewood. It was very warm and some passengers headed for the shade and cool of the bar, whilst others preferred to stretch out on the lawn in the autumn sun. A few of the children played ball games, but it was a lazy Saturday afternoon for most of us, relaxing and waiting for the little train to take us back to Port Elizabeth.

The Apple Express returns to 'P.E.'

The return journey was accomplished in slightly less time than the outward one, as we were travelling downhill and we were not given the opportunity to walk over the Van Stadens Bridge. As we turned the corner and the ocean came into view, I realised we were almost home. After a final few photographs I was walking back along Beach Road to the cosy lounge of the Humewood Hotel.

A ticket to ride - on the Apple Express

AUSTRALASIAN

JOURNEYS

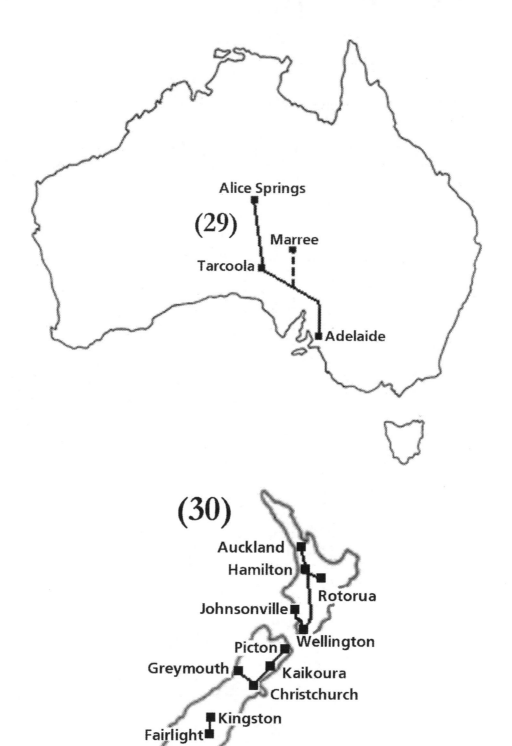

(29)

Alice Springs

Marree

Tarcoola

Adelaide

(30)

Auckland

Hamilton

Rotorua

Johnsonville

Wellington

Picton

Greymouth

Kaikoura

Christchurch

Kingston

Fairlight

January 10 - 11, 2004: Alice Springs to Adelaide

I spent the first nine days of 2004 on a Backpackers' Bus tour from Adelaide to Alice Springs. This took me along part of the old Ghan railway and past bits of the Overland Telegraph Line. One of the stops on this trip was at Marree, where the temperature was about 45°C (113°F). Whilst the others on the bus headed for the cool interior of Marree's last remaining shop, I walked over to the huge, derelict railway station to examine the old narrow-gauge diesel locomotives that were silently rusting there. Marree was once a flourishing railway town but is now little more than a ghost town. It was one of Australia's 'break-of-gauge' stations, like Albury between Sydney and Melbourne. The standard-gauge track never got any further north than Marree; here passengers had to disembark with all their luggage and worldly goods and transfer to the narrow-gauge, 16mph *Ghan* for Alice Springs. Marree station was abandoned in 1980 when the old line to The Alice was closed and replaced by a brand-new standard-gauge line on a completely different alignment. The old narrow-gauge tracks have been pulled up, but the course of the line is still marked by decaying wooden sleepers that are gradually being devoured by termites.

Remains of the old Ghan railway

Alice Springs is a nice place to chill out, a pleasant, medium-sized, middle-class town just plonked down in the middle of nowhere! As Nevile Shute says, it has an ice cream parlour and a cinema. It now also has traffic lights, a McDonalds and a KFC! It is one of the best places in Australia to get an understanding of Aboriginal culture. The Old Telegraph Station and Flying Doctor Service are well worth visiting, and there are plenty of shops, especially for those who like purchasing didgeridoos.

January 10th and I am off to the station for the train to Adelaide. Alice Springs railway station only comes to life twice a week when the *Ghan* train comes in, but it will be a bit busier from next month when the long-awaited extension to Darwin is opened. Then it will be the mid-point rather than the terminus of the line. The station was rebuilt when the line to Darwin was first planned, and is quite modern with little character.

Old Ghan locomotive at Marree

The train, on the other hand, is redolent with character, with the name proudly emblazoned on each gleaming stainless steel carriage. Inside it is comfortable, with a décor that was probably deliberately old-fashioned when it was built in 1981. I am in Red Kangaroo Class, with wide reclining seats. I have access to a Lounge Car, all panelled in wood inside, and to a dining-car that is pure Art Deco with plenty of chrome and blue plastic. As the train rolls out of Alice Springs, I see a row of telegraph poles from the Overland Telegraph line. But soon the suburbs of The Alice give way to the Outback, with trees, shrubs, red earth and the occasional cow and kangaroo. The scenery will remain much the same for the rest of the 520 or so miles south till we join the main east-west line at Tarcoola.

Opposite me I have been vaguely aware of two women chatting in German. The one seated by the window puts on earphones and starts listening to her Sony Walkman. The one in the aisle seat turns towards me and we start to talk. This young German lady is quite simply stunning. She says her name is Sissy, which, with my surname being what it is, rules out any hopes of marriage. But we have quite a nice chat. She's from Heidelberg and has been on a sabbatical in Australia. Her English is almost flawless. What is even more flawless is her face: big blue eyes, delicate little slightly upturned nose, full lips and long blonde hair that falls down her back in two tresses, with the odd curl escaping and winding itself seductively around her ears.

Conversation is not possible for very long, as the train management decide it's time to show some movies. Well, two movies in fact. *Harry Potter and the Philosopher's Stone* followed by *E.T.* I'm not a great movie goer so it's rather unlucky that I've already seen both of these more than once.

Sissy and I exchange glances and smile at some of the more amusing scenes.

Later I have dinner with three people from the Backpackers' Bus tour who are also on the train. Sissy seems to have her own food with her. I return to my seat from the diner, and find she's trying to sleep. As she wriggles around trying to get comfortable I find it hard to take my eyes off her beautiful long bronzed legs!

I wake up in the middle of the night and feel freezing! The air conditioning on this train is ridiculously cold! Luckily I have my backpack on the luggage rack above me, so I quickly pull out tracksuit pants and a sweater and pull them over my clothes. I wonder how Sissy is coping in her skimpy shorts and T-shirt. Later on I wake to find her vigorously rubbing her thighs. I wonder momentarily if I ought to offer to do that for her. I think about offering her a pair of my trousers, but worry it might be misconstrued. Anyway, she has the bright idea of getting some towels from the luggage rack and wrapping herself up in them. At last I can go to sleep properly!

The New Ghan at Alice Springs

We arrive in Keswick Terminal about 45 minutes late. It's a modern, impersonal transit centre about two miles from Adelaide city centre. Sissy dashes for the connecting train to Melbourne and my friends from the bus tour wait for their relatives to come and pick them up. I phone the hostel called *Backpack Oz* where I have reserved a room, and they give me directions to find their minibus, which is in the station car park.

Backpack Oz is an old Victorian pub, with a wrought iron balcony and some quaint period features. I dump my backpack and board a City Loop Bus for a free sightseeing tour of the city. After getting off the bus, I have a stroll, admiring the parks and the fine 19th-century architecture. It's Sunday so most shops are closed. But I have already made up my mind about what to do - I'm going to Glenelg for a day by the sea.

Glenelg is *the* beach for Adelaide, and *the* way to get there is by tram. And I don't mean a modern light-rail vehicle, but a proper electric tram, built in 1929. Reeking of oil and varnished wood it clanks and rattles to Glenelg, with the conductor issuing tickets. It terminates at right angles to the fine sandy beach. The scenery en-route is reminiscent of the Romney, Hythe and Dymchurch Light Railway, with suburban seaside bungalows and their neat front gardens, and the smell of the sea. But there is nothing lightweight about the Glenelg Tram. And Glenelg, although obviously a Victorian resort, is still very popular and seems to be undergoing a boom, judging by the smart new hotels and flats on the seafront.

I sunbathe, swim in the sea and look around the shops, then return in the evening to Adelaide. Here I have the ultimate Adelaide dinner - a *Pie Floater*. You can only get them at a Pie Cart, and I find one strategically placed outside the old city-centre mainline station. This peculiarly Adelaide delicacy consists of a square meat pie floating in a thick pea soup topped with tomato ketchup. It's surprisingly tasty!

I continued my journey from Adelaide by bus, but the Glenelg tram was not my last rail journey in Australia. After a short stay in Melbourne - the ultimate tram city of Australia, if not the world - I took an overnight *XPT* train to Sydney. I didn't have a sleeper booked, but the reclining seats on the XPTs are pretty comfortable, and I soon fell into a deep sleep…

WHAM! Crunch!

At 2.40am I am woken up by a sudden lurch of the train from side to side, as if negotiating a particularly bad set of points at 125mph (unlikely, as XPTs amble along at about 55mph).

Then follows a strange railway experience - it feels as if we are travelling over gravel. You can definitely hear something crunching under the wheels. The train slows to a complete stop.

The Adelaide - Glenelg tram

A guard with a torch walks through our carriage. "I'd better go and see if there's any damage!" he says.

My neighbour, a small elderly lady who up till now has not been very talkative, informs me she is a regular traveller and knows just what's happened - we've hit a kangaroo! A six-foot kangaroo hitting a train travelling at 55mph doesn't do it much good, and doesn't do much good to the kangaroo either!

After about an hour, we are on our way again, very slowly at first, then back up to cruising speed, and I fall asleep again. We get in to Sydney about two hours late, but according to the PA system our delay is attributed to 'a points failure at Spencer Street Station'. Still, we do get a free cup of coffee from the buffet.

The Old Railway Station at Marree

30. The Land of the Long White Cloud (and long-lost railways)

November 2000: Auckland to Greymouth with a few diversions

I have dual British and New Zealand nationality, so travelling to NZ is always a bit like going home. My first visit to my father's homeland was as a teenager, on holiday with my family. During the course of this trip we went on a red electric train from Melling to Wellington. This was my first introduction to the railways of New Zealand.

Some people consider New Zealand to be more British than Britain itself, but its railways do not particularly resemble those in the Old Country. Firstly, there is the difference in gauge: New Zealand's railways are all laid to the narrow 'Colonial' 3 foot 6 inches. The rolling stock and the station architecture are most unlike anything to be seen in Great Britain. Finally there is the dramatic contrast in the two systems' frequency of services. Apart from the suburban systems in Wellington and Auckland, most lines have a very sparse passenger service, if indeed they are fortunate to have one at all.

Of course, New Zealand has a tiny population when compared with the UK, and there are few large towns apart from Auckland and Wellington. But I still feel that a beautiful country with such 'green' credentials could do much better. The Kiwis have embraced the internal combustion engine all too enthusiastically, and the country's few remaining long-distance trains are now mostly used by tourists. With almost unlimited supplies of cheap hydro-electricity, New Zealand should by now have an efficient electrified rail network - yet electrification has been patchy and piecemeal, and some lines that were once electrified have had their catenary dismantled and are now operated by diesel engines burning expensive imported fuel. Since New Zealand Rail Ltd was privatised in 1993, the system has been split up, renamed, sold to foreign owners and now partially re-nationalised. For passenger trains, the last few years have been nothing short of disastrous. In 1997 New Zealand Post issued a beautiful set of stamps showing six of the country's long-distance trains in appropriate scenery, with a map of their routes. Today three of those journeys are no longer possible. Most developed countries have enjoyed a railway revival of sorts in recent years, but NZ has adopted a policy of railway destruction.

```
Tranz Scenic
                            Ref: 3734002
                            Super Saver Fare
Mr   R   Sissons
                                          ADL  1
from Auckland          to    Rotorua

Travel Date        time    Service
27 NOV 00 MONDAY   08:20am  The Geyserland
Report time        08:00am
                            Fare incl GST  $   34.00
                            and Extras      CAR:
REFUND CONDITIONS  SuperSaver/NoFrills
GST 56-132-864                              Seats:
Silent acceptance .................
Refer to Ticket Cover for Summary of Conditions of Carriage.
```

My ticket for the one daily train to Rotorua

My latter-day exploration of New Zealand's railways started with the line from Auckland to Rotorua. This was served by an elderly but extremely comfortable silver railcar set, known as the *Geyserland*. Auckland railway station was in a state of disarray: the majestic old station building was out of use and being converted into student accommodation, although trains still left from the original platforms behind, which had tatty Art Nouveau-style concrete shelters rather like those on Surrey's Chessington branch. The old station has now been decommissioned and replaced by a very smart, new, mostly underground facility that is much more convenient for the city centre and offers much better bus connections. Unfortunately many of the trains that served the old station were withdrawn before the new one was inaugurated.

None of Auckland's railways are electrified, and the suburban lines are operated by a fleet of rather basic stainless-steel diesel units. These serve shabby unstaffed halts, most of which have been defaced by graffiti. Auckland is undoubtedly a beautiful city in a lovely setting, but it is not seen at its best by train.

The almost-empty *Geyserland* passed the last of the Auckland suburban stations at Papakura, and then started following the Waikato river through a whimsical rural landscape that could have passed for Ireland. One of the most enchanting things about NZ is its capacity to mimic other countries: travelling by road or train one may start off in England, cross through France to Austria and pass through the southern USA before ending up in the Caribbean. The first stop of any importance came at Hamilton, the largest inland town in New Zealand. This is where the *Geyserland* branched off onto its own line, passing dairy farms, factories and the spa town of Matamata, which has its very own hot springs. Beyond Matamata there were some of those immense forestry plantations that cover so much of the interior of the North Island, until lovely Lake Rotorua came into view on the right-hand side.

The Geyserland train at Rotorua

The Rotorua branch was finally laid to rest in 2001. It had been a slow, lingering death. Rotorua, with its world-famous geysers, thermal springs and colourful Maori culture is a world-class tourist attraction, and Auckland is by far the largest city in New Zealand, so a railway linking the two should be a licence to print money. Sadly, *Tranz Scenic*, the operator of the country's long-distance passenger services, made a pretty good job of sabotaging the line. The convenient, centrally-located railway station in Rotorua was closed and its site sold for a shopping development, and trains were forced to terminate at a lonely platform a kilometre out of town. Then the passenger service was reduced to a single return journey daily. This was made worse by the fact that the train arrived at 12.25 and left at 13.05, forcing passengers either to overnight in Rotorua or to return to Auckland by bus, which is precisely what I did. Today there are no trains of any kind to Rotorua.

My cousin, who then lived near Auckland, took me to the Glenbrook Vintage Railway to experience some old-time North Island railroading. Just under four miles long, this line runs along a former New Zealand Railways branch closed in 1968. It is a perfect example of an enthusiast-run operation, with gleaming steam locomotives, sparkling carriages and a lovingly-maintained station with a buffet and well-stocked gift shop. The staff were very friendly and the man who sold my ticket proved to be a Londoner! The countryside served by the Glenbrook line is very pastoral and English-looking, but the locomotive hauling my train, with its spark-arrester, cowcatcher, huge headlight and tiny driving wheels, was a piece of classic Americana, built by the American Locomotive Company in 1912.

My next trip on *Tranz Scenic* was to Wellington on the overnight train, much to the dismay of my cousin, who said "But you can't do the Main Trunk by night! What about the Raurimu Spiral?" Still, he obligingly gave me a lift to the station and I grabbed a seat near the rear of the train, which left at 20.40.

Train at the old Auckland station

The *Northerner* was quite a basic train, its carriages dating back to the 1940s, and my fellow passengers were a mixture of international backpackers. Once you could have ridden along this line in a comfortable sleeping-car on the luxurious *Silver Star*, but that train was sold to a British luxury travel company and now operates as the *Eastern and Oriental Express*, which I saw on my travels in Thailand. Even the *Northerner* was withdrawn in 2004, and there are now no overnight passenger trains in New Zealand.

The first part of the *Northerner's* journey took me along the same rails along which I had started my journey to Rotorua. From Hamilton there were two changes: the diesel locomotive was uncoupled and replaced by an electric one, and we headed south on the North Island Main Trunk. There were occasional stops at dimly-lit stations with Maori names: Te Awamutu, Otorohanga, Te Kuiti and Taumaranui.

I managed to stay awake for the famed Raurimu Spiral. This remarkable feat of engineering enables the line to gain 220 metres in height, with two tunnels and a complete circle. By night it was far less spectacular than it would have been by day, but I still had the disconcerting feeling that the train was going in the wrong direction. National Park, the next station, still has a nicely-maintained main building, and I remember reading the nameboard before falling asleep, hoping that nearby Mount Ruapehu would not choose this night to resume its volcanic activity!

I slept through Taihape and Palmerston North, where we must have exchanged our electric locomotive for another diesel, and finally woke up at Levin, a town that I discovered is *not* pronounced as in Bernard.

It was 6 am and I got a coffee from the buffet. At Paraparaumu, overhead electric masts appeared again beside the tracks: we were now in the Wellington suburban area. The train now joined the coast, and for the final hour the scenery was magnificent, with the Tasman shore on the right-hand side for mile after glorious mile. After passing pretty Porirua with its harbour, the train left the coast, burrowed through two long tunnels and then emerged by Wellington Harbour, which, disconcertingly, was on the *left* side of the train!

Wellington station's grand facade

Wellington Station was still very grand: an immense brick structure with a massive colonnaded façade as befits a major terminus in a capital city. The grandeur was somewhat tempered by the fact that a farmers' market appeared to be taking place on the station concourse, and the formerly elegant railway hotel opposite the station had been converted to a backpackers' hostel. Wellington is a handsome, hilly city, with a somewhat convoluted ground plan: its public transport includes the metre-gauge Kelburn funicular railway, ferries and trolleybuses painted in Stagecoach livery!

Wellington has a well-served electric network, including that branch from Melling that I had travelled on long ago. One of its suburban lines is of special interest, and I decided to take a return trip on it before my ferry to the South Island. The line in question is a mere six-and-a-half miles long but offers wonderful scenery, with steep gradients, tight curves and seven tunnels. It runs to Johnsonville, and has two particular claims to fame: it originally formed part of the main line route from Wellington to Auckland, but was bypassed by a new line in 1937 and cut off as a branch; and in 1999 it was still served by English Electric multiple-units dating from the 1940s. These trains looked and sounded very British, quite unlike the more modern Hungarian-built Ganz trains that operated the other Wellington local services. I found the journey delightful, with fine scenery, wild flowers growing by the trackside and wooden posts supporting the overhead electric wires. If it had not been for the sea breezes I could have been in Switzerland.

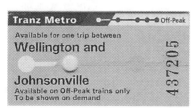

Ticket for the suburban train to Johnsonville

But the Johnsonville line was only a prelude to what was to come. I returned to Wellington's monumental station and then got a bus to the ferry terminal where I boarded the *Arahura* for the three-hour crossing of Cook Strait. *Arahura* is a Maori word meaning 'pathway to dawn'. At the time of my journey the inter-islander ferries were run by the railway company, and the timetable was in a state of flux as a newly-delivered state-of-the-art ferry, the *Aratere*, had just suffered a major breakdown. Some joker had chalked up a notice at the terminal reading 'It's a good job Tranz Rail only run trains and ferries - not aeroplanes!'

Old electric train at Johnsonville

On a fine day, the crossing of the Cook Strait is relaxing but still exciting. A helicopter passed overhead, with a telegraph pole suspended beneath it. The super-fast *Lynx* catamaran overtook us. I was delighted to find a 'squashed penny' machine on board - the only one I have ever seen in New Zealand - and I obtained an elongated five-cent piece with a picture of the ship. I opened a bottle of Lion Red beer and watched the scenery as we sailed into Queen Charlotte Sound. As we neared Picton I saw the decaying hulk of an old ship. This was the *Edwin Fox*, which served as a troop ship during the Crimean War and later took thousands of convicts from England to Australia. She survived many adventures, including running aground off Deal in Kent, and eventually finished her days in Picton. Efforts are now being made to preserve and restore this antique vessel.

Picton is a friendly little town, where I once stayed in a weird hotel room with a circular bed, and where my mother once attempted to leave a tip in a restaurant and found the waitress running after her saying "Hey, you've left some money on the table!" The railway station is just minutes from the harbour. I followed the procession of backpackers off the ferry and onto the *Coastal Pacific* train, with its red diesel locomotive hauling a rake of blue coaches. The first part of the journey south, as far as Blenheim, was among streams, mountains, fields of gorse and forests of pine trees: it had a distinctly Scottish appearance. South of Blenheim the scenery became more French-looking, as we entered wine country. The main north-south highway ran roughly parallel to the railway, and occasionally the two shared the same bridge when crossing a stream; one bridge had two decks, with trains using the upper level.

After passing the saltworks at Lake Grassmere, the railway reached the coast, with the Pacific Ocean now on our left, and snow-capped mountains on the right. Sitting with the backpackers, I looked out for signs of marine life: no whales, but a number of seals, lounging lazily on the foreshore like giant slugs. This remarkable stretch of railway, with its tunnels carved through cliffs and its track running almost along the beaches, was only completed in 1945, seventy years after the first rails had been laid south from Picton.

I descended from the train at Kaikoura, the largest town between Blenheim and Christchurch and a former whaling centre. People come here now to watch whales rather than hunt them, and the station has been renamed 'The Whaleway Station'. I registered here for a whale-watching cruise before heading off on foot to a nearby backpackers' hostel. On the way I saw a dramatic mural showing a steam train going through the town.

There was plenty to do in Kaikoura: I went for a boat trip in search of albatrosses and had my first-ever swim with dolphins (I would later swim with 'Davina', the friendly dolphin, just yards from my home in Kent!) The highlight of my stay was most definitely the whale-watching cruise. After three fallow days with none of the great mammals in sight, I was rewarded with some magnificent viewing opportunities on my final morning, before returning to Picton on the northbound train.

Kaikoura - the 'Whale Way' station

New Zealand's South Island is often seen as the poor relation, but it maintains that it is the 'mainland'; the delicious milkshakes I bought in Kaikoura were served in cups marked 'Mainland Shakes'. In railway terms the South Island has never been as well-served as the north, and now it boasts just two 'regular' passenger trains plus two tourist lines. The distinction between 'tourist' and 'regular' trains is difficult here, as the majority of the passengers on the surviving *Tranz Scenic* lines are tourists, whilst the unashamedly touristy *Taeri Gorge Railway* runs trains just as frequently, if not more frequently, than the main lines!

The last branch line in the South Island to retain a regular passenger service is the one across the Southern Alps from Christchurch to Greymouth. An old school atlas of mine has a full-page map of the world that shows this 145-mile railway as a tiny black line about a quarter-of-an-inch long, joining the east and west coasts of the island. It has been named as one of the world's greatest train journeys, and I knew I simply had to take it.

Christchurch is the most English city in New Zealand, with its stone and red-brick buildings, its stately mock-Gothic cathedral and its meandering River Avon. Only the regular grid plan of its streets has something un-English about it. Restored vintage trams run on a loop around the town centre; they are more a tourist attraction than a serious form of local transport, but are nonetheless the only trams running on city streets in New Zealand (although a tourist line runs on a railway-type track between the Zoo and the MOTAT transport museum in the Auckland suburbs).

Like that at Rotorua, Christchurch's old city-centre railway station has been demolished and its site sold for redevelopment. *Tranz Scenic's* trains now leave from Addington, nearly two miles away and the site of the former railway workshops. Yet whilst the *Geyserland* train to Rotorua was almost empty, the *Tranz Alpine* to Greymouth was packed. In fact, my first attempt at purchasing a ticket from a travel agency met with the response "Sorry, the train's full!" When I enquired at the station, however, I had no difficulty in procuring a ticket: I assume that the agency had been allocated a block of seats on their computer and that these had all sold. One wonders whether the *Geyserland* could have been saved if it had been promoted as enthusiastically as the *Tranz Alpine*.

The train consisted of the usual old New Zealand Railways carriages, thoroughly refurbished and equipped with panoramic windows. It was diesel-hauled, and in its centre was a generator car, with open balconies where many passengers would gather to view the scenery, take photographs and enjoy a crafty cigarette - smoking had for some time been prohibited elsewhere on New Zealand's trains!

The train followed the South Island main trunk for a short distance, then curved off on the branch and crossed the Canterbury Plain, with its vast numbers of sheep. The stations along this stretch had English-sounding names, which suited the countryside perfectly. One of them is called Sheffield, and another has a very appropriate name for a narrow-gauge railway: Hornby!

The Tranz Alpine at Springfield

After crossing the plain for about an hour, the train reached a station called Springfield. The guard told us about Rosie, the late lamented border collie, who used to meet every passenger train here to be rewarded with a meat pie from the buffet. It was just beyond Springfield that the landscape suddenly changed: the train started climbing towards the Torlesse Range, crossing the Kowai viaduct and then passing along the beautiful Wamakariri Gorge, where the formation has been cut out of the cliff on the west bank of the river, rather like the Tournon - Lamastre railway in France.

The railway has to climb about 2,400 feet between Christchurch and Arthur's Pass, and it is a pretty constant climb all the way. There are sixteen short tunnels and several lofty viaducts. I spent quite a lot of time on the generator-car balcony with some Japanese backpackers. Unfortunately most of the viaducts had high fences on one side, which blocked some of the best views! Our conductor explained that these were here for a very good reason: they acted as windbreaks.

The scenery was definitely Alpine when we reached Arthur's Pass, where even the railway station looks like a Swiss chalet. We had a short break here, enough time to take photographs and stretch our legs before we were all ordered aboard by a series of blows on the locomotive's horn. The conductor sternly warned us not to go out on the observation decks, as we were about to go through the Otira Tunnel.

This famous tunnel, over five miles long, links the stations of Arthur's Pass and Otira and was the last part of the line to be built: it was not opened until 1923. Otira had been linked to Greymouth since 1900 and the Arthur's Pass to Christchurch section was completed in 1914. The line through the tunnel was formerly electrified, trains changing from steam or diesel to electric traction at Arthur's Pass. Nowadays the big diesels go straight through. The tunnel has an incredible gradient of 1 in 33, and Otira station is almost a thousand feet below Arthur's Pass.

We emerged from the tunnel into brilliant sunshine, and I resumed my vantage point on the observation deck. The descent to Greymouth was peaceful and pastoral, with lakes, streams and wooded hills, but at one point we were switched to a siding while a gigantic coal train passed by. This was a reminder of the main reason the railway was built: to take coal from the Westland to the cities on the east coast and the port of Lyttleton. Yet not a slag heap is visible from the line; the coal train had originated from the Westport branch line that joins the Greymouth line at a place called Stillwater.

The stations beyond Otira have a strange mixture of Maori and British names; after Aickens, Jacksons and Inchbonnie, we passed through Poerua, Rotomanu and Ruru before reaching Stillwater and Dobson. At the tiny halt of Ruru, we stopped to let an elderly passenger board the train. He bought a ticket from the conductor and complained about the changes to the schedules to suit the tourists, and the closure of the old Christchurch station. It was reassuring to know that a few New Zealanders still use the *Tranz Alpine*.

View along the Tranz Alpine

Greymouth is a most attractive little seaside town, with fishing boats in the harbour and shops selling jade and gold jewellery. The railway station is beautifully-maintained, and nearby is another of those murals showing a steam train - I wonder if it was done by the same artist as the one in Kaikoura? Although it is the largest town and the only passenger railhead on the west coast of the South Island, it has a population of only about 7,000.

At the time of my visit, the only active steam railway in the South Island was at Kingston, on Lake Wakatipu. This beautiful lake is itself served by steam in the form of the gracious *TSS Earnslaw*, a genuine steamship dating from 1912, on which I went for a lovely evening cruise from Queenstown to Walter Peak

Farm across the lake. The *Earnslaw* must rank as the most staid and gentle of Queenstown's tourist activities, which include bungee-jumping, jet-boating, white-water rafting, hang gliding and skydiving. It is no surprise that this small but lively town bills itself as New Zealand's 'adventure capital', and that hardly anyone you pass in the street looks over 30.

Queenstown never had a railway station. In the old days the good folk of Queenstown would take the *TSS Earnslaw* down the lake to Kingston, where they would board the *Kingston Flyer* steam train to Invercargill. The train and its branch-line succumbed to buses in the 1950s, but since the 1970s it has been revived as a highly successful tourist operation, albeit on a mere nine miles of track between Kingston and Fairlight. I had to use a hire car to get there, and was greeted by the sight of an immaculate steam locomotive (of the Ab class, built in the 1920s) and a rake of green-painted coaches. One of these was a most unusual observation coach known as a 'birdcage': one side of it was completely open to the elements, with metal railings and wire netting to ensure that no passengers fell out! The train was well-filled and I was intrigued to discover that a fair proportion of those travelling were New Zealanders, although a tourist coach deposited a party of British visitors at Kingston and picked them up again at Fairlight, where a vast triangle of track enables the locomotive to be placed, facing forward, at the other end of the train for the return journey.

The Kingston Flyer

Taking half-an-hour each way, with half-an-hour's stop in Fairlight, this was a lovely journey and a fine conclusion to my stay in New Zealand. But as the whistle of the 'Ab' died away and I returned to my car, like all the other Kiwis who had travelled on this train, I reflected that perhaps all railways in New Zealand are just relics from the dim and distant past, like prehistoric stone circles or medieval castles in Europe. A few may be preserved as ancient monuments, but to the average Kiwi a train is not a means of transport. In the Land of the Long White Cloud the car is king. It must be admitted that motoring in New Zealand is still a pleasure; the roads are superb and generally uncrowded, and there is hardly ever any problem in finding a parking space (which is normally free of charge). Cars have an easy time here: a stroll down any street will usually reveal several specimens between twenty and thirty years old, and those are everyday runabouts, not cherished classics. Somehow I cannot see New Zealand's railways regaining their role as a major passenger mover unless traffic congestion reaches the levels it has in the larger cities of Europe.

BRITISH

JOURNEYS

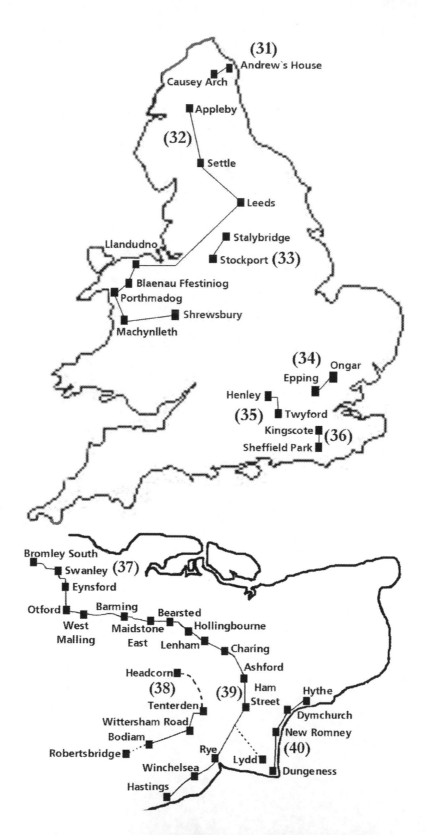

(31) Andrew's House
Causey Arch
(32) Appleby
Settle
Leeds
Llandudno
Stalybridge
Stockport (33)
Blaenau Ffestiniog
Porthmadog
Machynlleth
Shrewsbury
(34) Ongar
Epping
Henley
(35) Twyford
Kingscote (36)
Sheffield Park

Bromley South
Swanley (37)
Eynsford
Otford
West Malling
Barming
Maidstone East
Bearsted
Hollingbourne
Lenham
Charing
Headcorn
(38) Ashford
Tenterden
Ham Street
(39)
Hythe
Wittersham Road
Bodiam
Dymchurch
New Romney
Robertsbridge
Rye
Lydd
(40)
Winchelsea
Dungeness
Hastings

February 22, 2004: A Winter Ride on the Tanfield Railway

Many preserved railways run steam trains in the summer months only. This leaves the winter free for maintenance and restoration, and ensures that visitors can enjoy a train ride when (theoretically) the weather should be at its best. But it does not recreate the daily experience of running a steam railway throughout the year, in all kinds of conditions.

Luckily a number of railways do offer visitors the chance to travel behind a steam locomotive in the depths of winter (and not just on a 'Santa Special' train). The Bluebell Railway is one, and another, at the opposite end of England, is the Tanfield Railway.

The Tanfield Railway is a dinosaur among railways. The very first book on railways I ever had, the Ladybird 'Achievements' book *The Story of Railways*, has an opening chapter describing how short railways with horse-drawn trucks were used at coal mines 'between 1790 and 1820'. But the Tanfield goes back much further than that.

The 18th-century Causey Arch

Bryan Morgan's book *Early Trains* describes how simple wooden 'tramways' using trucks with flanged wheels were in use in Silesia as long ago as 1520. He also mentions the grooves found on Maltese paving slabs that some archaeologists have dated back to 2000BC, and which could have been a very early form of guided transport! I have seen these grooves, in the company of a group of rather unimpressed American tourists, but I was much more impressed by the Tanfield.

The present-day Tanfield Railway is only a small portion of an extensive network of colliery waggonways that were developed in the seventeenth and eighteenth centuries. The line included massive embankments, cuttings and the largest single-span bridge yet built in Britain - the Causey Arch. This 105-foot structure stands 80 feet above the Causey burn and took two years to build, at a cost of £2,253.

Andrew's House station

It was a cold winter's morning when my friend Ian took me to Andrew's House station, the main joining-point of the railway for those coming by car. The station looks 100% authentic, but was actually built in the 1980s for the tourist operation. We sheltered in the buffet from the blizzard that had started as soon as we had arrived. The first train we took was the 11.30 to Sunniside, the present-day northern terminus of the line. We were travelling on a line opened in 1725, a whole century before the Stockton & Darlington that is commonly identified as the world's first railway.

Stagshaw hauling a passenger train

Our train consisted of a little tank engine called *Stagshaw* hauling Victorian-style four-wheel carriages. The Tanfield Railway does not run the ex-British Rail Mark I stock that is the bread-and-butter of most preserved lines; it actively tries to recreate the atmosphere of a minor passenger railway in Victorian times. The former industrial tank locomotives are perfectly at home here. And whereas some spick-and-span preserved railways are spoilt by lines of rusting locomotives and decaying carriages in sidings, the large collection of superannuated rolling stock at Marley Hill adds to the Tanfield's atmosphere. It comes as no surprise to learn that film adaptations of several Catherine Cookson novels have been shot here.

Our train returned from Sunniside to Andrew's House and then started heading south over the massive Causey embankment, perhaps the largest work of pure engineering to have been constructed in England since Roman times. The snow had stopped and the sun came out, allowing us views of the winter countryside. The train started slowing down so soon after leaving Andrew's House that we wondered whether the next station would be called 'Andrew's Back Garden'. In fact it was Causey Arch itself.

The Tanfield Railway does not actually cross the Causey Arch any more; it veers away from the original waggonway and terminates at East Tanfield, site of a former colliery. Ian and I got off here and took some photos while *Stagshaw* ran around her train. We rejoined the train for the eight-minute trip back to Causey Arch, where we got off and investigated the station site. There was just a simple platform here, but interesting information boards had been erected to tell the story of the area. A replica of an early horse-drawn colliery wagon was on display, and, of course, the greatest attraction of the stop was the opportunity to walk across the Causey Arch itself. Even today it looks impressive, and one advantage of travelling in winter was that the views were not too obscured by foliage and undergrowth.

We had 45 minutes at Causey before rejoining the train to Andrew's House. Here we explored the Marley Hill engine sheds, where we saw locomotives and other rolling-stock in various stages of restoration. The original shed dates from 1854, but it has been supplanted by larger workshop facilities to cater for a growing stud of locomotives. I can't remember ever having seen so many tank engines in one place! Other exhibits included steam cranes, a few diesels and a remarkable ancient electric locomotive.

Old National Coal Board locomotives

The fading initials 'NCB' on much of the stock were a reminder that this was once the greatest coal-producing area in the world. Today tourists have replaced coal as the main cargo, but perhaps this is just natural progression, as the Tanfield could be described as the world's first tourist railway. Eighteenth-century visitors to the area were astonished by the bridge and the mighty embankments, and engravings of the Causey Arch were sold in much the same way that postcards are sold by present-day tourist lines.

32. A Pass, a Petition, a Blonde in Blaenau and a Diesel around the Deviation

July 8 - 9, 1988: Leeds to London via Appleby and Porthmadog

In the late 1980s I worked with a major tour operator in Bromley in Kent. Our company also had an office in Leeds, and occasionally someone would ask for volunteers to deliver parcels of brochures, lost property or customers' passports between the two offices. For these purposes the company had a number of British Rail all-stations passes, which were endorsed with the words that they were to be used for business travel only.

I took the habit of coming to the office on Fridays with my camera and a small overnight bag, just in case the opportunity arose for a trip up to Leeds that I could extend into a weekend away. I was not unduly worried about the 'business travel only' wording on the passes. Our company worked with travel agents and hotels all over the UK, and I could surely come up with a cover story if I were discovered on some obscure branch-line with an all-stations pass. Besides, on the numerous occasions that I had used the passes for genuine business reasons, nobody had ever asked me who I was or why I was travelling.

One day my dream came true. "I'm sorry about this, Robert, but would you mind taking this pack of stationery to Leeds?" my boss said, "If you leave now you should be able to make it home this evening!"

Not telling him that I had absolutely no intention of going home that evening, I seized the pass and the parcel and hurried off to Bromley South station. Arriving at Victoria, a quick taxi-ride took me to Euston, and then it was Inter-City luxury all the way to Leeds.

Ribblehead Viaduct

The business of delivering the stationery was soon accomplished, and, after checking that there was nothing to take back to Bromley, I set off back to Leeds railway station. It was still early afternoon and I wondered where to go. Of course, Leeds was the starting-point for one of England's greatest railway journeys, the Settle & Carlisle. Could I travel on it that afternoon? A glance at the timetable showed that a full return journey would be impossible, but if I took the next northbound train as far as Appleby I would be able to return on a southbound train from Appleby to Leeds. All the books and articles I had read agreed that the stretch south of Appleby was the finest part of the line.

So many books have been written about the splendid Settle & Carlisle that no description of its history or its beauty is required here. The most important thing to remember is that back in 1988 the line was threatened with closure. When I boarded the locomotive-hauled train of corridor coaches at Leeds, it filled up quickly, and by the time we reached the excitingly derelict-looking station of Hellifield, with its acres of disintegrating Victorian canopies, most of the seats had been taken. When at last we pulled into a lovingly-maintained station with the nameboard 'Settle', there was a final rush for the remaining places. The Settle & Carlisle may have been 'uneconomic', but such a thought was incredible when one looked at the crowd on this train!

A group of young people passed along the corridor with a clipboard. "British Rail are going to close this line. We need your signatures here to make sure that doesn't happen!" We all dutifully signed the petition and they moved along to the next compartment. Just too late, a plump gentleman with a camera shouted after them "Excuse me, please could you tell me where Ribblehead Viaduct is? I don't want to miss it!" His blonde wife reassured him "Don't worry, love. I'm sure they'll tell us!" They didn't. The approach to the viaduct was marked by a rush of those 'in the know' towards the windows, and the track changed from double to single. We passed through the desolate Ribblehead station and then crossed the mighty viaduct. Two of its piers were encased in scaffolding and it was looking a little sorry for itself. British Rail claimed that the increasing cost of maintaining this viaduct was the main reason the line had to close.

Appleby Station

The viaduct was soon followed by the long Blea Moor Tunnel, which none of the passengers on the train could fail to notice. Beyond the tunnel, the S&C crossed vast open spaces that came as a surprise to me. When you live in Kent, although the county is blessed with some magnificent scenery, civilisation is never far away. Here there was virtually no sign of any human impact on the landscape other than the railway on which we were travelling. I wondered what life had been like for the Midland Railway's navvies who had driven the line through this remote area in mid-Victorian times.

After passing several seemingly abandoned village stations (since happily restored to life), our train came to a halt at the living station of Appleby. Here I forced my way through the people standing in the corridor and jumped off the train. I had time to examine the well-maintained country station with its plaque commemorating the Reverend Eric Treacy, the great railway photographer (and bishop of Wakefield) who had dropped dead here while photographing a steam special ten years earlier.

I went for a short walk to visit the interesting parish church, with its graveyard where some of the railway navvies are buried. As I returned to the station, I wondered whether this was the first time in my life that I had set foot in the erstwhile county of Westmorland.

The train that took me back from Appleby to Leeds was just the same as the one that had brought me there - a Class 47 diesel and BR Mark I corridor coaches - and it was equally well-filled. I signed another petition and enjoyed the scenery, just in case it was the last opportunity I would get to travel over the line.

I then planned my journey south. How about a ride on the Ffestiniog Railway? I had never travelled on this famous line. Checking the timetables, I discovered that there was a Fridays-only train called a 'Holidaymaker Express' that would take me south from Leeds, and that by changing in various places I could end up at Llandudno Junction, where I could get the Conwy Valley line to Blaenau Ffestiniog.

I spent the early morning at a cold and deserted Llandudno Junction waiting for the first train of the day to Blaenau Ffestiniog. When it came, it was a three-car diesel-multiple unit and was practically empty. I joined the leading coach and sat behind the driver. The guard started at the other end of the train and seemed exhausted when he got to me. He gave my all-stations pass a respectful glance and didn't comment on what sort of business I could be doing in North Wales on a Saturday morning.

The Conwy Valley train wound and climbed for an hour from the North Welsh coast to Snowdonia, and although it was a bit misty it was still a memorable journey. We ran alongside the broad Conwy, stopping at little halts whose names were unpronounceable to an Englishman. The modest station at Llanwrst was the original southern terminus of the line. Here the train driver reached out to take a huge brass token from the signalman, and placed it on the dashboard. At Betws-y-Coed, a number of old items of rolling-stock were on display: I discovered later that these belonged to the Conwy Valley Railway Museum, based in the old goods yard at the station.

Half an hour beyond Betws-y-Coed, the train appeared to be heading straight for a wall of rock. There was an abrupt curve and suddenly we were in the two-mile Moel Dyrnogydd tunnel. Despite its length, the tunnel was so straight that from my vantage point at the front of the train, I could see the small pinprick of light at the end almost as soon as we entered the tunnel.

Conwy Valley train at Blaenau

We left the tunnel and almost immediately pulled up at the new Blaenau Ffestiniog station, shared jointly between British Rail and the Ffestiniog Railway. The station and indeed the whole town seemed to be hemmed in by great grey cliffs - the spoil heaps from the slate mines that made Blaenau the slate capital of the world, and the reason its railways were originally constructed. The narrow-gauge Ffestiniog railway opened way back in 1836 to carry slate down to the harbour at Porthmadog, and the standard-gauge Conwy Valley line was extended from Llanwrst to meet it in 1879.

I had an hour and a half before the first Ffestiniog Railway train, so went for a stroll around the town. It looked as if it were in need of a facelift. Quite a few shops were empty, and there was a general air of poverty. Looking in an estate agent's window I could hardly believe my eyes when I saw a terraced two-bedroom house for sale for £7,000 - about one-tenth of what a similar property would have then fetched in my home town in Kent!

I was quite glad to return to the station, where I had to buy a ticket, as my BR pass was not valid on this independent line. The ticket came out of a hi-tech computer printer and was devoid of any character. When travelling on heritage railways I prefer to get historic-looking tickets, but this looked more like the sort of thing one got from a machine in a car park! But then I suppose the Ffestiniog has always been an innovator: it was the first narrow-gauge railway to run steam locomotives and to operate passenger trains. It is also wrong to dismiss the Ffestiniog as 'just another preserved railway'. Although closed in 1946 and re-opened in 1955, the line is still run by its original operating company, created by an Act of Parliament in 1832! And, as I was to discover, the railway does see genuine use as a form of local public transport.

Ffestiniog Railway diesel train

I had another slight disappointment when the train arrived, as it was diesel-hauled. Still, I was here for the journey, and I boarded the 1'11" gauge carriage and prepared myself for a spectacular ride. Almost immediately I realised I was doing the trip the wrong way - the leaflet I had picked up at the station, in addition to all the articles I have ever read on the line, described the journey as starting from Porthmadog. Of course, for a true steam enthusiast the journey must be done from Porthmadog, as then the journey will be uphill all the way and the engine will be working hard up the gradient. You hardly even need a locomotive to travel down the Ffestiniog - the line was originally designed so that laden slate-wagons could run down to the port by gravity! They were then hauled back up to Blaenau by horses, which were replaced by steam engines in 1863.

The first mile or so from Blaenau is on an embankment and is fairly straight, with views over the town. There were half-a-dozen passengers in my carriage, including one stunning blonde who appeared to be unaccompanied. She didn't have any luggage with her and wasn't taking a particular interest in the scenery. At Tan-y-Grisiau a tall, dark, bearded man got on and took the seat beside her. They started talking animatedly in a beautiful but incomprehensible language. Foreign tourists? Of course not! As an Englishman *I* was the foreign tourist. As we continued along the line I was impressed by the number of locals who used it, and I began regretting that I had not taken the trouble to learn just a little bit of Welsh. I did work out that *rheilffordd* must mean 'railway'.

The most unusual feature of the Ffestiniog line is also its most modern part. When the line lay derelict, part of the original trackbed was flooded by a new hydro-electric scheme. This meant that the largely volunteer workforce had to build a two-mile diversion from the old route, on a higher level. The volunteers who worked on this new stretch of the Ffestiniog called themselves the 'deviationists', and their work also included a substantial tunnel through the Moelwyn mountains. Just before this I could see the old trackbed emerging from the reservoir on the left, far below.

To enable the trains to reach the lower level a complete spiral was built, the only one in Britain. Approaching Dduallt station I had the impression that my train was crossing over another narrow-gauge line. Leaving the station we appeared to pass underneath yet another. The only similar experience I have had was on the Bernina railway in Switzerland, where the train does a complete open-air spiral between the stations of Brusio and Campocologno. But the Ffestiniog line is different as it has a station in the middle of the spiral! South of the spiral, the line rejoins its original alignment.

We went through a short tunnel, passed another artificial lake, Llyn Mair, and arrived at Tan-y-Bwlch station, where our train had to wait in the loop for another coming in the opposite direction. After checking with the conductor that I had sufficient time, I got off here to take some photos. The station was lovingly maintained with Victorian lamp-posts and pots of flowers on the platforms. I got out and waited on the station footbridge for the other train to arrive. I could hear it whistling long before it came into view - a proper steam-hauled train, with its locomotive bearing the headboard *Mountain Prince*. I had time for several photos before re-boarding the diesel train for the second half of the journey.

Steam train on 'The Cob'

The section of line around Tan-y-Bwlch passes through Snowdonia National Park; the railway goes in a big loop around Llyn Mair and even starts heading north again, running along a shelf cut into the hillside. We rounded the sharp Tyler's Curve (named after a Captain H W Tyler rather than Bonnie!) and from then the line was much straighter, running south-west with numerous cuttings and embankments. We stopped at Penrhyn station about fifteen minutes after leaving Tan-y-Bwlch, and at Minffordd some five minutes after that, where we crossed over the British Rail line and the road to Portmeirion.

I knew that the end was nigh, but it came in style. We passed other locomotives and stock outside the sprawling Victorian workshops at Boston Lodge, and then crossed the 'Cob' - a 1,600-yard causeway across the Glaslyn estuary that predates the railway by a quarter of a century. It was originally built for land reclamation, but it had the bonus effect of creating a safe harbour from where Welsh slate could be exported. The harbour - Porthmadog - took its name from William Madocks, its builder.

At Porthmadog Harbour station I left the train and visited the interesting museum. I got some pictures of a steam-hauled train crossing the Cob, and went for a walk to the Welsh Highland Railway at the other side of the town. Here an immaculate little tank engine named *Karen* was taking passengers for rides on a few hundred yards of restored track, all that remained of the 21-mile WHR that had closed in 1937.

Unfortunately, I did not have time for a ride behind *Karen*, as I was now concerned with getting home. I found Porthmadog BR station and got a train to Machynlleth, along the lovely Cambrian Coast Line past Harlech Castle and over the long Barmouth viaduct. At Machynlleth I changed trains for Shrewsbury and from there I returned to London after a wonderful but exhausting day.

Loco-hauled train at Machynlleth

Two decades on, much has changed for the better. The Settle & Carlisle Railway was reprieved and its future now seems more secure than ever: most of the intermediate stations have re-opened, and the line sees an increasing amount of freight traffic. Hellifield station has been lovingly restored. The Ffestiniog Railway is proceeding with an incredible scheme to revive the moribund Welsh Highland line; already over twelve miles have been relaid, and when the project is complete it will result in a 40-mile, 1' 11" gauge railway from Caernarfon via Porthmadog to Blaenau Ffestiniog. On the main lines, the Class 37 and 47 locomotives and Mark 1 corridor coaches that were still ubiquitous in 1988 have passed into history, and have been replaced by modern multiple-unit stock, not necessarily an improvement on the trains they replaced. Sadly the all-stations British Rail pass is also a thing of the past, a victim of the privatisation and fragmentation of our national railway system by John Major's government in the 1990s.

33. Riding the Ghost Train

November 27, 1998: I travel on Network Rail's most infrequent passenger service

For nearly 20 years there has been a railway line in the UK that is served by one passenger train a week. This is not a seasonal tourist railway, but a short suburban line in Greater Manchester. The train runs in one direction only, from Stockport to Stalybridge; there is no train service from Stalybridge to Stockport. For several years the train left Stockport around 3pm on Friday afternoon; more recently it has been retimed to leave at 11.28am on Saturdays, which probably attracts a few more railway enthusiasts.

The Stockport - Stalybridge train is the most infamous of Britain's so-called 'Ghost Trains' or 'Parliamentary Services'. Since privatisation, it has become virtually impossible to close a railway line, even one that has outlived its useful purpose. By running a train once a week, the train operator is let off the hook, and is able to avoid the lengthy and costly procedures that a line closure entails.

The Ghost Train at Stockport

The line was once reasonably busy, for in addition to serving local commuters it provided a useful service to travellers going from the south to the north-east. Someone travelling, say, from Stoke-on-Trent to York in the 1970s, would arrive at Piccadilly station in Manchester and then have to cross the city by bus or taxi to catch the York train at Victoria. By changing at Stockport and Stalybridge, such travellers could avoid Manchester altogether. But the 1980s saw the introduction of through trains from the south of England to the north-east, and the death knell of the line came in 1992 with the opening of the Tramlink network, which provided a rapid and reliable link between Piccadilly and Victoria.

I was planning a weekend with a friend in Newcastle, and decided for fun to travel via Stockport and Stalybridge. Reaching the busy and modern Stockport station, with fast electric Virgin trains passing every few minutes, I located the neglected bay platform 3A for the Stalybridge train.

An elderly diesel multiple unit appeared from nowhere and a handful of passengers somehow melted out of the background to join the Ghost Train. None of them seemed to be railway enthusiasts. I chatted to an elderly lady who said that she had been using the line for years and always tried to get this train on Fridays as she then didn't need to change in Manchester. I managed to get a front seat with a panoramic view through the driver's cab, something more modern trains do not permit.

The journey started in quite a spectacular way with a ride across the 111-foot high Stockport viaduct, which dates from 1842 and was the largest in the world at the time of its construction. With its 27 arches, it is still one of the biggest brick structures in Europe. Its 11,000,000 bricks would stretch for 1,500 miles if laid end-to-end. Although Lowry immortalised the viaduct in a number of his paintings, it would certainly be better known if it traversed a bleak empty moor rather than a swathe of post-industrial cityscape. But there is an interesting sight from the viaduct in the form of a huge blue truncated glass pyramid, which houses a call centre for the Co-Op Bank.

Shortly after the viaduct, the Stalybridge line branches off to the east, with views across to the Pennines on the right-hand side. Four minutes after leaving Stockport, the train pulled into Reddish South Station. There was nothing to be seen except an overgrown platform, some broken lights and a solitary nameboard. After the guard had made absolutely sure no-one was waiting, the train set off again.

This railway gives its rare passengers a rather misleading impression of rural tranquillity, with trees and undergrowth obscuring any sign of urbanisation. Beyond Reddish South the railway crosses the M66 motorway and then dives under the M67. Passing under the ugly concrete bridge that carries the motorway over the line, the Ghost Train reached Denton, another semi-derelict station. Once again, nobody got on.

Beyond Denton, our train suddenly came to a halt in the middle of nowhere. The guard got out and started talking to someone on a lineside telephone. Some of the passengers speculated on whether there were any leaves on the line. The elderly lady told me that the train might be diverted to Manchester Victoria - apparently this had happened before.

Denton station wilderness

But our next stop was at Guide Bridge, where we joined the Manchester - Glossop line. The station here had obviously once been quite impressive, but its buildings were now mostly boarded-up and dilapidated. But there were several passengers waiting here, and a few of them joined our train to Stalybridge.

The Ghost train terminated in Platform 3 at Stalybridge station. The main station buildings here are well-maintained, with a Victorian cast-iron canopy, a large clock and a famous buffet that is one of the few free houses on the rail network. It is decorated with old railway signs and locomotive number and name plates, has an open fire, and serves all kinds of unusual fare such as black peas, perry and wheat beer.

The Ghost Train at its destination

Stalybridge Station Buffet seemed the best place to wait for the Trans-Pennine Express, which was to take me on the next stage of my journey. Looking out of the window, I was intrigued to see the Ghost Train disappear back along the same set of tracks that it had come on. Was it going all the way back to Stockport, or to some mysterious hidden siding somewhere en-route? Thoughts of dark tunnels with dangling skeletons came to mind…

Amazingly, the farce of the once-weekly Stockport - Stalybridge train has endured for the best part of two decades. A formal proposal to withdraw the passenger service was made by Network Rail late in 2006, but, after a concerted campaign led by the local MP, councillors and hundreds of local people, the line has won a reprieve. At the time of writing, Andrew Gwynne MP, Member of Parliament for Denton and Reddish, is proposing the introduction of a frequent shuttle service from Stockport to Manchester Victoria, calling at Reddish South and Denton stations. Perhaps there is a real chance that this ghost line can return from beyond the grave.

34. *Don't Look Back in Ongar*

September 30, 1994: On the way north to a friend's wedding I am distracted by the last tube train from Epping to Ongar…

If there is one railway system in the world that I dislike, then I am afraid it has to be the London Underground. Crowded, dirty and expensive, the Tube is also quite frightening. One may worry about getting crushed in the crowd, mugged or blown up by a terrorist; there is also the risk of being mistaken for a Brazilian electrician and shot by the Metropolitan Police. And the most terrifying situation is to be all alone late at night on the platform of a deep-level station. When the 'whoosh!' and the rush of air tells me a train is coming, why do I have this self-destructive urge to jump out onto the track in front of it?

Of course, the Tube is full of curiosities, and I would enjoy the long open-air stretch of the Piccadilly Line were it not for the fact that I usually travel along it on my way to or from Heathrow airport for a holiday or business trip, so I am usually thinking or dreaming about somewhere much further away.

A friend of mine was getting married on Saturday October 1, 1994 and I decided to drive to York for the wedding. I planned to leave work at 5pm on the Friday and head up the M20, M25, M11 and A1. Another friend then pointed out that London Transport was closing the Holborn - Aldwych and Epping - Ongar lines that day. I knew I couldn't make it to Aldwych, but Ongar was just off the M11. I might just be able to travel on the Epping - Ongar line or at least get some photos of it in action.

Ongar station in 1994

The Epping - Ongar line had fascinated me for a long time, although I had never travelled on it. When I was very small my parents gave me a *Ladybird Book of London*, which had a slightly abbreviated map of the Tube inside the back cover, and I remember being intrigued by the arrow pointing off to the top right with the caption 'To Ongar'. Later I attended a boarding school in Essex and we would always drive past Ongar station on the way to and from school. It was somehow reassuring to know that within striking distance of the school there was a Tube station and I could escape to London if I ever wanted to. My greatest interest in those days was old churches, and it seemed quite bizarre to me that the wooden Saxon church at Greensted-juxta-Ongar should be on the Central London Tube!

By September 30, 1994 the Epping - Ongar service had been reduced to a peak-hour shuttle. As I headed up the M11 I wondered when the last train would be. I assumed that there would be a special service for the last day, with trains running until late in the evening.

When I got to Ongar station, just after half-past six, it was quite crowded with photographers and sightseers. A single London Transport official was on duty. I asked him if I could get a return ticket to Epping. He said it was too late: the last train from Epping to Ongar was leaving Epping at 18.39 and would be arriving at Ongar at 18.56, whence it would return to Epping and terminate in Loughton. There were no additional special trains: it was as per the normal timetable.

I considered waiting at Ongar and just doing a single journey to Epping, but I was worried that I would not be able to get back to Ongar afterwards to pick up my car. Then I had a thought: the train would presumably be stopping at the intermediate station of North Weald. Could I get to North Weald before the train arrived from Epping?

I got back in my car and drove, not quite dangerously, to North Weald. I missed the turning to the station, did a three-point turn and got there. Parking in the station car park, I walked to the platform. The sight of a large number of men with cameras on the footbridge raised my hopes: the last train had not yet come. But had it now reached Ongar and already turned back?

Enquiries revealed that the train from Epping had not yet arrived, so I went into the ticket office and bought myself a return ticket to Ongar from the machine, which cost the grand total of 70p. Seconds later, out of the Essex twilight a three-car red tube train crept into the station. Would I get on? The train was as crowded as any central London rush-hour tube, but somehow they managed to find room for one more.

Passengers on the last train to Ongar

The train was packed and the light was fading, so I couldn't see much of the countryside through the windows. But I *was* interviewed by two people from a local community radio station! All too soon the train reached Ongar, where we made a short stop. I remained on the train. A few other passengers were shoe-horned in and the guard announced "Well done! You've made it! This is the last train from Ongar".

As the train pulled away from Ongar, there were a few small explosions - someone had placed detonators on the track. The train whistled - something you don't often hear a tube train doing - and there was quite a festive atmosphere on board, with some of the passengers singing "Last Train to Chipping Ongar" to the tune of *Last Train to San Fernando*! One enthusiast was upset by this - "It's supposed to be a sad occasion!" he said.

The last train leaves North Weald

The train made a special stop at Blake Hall station, which had closed some 13 years previously. The station had been converted into a private house and the platforms demolished.

I think I was the only passenger to get off at North Weald, although quite a crowd had gathered on the platform. I asked the driver and guard to sign my ticket, and then watched the little red train fade away into the night, used the now-derelict station loo and went to find my car. It was quite emotional to participate in the death of a railway.

I have never been the first person to do anything in the world, but I can truthfully say that I was the very last person to make a return journey with London Underground from North Weald to Ongar!

Traditionally I always say a wish when I travel on a railway line that I have not been on before. On this occasion my wish just had to be for the couple whose wedding I would be attending the next day.

My return ticket from North Weald to Ongar, issued at 18.43 on September 30, 1994

After my trip, the line remained dormant for a decade, succumbing to weeds and vandalism. There was a great deal of controversy regarding London Underground's sale of the line, and arguments between those who wanted to restore an electrified commuter service and those who preferred running a tourist railway. Eventually, in October 2004, a group of enthusiasts started operating diesel trains on Sundays between Ongar and North Weald. Further restoration is in progress, but the electric third-rail has been permanently disconnected, and the line no longer serves a public transport function or provides a connection with tube trains from Epping to Central London.

35. A Beautiful Berkshire Branch Line - and Cakes with the Women's Institute

June 16, 1987: I take the train to Henley-on-Thames

During the late 1980s, when I was working with a Bromley-based tour operator, one of my occasional duties was to visit various travel agents and other interested groups around the country to give talks on our programme of holidays. In June 1987 I was asked to give a presentation to Mrs Markham of the Berkshire Women's Institute in Henley-on-Thames.

"It's very near the station", Mrs Markham said as she gave me directions; "you'll have to change trains at Twyford - there are no through trains to Henley."

This should have made me realise that I was about to undertake a rather special journey, but it didn't. As far as I was concerned it was a work trip that was just going to take me over boring suburban railways with anonymous trains in Network South-East livery. I soon discovered how wrong I was.

June 16 was a beautiful warm and sunny day in what was not an especially good summer. My train on the GWR main line passed through the traditional station at Taplow, crossed the Thames on Brunel's famous flat-arched bridge and halted at Maidenhead, junction for the Bourne End and Marlow line. When I alighted from the mainline train at Twyford I found the branch train to Henley waiting in its bay.

The Henley branch train at Twyford

The Henley branch motive power was quite different from most Network South-East trains. It was not an electric multiple-unit. It was not even a diesel multiple-unit, but was a single diesel unit, of the type known by enthusiasts as 'bubble-cars'. I took my seat at the front behind the driver, who obligingly had not closed his blinds, allowing me a clear view through the cab to the track ahead. Soon there was a 'toot' from the horn and we were off on the 13-minute, four-and-a-half mile journey to Henley.

Within a minute the east - west main line could have been a world away. With the characteristic squeal of the wheel flanges against the rails, we rounded a sharp curve, brushing foliage on both sides, and then headed north in an almost-straight direction. The first station on the branch was called Wargrave. The name to me conjured up images of cemeteries on the Somme with dozens of stone crosses, but in actual fact it proved to be a very pretty riverside village with a fine church. Beyond the station we crossed the wide Thames, which thereafter remained just to the right of the railway. We also crossed from Berkshire into Oxfordshire, although there was no sign by the railway informing passengers of this!

The Thames was lined with expensive-looking houses and equally expensive-looking houseboats. The next station was called Shiplake, quite an appropriate name for a settlement on a wide and placid river. It had been reduced to an unmanned halt and had obviously come down in the world, but the Victorian station buildings were still in good condition.

After Shiplake we passed over a level-crossing, where a large number of motorists were waiting, and continued through beautiful scenery to Henley. The line was hemmed in by trees on both sides, but on the right there were occasional glimpses of the Thames.

Henley Station

At Henley, the station proved to be right in the town centre. It had a single platform that retained a fine Victorian canopy. I now opened my briefcase and got out the directions to Mrs Markham's. For not the first time of the day I regretted that I had not brought a camera with me.

The Berkshire Women's Institute were having their meeting in the drawing-room of a large Edwardian house about five minutes' walk from the station. I did my presentation on the various European coach tours offered by my employers, handed out brochures, answered questions and took notes. The French windows were open, giving views of a charming back garden where birds were singing merrily. My hostess served delicious tea and home-made cakes, and I told her how enchanting I had found the railway journey from Twyford to Henley. I never did ask why the Berkshire WI had chosen to hold their meeting just over the border in the neighbouring county of Oxfordshire!

After I had said my goodbyes, I went for a stroll around the centre of Henley. The five-arched stone road bridge across the Thames is elegant and attractive, and the waterfront is dominated by the tall west tower of St Mary's Church. It dates mostly from the 15th century and is a fine example of the Perpendicular Gothic style, although it has been much restored. But the real attraction of Henley is the river itself - small vessels of all kinds kept going past on this beautiful midsummer afternoon.

Henley-on-Thames

I had a quick look around the shops and was delighted to find a disposable camera. I bought it and took a few pictures of the town and church. Returning to the station, I took a photo of the 'bubble-car' before boarding it for my return trip. I attempted a few shots through the driver's cab along the way back to Twyford, but unfortunately the blurred prints I got back from processing were not worth saving in my album. After another idyllic 13 minutes I was back at Twyford waiting for the mainline train.

Sometime later I read a book about the history of the Henley branch. It was opened by the Great Western Railway in 1857 and was originally broad-gauge, being converted to standard-gauge in 1876. I find it hard to imagine a giant 7-foot gauge steam locomotive making its way along this little rural line where vegetation had brushed against the sides of my 'bubble-car'. But I suppose in steam days the trees would not have been allowed to grow so close to the line. The Henley-on-Thames railway probably offered a more picturesque rural journey to me in 1987 than it would have done to a traveller 130 years earlier, when no doubt it cut like a fresh scar through the landscape and its stations were busy with freight as well as with passengers.

The Henley line does have one notable claim to fame: in 1906 it was the first railway to be equipped with automatic train control (ATC). In its primitive form, this consisted basically of a third rail between the running rails, which made contact with a shoe on the underside of the passing locomotive. The rail was divided into separate lengths, each of which was connected to a particular signal. When the signal was at danger, the rail was 'energised', ringing a bell on the engine's footplate. If the driver failed to acknowledge this warning within a preset time, the brakes of the train would be applied. Updated and refined over the past century, ATC is now standard practice on modern railway systems throughout the world. And it all started on this little four-and-a-half-mile English branch line.

My diary entry for June 16, 1987 states 'The Henley - Twyford branch line is the most beautiful railway I've been on for ages!' I can't promise that you will get any of the Berkshire WI's delicious home-made cakes, but, if you ever get an invitation to Henley, perhaps to attend the Royal Regatta, make sure that you go there by train!

June 5, 1999: My Brother learns to drive a steam locomotive

A one-day course to drive a steam engine seemed an appropriate 50th birthday present for my elder brother Richard, who is far more knowledgeable about railways than I am but spends more of his time with miniature versions than with the prototypes. His business of selling model railway items keeps him so busy that it was more than a year before he was able to cash-in the voucher I had sent him for a footplate experience on the Bluebell line. Naturally, I had to take my parents along to witness this historic occasion. My mother still cherishes a silver cup that Richard won in a 'Learner Driver of the Year' competition when he was in his late teens. So how would he cope with the iron road?

The Bluebell Railway in Sussex is the doyen of England's preserved lines. It has achieved far more fame and carried far more passengers as a tourist line than ever it did before closure. Originally linking the towns of East Grinstead and Lewes, it was a classic example of the Victorians' over-provision of railway facilities. Winding their way between the London, Brighton & South Coast Railway's double-track London to Brighton line and the South-Eastern Railway's double-track London to Hastings line (not much more than twenty miles to the east), there were once no fewer than three secondary north-south lines: the Bluebell, the Oxted - Uckfield - Lewes and the 'Cuckoo Line' (Eridge - Polegate - Eastbourne). These minor lines were all promoted by independent organisations - the Bluebell by the Lewes & East Grinstead Railway Company - but were invariably bought out by the SER or the LB&SCR, each anxious to have a finger in the other's pie. At the time of Grouping in 1923, both companies became part of the Southern Railway, and competition between rival railways was replaced by competition between trains and the new rural bus services, and the growing threat of private motoring. For these Sussex railways had chosen the easy routes through the Weald, following river valleys; the main roads and the larger villages were usually on the crests of the sandstone hills. Many a station was two or three miles from the centre of population whose name it bore; others, such as Eridge or Kingscote, were named after insignificant hamlets or nearby country houses. By the 1930s wealthy commuters were eschewing their local branch lines and driving to mainline stations such as Hayward's Heath or Tunbridge Wells for their daily trains to London.

When British Railways announced the closure of the East Grinstead - Lewes railway in 1955, it can hardly have inconvenienced many travellers. But a determined local resident named Miss Bessemer (England's first female railway enthusiast?) pointed out that the Act of Parliament that constituted the Lewes & East Grinstead Railway had guaranteed a service of four trains a day, and this guarantee had been inherited by the LB&SCR, the Southern Railway and British Railways. She took British Rail to court - and won! The national institution responded with bad grace, putting on four return journeys at inconvenient times. Since Kingscote and Barcombe stations had not been named in the original Act, the re-instated services did not stop there, even though Barcombe had developed into the busiest station.

British Rail eventually had to get a second Act of Parliament passed before they could close the line. But the interest that had been aroused in the 'Bluebell Railway', as the press had dubbed the line, inspired a group of local volunteers to step forward and preserve a section of it. BR were closing railways and scrapping obsolete rolling-stock all over the country, and nobody seemed to be taking any action to preserve this vanishing part of our heritage. With the birth of the independent, volunteer-run Bluebell Railway in 1960, there was at last a safe refuge for trains that would otherwise have gone to the scrapyard.

One of my earliest childhood memories may well be of a station on the Bluebell Line. I was in the car with my parents and brother, and we were no doubt travelling back to our home in Kent after a day at the seaside. Probably at my brother's suggestion, we pulled off to investigate a derelict railway station. It had two platforms, with awnings supported by faded green-painted columns. There was a footbridge across the tracks, which were still *in situ* although overgrown and obviously disused. From photographs I have seen since, I am convinced that this station was West Hoathly on the Bluebell Line.

A few years later my parents took my brother and I for a ride on the Bluebell, and I remember the little tank engines *Bluebell* and *Primrose* in their dark blue livery. We travelled in the beautiful Observation Car and I remember being most impressed by the vast Victorian station at Horsted Keynes with its subway under the platforms, its refreshment room and its period urinals!

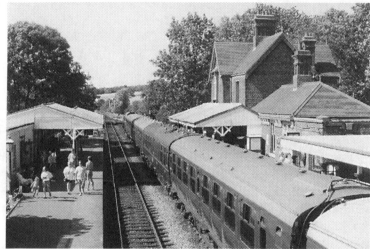

The Bluebell's Sheffield Park station

In its early days one suspects that the Bluebell volunteers were just happy to play with trains on a full-size railway; they painted locomotives in their own made-up liveries, gave them names they had never carried in service, and operated items of stock (like a bizarre Aveling & Porter industrial flywheel locomotive) that were most inappropriate to a Sussex branch line. As time went by, the railway developed into a more faithful recreation of the days of steam, with Sheffield Park station restored to late Victorian condition and Horsted Keynes to the green-and-cream colours of the Southern Railway. But the Bluebell did not rest on their laurels; they built extensive facilities for restoring locomotives at Sheffield Park, they erected an equally impressive coach repair works at Horsted Keynes, and then they started to extend their line north with the long-term aim of meeting up again with the national network at East Grinstead. Another of their innovations was the introduction of train-driving courses.

On June 5, 1999, my parents and I travelled through Sussex on the A272, turned off for Sheffield Park and parked in the station car-park. There is no village of Sheffield Park; the station gets its name from the nearby stately home of the Earls of Sheffield, the gardens of which now belong to the National Trust.

The Bluebell Railway is still 100% steam, and our train was headed by one of the strangest and ugliest steam locomotives I had ever set eyes upon: a Southern Railway 'Q1', built during the Second World War and designed to be economic and easy to maintain. It certainly made short work of the line to Horsted

Keynes. We could see the 'learner drivers' gathered here on the far platform, but we decided to stay on the train for the ride to Kingscote.

The Southern Railway 'Q1' locomotive

When I first rode on the 'Bluebell', the rails finished just north of Horsted Keynes station, although the way the track curves sharply under a brick arched bridge meant that this was not obvious. The section of track north from Horsted Keynes to Kingscote was for 30 years just a derelict, overgrown trackbed. It was therefore quite exciting to be riding on this part of the line, which even my fairly recent Ordnance Survey map marked with a dotted line and 'cse of old rly'. The track appeared smoother-riding north of Horsted Keynes, and the vegetation had yet to gain a foothold on the recently-cleared embankments, giving us sweeping views across the Sussex Weald. Then all became dark as our train plunged into Sharpthorne Tunnel, 730 yards long and one of the longest in preservation. The tunnel was notorious in the old days as the line is on quite a steep gradient and the rails could often become slippery in wet weather, but our 'Q1' had no problems. Immediately after the tunnel we slowed as we passed through the platforms of what had been West Hoathly station.

Kingscote station from the train

Ironically, although West Hoathly station survived the closure of the line by many years, it was subsequently demolished, and there has been little support among local residents for its reinstatement, many villagers fearing an influx of camera-wielding enthusiasts blocking the narrow local roads with their cars. Reconstruction is still a long-term possibility, but for the moment the 'Bluebell' management is more interested in pushing ahead to East Grinstead.

From West Hoathly the rebuilt railway continues north in a relatively straight line to Kingscote, a gem of a station and the current northern terminus. Here we got out and had a few minutes to look around while our engine 'ran around' the train. Amazingly for a country station that cannot ever have had much traffic, there was a pedestrian subway under the tracks. Kingscote station was immaculate; the waiting-room was straight out of the 1950s, and the ticket-office was furnished with old desks, racks of tickets and important-looking pieces of equipment including a large, ancient typewriter. It all looked as if it must have been in a state of suspended animation since closure in 1955, but, remarkably, the station had been sold by British Rail in the 1960s and converted to a private house. It survived 20 years of domestic use before fortuitously coming on the market and being snapped up by the railway. Large numbers of old railway stations all over the country have been converted into private houses, but there cannot be many private houses that have been turned back into working railway stations!

My parents and I returned by train to Horsted Keynes, where we enjoyed a meal in the delightful little Victorian refreshment room on the island platform. We now looked out for my brother and his fellow 'trainees'. There was no sign of them: since the departure of the 'Q1' towards Sheffield Park the vast station was so quiet that one could hear birds singing and the bells of Highbrook church chiming in the distance. Then, suddenly, out of nowhere, came the 'toot' of a steam whistle, and a little green tank engine appeared, attached to a brake van. I recognised my brother as one of the van 'crew'. He explained that each of the trainee drivers had to take the locomotive through Horsted Keynes station and continue north towards Kingscote, trying to stop the engine level with a snow-plough on a parallel siding. When it came to Richard's turn, I was invited to climb aboard and travel in the van. I hope that my presence didn't make him nervous, but in any case he performed the operation faultlessly, aided by a most efficient young 'firewoman'. My parents meanwhile waved to us from the platform and took a few photos.

Pause for water during driver-training

My parents returned to Sheffield Park by one of the service trains, but my brother had arranged a treat for me - a ride back on the brake van! Although I had travelled on the Horsted Keynes - Sheffield Park section numerous times before, it had always been in a comfortable upholstered coach riding on bogies. The four-wheel brake van was something else. There were, of course, no seats; one end was open to the weather, and I could feel every single rail joint. But it was a most memorable five-mile trip and remains my only brake-van ride as well as my only journey on the 'Bluebell' on other than a scheduled passenger train. And the locomotive that my brother had driven was none other than *Bluebell* herself, although nowadays she has regained her original identity as South-East and Chatham Railway no. 323.

Locomotive 323 and its brake van

Since my brake-van ride, the Bluebell Railway has pressed on with its ambitious programme of expansion. Track-laying north of Kingscote towards East Grinstead is well under way, and one day in the not too distant future steam trains should be crossing the mighty red-brick Imberhorne Viaduct. The only obstacle (now being cleared) is a large quantity of domestic waste that was tipped into a railway cutting south of East Grinstead after the line closed. The Bluebell has also acquired the trackbed of the former branch line from Horsted Keynes towards Ardingly, and volunteers have already laid a short length of track along part of this line. If the Ardingly branch were relaid, connecting with Network Rail's goods spur to Haywards Heath, it would open up the possibility for all kinds of special trains, and give the Bluebell back its role as a north - south link through the Sussex Weald. Miss Bessemer would be proud!

Bluebell Railway ticket

A Snowdrift, a Hurricane, the Beauty of Barming and the Ghost of Hollingbourne

When I was a very small boy there was only one road and one railway. The road was the A20, running to Maidstone and London in one direction and to Ashford and Folkestone in the other. Its steel equivalent was the Ashford - Maidstone East - Victoria railway line, and its heart was Bearsted & Thurnham station. One of my earliest memories is of my mother taking me with her in the car when giving my father a lift to the station, and watching a little black tank engine shunt in the coalyard. But even then the passenger trains consisted entirely of green electric multiple-units, which would occasionally take us to London for a visit to the theatre or a pre-Christmas shopping treat.

As I got older, I would use the railway to travel to Harrietsham and Lenham to visit friends, and sometimes even ventured as far as Ashford. The Number 10 bus provided an alternative, and slightly more convenient, form of inter-village transport, but travelling by train somehow felt much more grown-up.

Bearsted's 1884-built railway station

Until the early 1970s Bearsted & Thurnham station was a Victorian jewel. Built of yellow brick, with red-brick arches over the doorways and windows, both the main building and the shelter on the down platform had broad, dog-toothed canopies supported by ornate wrought-iron brackets. All the ironwork was painted in Southern Railway green and all the woodwork in cream. The station was lit by gas, both inside and outside, and in winter the waiting room always had a welcoming fire.

I moved away from Bearsted in 1973, by when the station had been modernised, with electric lights, new nameboards and paintwork in the dull corporate British Rail colours. The tracks into the coal yard had been pulled up and the electric trains had changed from green to blue. For many years I never travelled on the Maidstone East line. Then in 1986 I started a job in an office next-door to Bromley South station, and the line that I had travelled on as an occasional treat became my daily commute for two years.

Whilst it does not feature in any aficionado's list of great railway journeys, the Ashford-Maidstone East-Victoria line is nonetheless a pretty trip and is well worth a detour. The line was one of the last to be built in South-East England, seeing the light of day only in 1884, when it was completed by the LCDR (London, Chatham and Dover Railway), incorporating several smaller local companies, as a rival route to the SER's (South-Eastern Railway's) main line through Sevenoaks and Tonbridge. It has quite steep gradients and was never intended for high-speed running, although in the 1990s it frequently served as a diversionary route for Eurostar trains!

Ashford station, where my journey begins, was rebuilt out of all recognition to cater for the Eurostars, although sadly most of them no longer stop there. Back in the 1980s the station had just four platforms and a rather nondescript 1960s booking office on a bridge over the tracks. The platform buildings and canopies were of a similar vintage. The only things worthy of note were the station lamps; great, sausage-shaped fluorescent lights with 'ASHFORD' on them. The only other station on this line that I remember having similar lamps was St Mary Cray, further along towards London.

A steam special at Ashford in 1991

Ashford has always been rather a complicated station where it is all too easy to get in the wrong train (or the wrong half of the right train!), but, assuming one found the Maidstone East train, it would leave in a westerly direction, passing old freight yards and sidings as it branched off to the north of the ruler-straight Tonbridge line. The construction of the high-speed Channel Tunnel Rail Link (CTRL) has completely changed this part of the journey, and there is now a concrete cut-and-cover tunnel, whilst the old and new railways now run parallel as far as Hollingbourne, although the CTRL is not always visible.

The first station out of Ashford was originally Hothfield, but this was closed many years ago, although there is still an Amey Roadstone freight depot on the site. During the construction of the CTRL, a large 'temporary permanent-way' yard was laid near here, connected by rail to the Maidstone East - Ashford line. The yard went by the name of Beechbrook Farm, but the site has now been completely cleared and grassed over, and a casual observer would never know it had existed.

A half-timbered medieval house is passed on the right, and, soon afterwards, the train reaches Charing station. This is one of the largest on the line, although it is some distance from the village centre, which is across the A20. The station has recently been most tastefully refurbished with imitation Victorian lamps.

Well-maintained station at Charing

This railway is great for church-spotting. Charing once had an archbishop's palace and its church has a fine and very prominent 15th-century West Tower, of the typical battlemented Kentish design with a small stair turret on one corner. Egerton Church, visible in the distance to the left shortly after Charing, has a tower of the same design. Meanwhile, on the right-hand side are fine views of the North Downs. On both sides there are a fair number of oast houses, relics of the days when each farm had a few acres of hops.

During my commuting days the track between Charing and Lenham was blocked by snowdrifts for a week in January 1987. When train services resumed on the morning of January 19, the views from the carriage windows were incredible, as the train forced its way between great walls of snow on each side. Returning home that evening, the journey was even more spectacular, with pyrotechnic flashes from the electric conductor shoes as they touched the icy live rail.

The snowfalls of January 1987

Lenham station is almost identical to those at Harrietsham, Hollingbourne and Bearsted, with a pleasant Victorian station building on the down platform and a solid brick shelter with a decorative canopy on the up. In 1987 the station boasted the obligatory Network South-East clock, noted for the loud ticking it made as the numbers flicked over. During the Network South-East era of the late 1980s and early 1990s, the lamp-posts on all stations in the region were painted red, causing some railwaymen to refer to the area as 'the red light district'. Lenham is a most attractive little town with an interesting church and a lovely main square.

Harrietsham is the next village, and its church is visible on the right-hand side of the train as you approach the station. The church has another typical Kentish tower, but this is not its main claim to fame: there is a strange tall chapel on the north side of the building that is believed to be of pre-Conquest date, making this one of England's oldest church buildings.

Between Harrietsham and Hollingbourne the 1884 railway, the new high-speed line, the A20 trunk road and the M20 motorway run virtually parallel to one another, and the old Pilgrims' Way is just a little to the north. This valley has been a corridor for hundreds of years. Yet just to the south is Leeds Castle with its beautiful grounds. The castle is just out of sight of the railway, but can be reached by a pleasant walk from Hollingbourne station. This area lost a huge number of trees in the Great Storm or 'Hurricane' of October 16, 1987. It was quite remarkable that Network South-East managed to run a service of any sort the following Monday - I wonder how our new, fragmented railway system would cope with a hurricane? I can even remember a fellow commuter complaining that the train was reduced to only four coaches that day! Considering the great damage that had been done to infrastructure and rolling-stock, it is amazing that the trains were running at all just three days later. The devastation of the storm was all too visible from the train - many mighty trees were uprooted and most houses showed some signs of damage.

The railway station at Hollingbourne is lost in the leafy Kent countryside about a mile from the centre of the long straggling village. The parish church, mostly 14th-century, is quite near the station and can be clearly seen from the train.

At the time of writing there are plans to cut the number of trains stopping at Hollingbourne, which I think is a great pity, as the station has been useful to me on a number of occasions. Once I even got quite a fright there. One Sunday in the summer of 1994 I had a guiding job for a French group: I had to meet them at Dover Eastern Docks, accompany them to Leeds Castle and take them on a tour of the castle, and then check them in at the Great Danes Hotel on the A20 at Hollingbourne, where my duties would finish. I decided to drive to the Great Danes early in the morning, leave my car in the car park and get a train to Dover to meet the group; my car would then be there ready at the hotel for me to make a quick getaway in the early afternoon.

I parked at the hotel, crossed the A20 and headed up the road towards Hollingbourne. There was hardly any traffic about, but a couple of young women were exercising horses in a field just across the main road. I was quite surprised (and flattered!) when one of them called me and said "Come and join us!" I am sure it was meant in jest, and in any case I had a train to catch. The field with the horses was totally obliterated a few years later when the high-speed rail link was constructed.

If you are on foot and have a train to catch, Hollingbourne's long, narrow high street seems to go on forever, but at last I came to the bridge and bottle-bank and headed up the sloping approach road to the station. Although the station's buildings were still in good condition, it was unmanned and tickets were sold by a machine. I crossed the footbridge to the down platform. I had made it with about five minutes to spare.

I had thought I was alone, but then I spotted the other traveller. He was wearing a top hat and a Victorian frock-coat with a high collar. His skin was unusually pale but his lips were a deep red. Trust me to be getting on the same train as a weirdo, I thought. I walked about as far down the platform as I could. The strange gentleman just carried on gazing across the tracks. I wondered if he had been to a fancy-dress party the night before?

The old slam-door electric train crept into the station and I got on. Looking back along the platform, the Victorian gentleman was still standing there, gazing into space, making no effort to join the train. As we pulled off, I looked back and saw he was still on the platform. If he wasn't a ghost he must have been a mime-artist, but surely Hollingbourne station on a Sunday is not the best place to tout for business.

The station after Hollingbourne is my former home stamping-ground, Bearsted. The old station nameboards bore the name 'Bearsted & Thurnham'. The village centre and green are passed on the left before the train enters the station. The church has another Kent tower, but this one is unique because of the statues of 'beasts' at its corners. Thurnham is hidden among the North Downs on the other side of the line. It has the remains of a Norman castle, but these cannot be seen from the train.

Leaving Bearsted, the train passes the old goods shed on the left, still intact but unoccupied, and then goes under a fine brick three-arched bridge. A few converted oast houses reassure the traveller that he is still in Kent, but the anonymous suburbs of Maidstone soon take over, and then the line's first tunnel brings us into the county town. Unfortunately, Maidstone East is a most unattractive station, and it was hardly improved on September 6, 1993 when a goods train derailed and badly damaged the platform buildings. The main entrance and ticket office are on a bridge above the tracks, with covered stairways down to rail level. There are plans at the time of writing for the whole station area to be redeveloped in a scheme that will involve the construction of an Asda superstore.

Slam-door train at Maidstone East

The climax of the journey comes just after Maidstone East, when the train crosses a fine girder bridge across the Medway, the river that divides Men and Women of Kent from Kentish Men and Women. Just after the bridge, the line crosses the Medway Valley line, and the very basic Maidstone Barracks station can be seen on the left. The Medway Valley line runs from Strood to Paddock Wood, and its southern stretch, from Maidstone West to Paddock Wood, is a real treat - a proper rural branch line. It was in fact the first railway to serve Maidstone, opened in 1844.

Unlike those to the east, the stations west of the Medway have no 'house style'. The first is at Barming, a charming village station that was always busy with commuters when I rode the line. By the time the 07.27

from Ashford reached Barming it was already getting quite full, and among the passengers boarding this particular train would always be an especially stunning young blonde woman with long frizzy hair. Smartly dressed and heading for the big smoke, the Beauty of Barming would normally take a corner seat and pull out the latest Jackie Collins paperback to while away the journey. I have the feeling that male commuters from Maidstone used to have bets on where she would sit. I don't think I ever spoke to her apart from the occasional "excuse me" when I needed to squeeze past her to get out of the train at Bromley South. I did once see her board with a gentleman friend; they sat opposite me and, from snatches of their conversation, I gathered that her name was Maggie. Somehow it didn't seem to suit her delicate, gentle beauty - but then Maggie *was* a good name for high-powered blonde ladies in the 1980s!

But I have been concentrating too much on what might be seen inside the train, and not enough on what can be seen outside. After some pleasant countryside with farmyards and orchards, the little halt of East Malling comes, with the square-towered East Malling Church just to the right. West Malling, quite a substantial little town, comes only a mile later. On the left, just beyond the station, a ruined Gothic tower survives from the medieval Malling Abbey, dissolved by King Henry VIII in the 1530s and now restored to monastic use.

There follows a comparatively long stretch without any stations, as the railway cunningly contrives to miss the villages of Leybourne, Addington and Offham altogether, although Offham Church is visible in the distance to the left. The line temporarily loses its tarmac neighbour, the A20, which veers to the north, and stops at the station of Borough Green, formerly known as 'Borough Green and Wrotham'. Wrotham (pronounced 'Rootem') is an old village on the Pilgrims' Way, a mile to the north, but Borough Green is a rather unexciting post-railway residential development.

Although we are getting nearer London, the countryside seems to be getting more and more rural. Kemsing, the next station, is about the most perfect example of a rural halt that can still survive in England: hardly a house is visible from its platforms. Just beyond the halt, over to the left, is the impressive Kentish tower of Seal church. It has interesting brasses and is well worth a visit.

Quite suddenly and unexpectedly, you come to the junction. The Maidstone East line joins the older former LCDR line from Bat & Ball and Sevenoaks. There is no station at the junction: any passengers wishing to travel to Sevenoaks have to change at the next station, Otford.

Otford, like Charing, was once a place of some importance: the Archbishops of Canterbury had a palace here in medieval times. When I was very young I imagined it must still be very important, as the station seemed impossibly grand; all the platforms were covered by broad Victorian canopies supported by a forest of green-painted cast-iron columns, and there were lots of notice-boards and gas lamps. Sadly, modernisation has swept away most of the canopies, and there remains just the main station building and a 'bus-shelter' on the down platform. In the days of the old slam-door electric trains, a member of the station staff had the clever idea of painting on the wall a list of the various train headcodes together with the destinations they served. I could never quite understand the Southern Region's love for headcodes; they meant absolutely nothing to the everyday passenger and were not normally shown in the timetables. One good thing about the new sliding-door stock is that it actually shows the destination of the train!

Shoreham station, another tiny halt, follows Otford. The village church is a few hundred yards down the road on the left. I remember being rather startled by the sight of an ostrich poking its head above a hedge somewhere near here in the 1980s.

A white chalk cross carved on a hillside here serves as a war memorial: there is another at Lenham but it is not clearly visible from the train. Over to the left is the Tudor red-brick Lullingstone Castle and the modern shed that protects the remains of the 1,800-year-old Lullingstone Roman Villa. Lullingstone nearly had its own little halt, but work on it was abandoned at the start of the Second World War. The next actual station is at Eynsford, on the southern edge of the town and only half-a-mile from Lullingstone.

The rural ride is almost at an end. Just after leaving Eynsford, the train crosses a magnificent red-brick viaduct, which must appear like a Roman aqueduct to the ghosts of the occupants of Lullingstone villa, if they still haunt hereabouts. A longish tunnel follows, after which the railway passes under the M25, over the A20 and joins the main London-Chatham-Dover line at Swanley station.

Swanley is a busy suburban station, and the settlement around it is entirely post-railway: the old Swanley village is a mile-and-a-half to the north-east. Both Swanley and the next station, St Mary Cray, were rebuilt in a rather unlovely style in the 1960s, and have their main buildings and ticket offices on a bridge above the tracks. Between the two stations the train passes over the River Cray; the tiny and rather battered medieval church of St Mary can be seen by the river on the right, just below the railway.

Another suburban junction follows, and the next station is Bickley. In the 1980s, although it was rather dilapidated, it still retained its Victorian canopies and platform buildings, and was a stark contrast to the rebuilt stations on either side. There is nothing much to see around here apart from suburban sprawl, although there is rather a fine neo-Perpendicular church to the left, if you are able to glimpse it between the office blocks. The section of track between St Mary Cray and Bromley was opened back in 1858 and was then called the Mid-Kent Railway! Bickley station was originally known as 'Southborough Road'.

Bickley and Bromley South stations are so close together that one suspects that the first coach of the electric multiple-unit will just be entering Bromley as the last coach leaves Bickley. The train carries on, of course, to Victoria, but I get out at Bromley, pick up my briefcase, walk up the stairs to the ticket barrier and then turn right into Elmfield Road for another day at the office. For, if the train is on time, it is 8.57am, and I start work at nine!

Bromley South in NSE days

220

38. A Railway Revival in the Rother Valley

1979 - 2007: Summer trips on the Kent & East Sussex Railway

When I was very young my family would sometimes go down to the seaside on the A21. When we passed through a village called Robertsbridge, my father would always shout out "Look, Robert, it's your bridge!" I remember feeling very proud that a bridge should have been named after me, even though I was not actually sure which was *my* bridge - the road seemed to cross so many small streams on its way through the long, straggling village. There was also one level-crossing, and I remember my brother Richard saying "They're talking about getting that railway running again!"

In fact, Robertsbridge is a corruption of 'Rother Bridge', and the railway in question was the Rother Valley Railway, also known as the Kent & East Sussex. And yes, they *did* get it running again, although so far not across that level-crossing at Robertsbridge!

The story of the Kent & East Sussex is one of the most romantic in railway history. The line's main purpose was to serve Tenterden, the small town in the Weald that had been left high and dry in 1851 when the route via Rye was chosen for the Ashford - Hastings railway. The first stretch of the line, from Robertsbridge to the site of the present Rolvenden station, was not opened until 1900, some 15 years after Karl Benz had demonstrated the first practical motor car. The line was extended through Tenterden Town to Headcorn in 1905, but a planned extension to Maidstone never saw the light of day.

The Kent & East Sussex was built on a shoestring by the famous and somewhat eccentric Victorian engineer Holman Fred Stephens. Taking advantage of the Light Railways Act of 1896, this former colonel with the Royal Engineers built and managed a whole empire of minor lines, which he controlled from his office in Tonbridge. Although Colonel Stephens' lines could be seen as a quaint anachronism, appearing on the scene at the same time as private motor vehicles, they also showed a novel approach towards the provision of local transport. Stations were single-storey corrugated-iron structures, rolling-stock was usually purchased second-hand, signalling and staffing were reduced to a minimum and heavy engineering works were avoided. The colonel was also a pioneer in the use of diesel railbuses.

The K&ESR was never a very profitable line, and became insolvent on Colonel Stephens' death in 1931. The colonel's assistant, William H Austen, was appointed Official Receiver and managed the line until the Second World War, when it came under government control. Travellers' tales from the 1930s report unkempt stations, an uncomfortable ride in obsolete rolling-stock over decaying track, and a timetable apparently designed to discourage all but the most determined passengers.

After the war the line briefly regained its independence, and was celebrated in verse as 'The Farmers' Line', with a poem and sketches by Rowland Emett appearing in *Punch*. In 1948 the railway was nationalised and became part of British Railways, who withdrew passenger services and ripped up the Headcorn - Tenterden section in 1954. Goods trains and occasional hop-pickers' 'specials' continued to run from Tenterden to Robertsbridge until 1961, when the line was closed completely. A preservation society was founded in April 1961, but it was to be nearly thirteen years before they could run their first train.

In a way I have grown up with the K&ESR. I have witnessed it change from a disused, overgrown freight line to a prime passenger-carrying railway that is one of South-East England's major tourist attractions. Progress has been slow and the line has taken far longer to restore than it took to construct in the first place. But volunteers have done all the work, and modern safety regulations mean that it has been done to a far higher standard than that achieved by the line's original builders.

My first ride along this line was in 1979, in the company of my friend Charles from Zimbabwe. At the time all the trains in Charles' home country were still steam-hauled, many by mighty Garratt locomotives, but he still seemed happy to come with me on a short ride behind 'Hunslet Austerity' tank engine No. 23, appropriately named *Holman F Stephens*. In those days the railway's coaching stock was painted in a brown-and-cream Great Western-style livery, the locomotives were dark green and the stations were painted in the old Southern Region cream and green colours. Since then the K&ESR has standardised on a distinctive K&ESR livery, with most of its smaller industrial locomotives painted dark blue.

Engine No. 23, Holman F Stephens

Former mainline locomotives on the Kent & East Sussex are normally restored to one of the liveries that they bore while in service, which means that some of them have appeared in several different guises during their K&ESR careers. The most amazing survivor is locomotive No. 3, *Bodiam*, one of the London, Brighton & South Coast Railway's famous 'Terrier' tank engines, built in 1872. Originally numbered 70 by the LB&SCR and named *Poplar*, it was purchased second-hand for £650 by the original K&ESR in 1900 (with a £500 loan from Barclays Bank) and named after one of the villages on the line. It spent much of the 1930s lying in pieces on a siding at Rolvenden station, but fortunately was reassembled and put back to work. When the K&ESR was taken over by British Railways, the locomotive became BR number 32670, and continued to haul trains on the line right up until its final closure. In 1964 two benefactors purchased the engine from British Rail for £750 for the preservation society; the cost of its recent restoration was many times that figure!

Tenterden has a charming red-brick station building, relatively small but still the largest on the line. In 1979 the buffet facilities were in a grounded Pullman car, but now there is a proper station buffet. This has an impeccable 'vintage transport' pedigree as it was once the ticket office-cum-waiting room at Maidstone bus station! The town of Tenterden, incidentally, is absolutely delightful, with its wide, tree-lined High

Street, weatherboarded cottages and the magnificent parish church of St Mildred with its splendid tower. There are some nice pubs and a fine selection of shops for those who like to browse.

The departure from Tenterden is quite attractive, as the train passes almost immediately into the countryside. There are a few smart modern houses on the left, whose owners usually wave at the train as it goes by. There is a signal, a gated level crossing and a sharp descent down Tenterden Bank. At the foot of the hill, the train crosses another road, passes a picturesque old watermill and then pulls into Rolvenden station, nowhere near the village of Rolvenden. The station has always been the location of the railway's main locomotive works, although the present structures are all new, since British Rail razed the original buildings to the ground after withdrawal of the passenger service in 1954.

Signals near Rolvenden

Leaving Rolvenden, the line makes a graceful curve around a signal-box (re-erected by the preservation society), and begins its pastoral journey along the Rother Valley. A number of overgrown watery ditches on the right mark the site of a former crayfish farm; it is quite common to see herons here. Away in the distance you might catch a glimpse of the spire of St Michael's Church, one of Kent's loveliest Victorian churches. It looks as though it has been there for centuries.

When I took Charles on the line, our journey ended at Wittersham Road station. There is a simple station building at right angles to the track, and a signal-box was under construction at the time of our visit, while rusting rails continued west towards Northiam. Now the signal-box is fully operational and it is not unusual for two trains to cross at Wittersham Road, although there is only one platform. Anyone wishing to alight here and walk to Wittersham should note that the distance between the station and village is approximately three miles!

After two miles of quiet countryside, the passage from Kent into East Sussex is marked by the crossing of the River Rother, on a bridge that had to be rebuilt before the preservationists could re-open the line. Flooding was a major problem here in the old days: there are stories of locomotives sinking up to their axles in a muddy quagmire whenever the river burst its banks. Shortly after crossing the Rother, the train passes one of the last operational hop-gardens in the area (hop-pickers were once the line's chief patrons) and enters Northiam station.

Northiam station was reopened on a grand scale in 1990, with television personality Anneka Rice doing the honours as part of her *Challenge Anneka* series. The station building has been lovingly restored and a brand-new 'loo' block erected alongside to match it!

Leaving Northiam, the sharp-eyed traveller will spy on the right, in the distance, the white weather-boarded tower of Sandhurst mill, the only windmill in Kent to have five sweeps (as sails are known in the South-East). A smock-mill (so-called as its silhouette was supposed to resemble a countryman in a smock), it was built in 1844 for a Mr James Collins by Warren's, a firm of millwrights from Hawkhurst, and was considered a wonder at the time. The mill fell into decay between the wars and was demolished in the late 1940s, leaving just the octagonal brick base. In 2001 a new owner decided to rebuild the mill as a private residence, and it has now regained its prominent position on the horizon.

Just beyond Northiam station is the half-timbered Great Dixter house, with its world-famous gardens. In May 1981, long before this stretch of the line had been officially re-opened, the K&ESR erected a temporary halt just below the house and operated a shuttle service between there and Bodiam station on selected bank holidays. The motive power used was a four-wheeled diesel railbus. Sadly 'Dixter Halt' did not become a permanent feature of the railway. The house itself is not visible from the train, which follows the river to its current passenger terminus at Bodiam.

Railbus at Dixter Halt, May 1981

Bodiam station is a small, corrugated-iron structure similar to that at Northiam. It also has a modern wc block, cunningly disguised as a goods shed. From the station it is a pleasant walk of about half-a-mile to the fourteenth-century ruins of Bodiam Castle, built to fend off a possible invasion from France. The castle has been much more successful as a tourist attraction than ever it was as a fortress: it even featured in early publicity posters issued by the promoters of the Rother Valley Railway!

I have travelled on this delightful ten-mile line more times than I can remember. I have sometimes escorted groups of tourists on its trains as part of a guided tour, and I often take my visitors there. I once took a good friend of mine, a lovely South African girl, on a return trip from Tenterden to Bodiam, where we walked to the castle; she was a bit disappointed by the diesel multiple-unit that we took to Bodiam - "It's just like a bus on rails!" she said, but she was more impressed by the steam locomotive that hauled our return train (No. 10, the *Norwegian Mogul*). Another memorable journey I made on the K&ESR was on October 1, 1993, when I was asked to take a group of French travel agents and tour operators on a tour of Kent and Sussex, and our trip concluded with a ride on the *Wealden Pullman*, the railway's luxurious dinner train. I am pleased to report that this group of passengers, from a land renowned for its railways and its cuisine, had no complaints whatsoever about either their transport or their meal!

Bodiam Castle from the Train

I have one very special connection with the Kent & East Sussex line. In the mid-1980s I was involved with the rescue of four old railway carriages from Kingsnorth, south of Ashford. Withdrawn by the Southern Railway in the 1920s, the carriages had been roofed over and converted into a bungalow. A developer, who had bought the plot and was planning to build a modern house on the site, offered the carriages free of charge to the K&ESR on the condition that they removed them! Over two days I joined a team of volunteers who stripped the exterior weatherboarding and roof, ripped out wiring and dismantled interior partitions to reveal the carriages. They had obviously been much knocked about since they had last been on the rails, with the insertion of a number of large picture windows and the removal or boarding-over of some of the original doors. But incredibly two of these coaches have been restored and now form part of the railway's Victorian Train. It is always especially enjoyable for me to ride on one of them.

Level-crossing on the K&ESR

The Train that Passes Windmills, Herons and Sheep
on its way from Ashford to Hastings

If there is one railway that was always destined to make it into this book, it had to be the Ashford - Hastings line. This line has almost everything: pleasant scenery, a beautiful halfway-stop, a fascinating history and an incredible ability to survive closure attempts. It is even a useful means of transport: most of the journeys I have taken along its metals have been for practical purposes rather than for pleasure.

The Ashford - Hastings line was planned back in the late 1840s, when railways were still in their infancy. It was the time of the railway mania, when schemes for different lines were being dreamed up by rival companies. The London, Brighton & South Coast Railway (LB&SCR) built a line along the coast from Brighton to St Leonards in 1846, later extending it to Hastings. They were not amused when the South-Eastern Railway (SER) announced the construction of lines from Tunbridge Wells and Ashford to Hastings. In fact they attempted to have the Ashford - Hastings line closed even before it was opened, claiming it was unsafe. On the opening day, February 13, 1851, the SER retaliated by preventing the LB&SCR's trains from entering Hastings Station!

To make matters worse, the line was built in the wrong place. A glance at a map shows that the only town of any importance along the route is Rye. Had the railway been built just a few miles further inland, a whole string of villages and small market towns could have been served; such a line would also have avoided the steep gradients, sharp curves and two tunnels on the descent into Hastings. The route taken by the railway can be blamed on the Duke of Wellington. In 1848, when Louis-Napoleon Bonaparte was elected French president, there were fears of another war with France. The coast of South-East England was unprotected against a possible attack: William Holman Hunt's painting, *Our English Coasts (Strayed Sheep)* was not just a pretty picture of sheep on a clifftop: it was a political statement about the lack of proper defence on the Kent and Sussex coasts. As Lord Warden of the Cinque Ports and a senior statesman, as well as a military hero, the elderly duke's views were taken extremely seriously, and he persuaded the railway company to build their line nearer the coast so that large numbers of troops could be conveyed to Romney Marsh in the event of a French invasion.

In the event, Louis-Napoleon Bonaparte, who later declared himself Emperor Napoleon III, turned out to be an Anglophile, and a new enemy was emerging to the east in the form of Prussia. England was left with a chain of useless and expensive forts along the south coast ('Palmerston's Follies') and the South-Eastern Railway was left with a line that could not possibly make a profit. In despair they pandered to the lowest common denominator, taking hundreds of spectators in special trains to watch bare-knuckle prize-fighters pummel each other to a pulp in a field near Appledore station.

It was the late nineteenth-century boom in seaside tourism that really saved the line. Branches were built to New Romney, Rye Harbour and Camber (the latter a 3-foot gauge tramway), and thousands of well-heeled Victorian and Edwardian visitors would pour out of the Italianate portals of Rye station, to explore the little town that writer E F Benson was to immortalise as 'Tilling' in his *Mapp & Lucia* novels.

Ore station, serving the expanding suburbs of Hastings, was opened in 1888, and three diminutive halts followed in 1907: Snailham, Doleham and Three Oaks & Guestling.

The line became part of the Southern Railway in 1923, but this had little immediate effect. Although it forms part of a long coastal link that permits journeys such as Ramsgate - Portsmouth or Canterbury - Worthing, there has never been much effort to exploit this. Originally built to main-line standards, for most of its existence it has been operated and treated as a self-contained branch. It was one of the few lines in Kent or Sussex to escape electrification.

The early 1960s saw the withdrawal of steam locomotives (the last used in regular service on the route were the Southern Railway's handsome 'Schools' class) and the replacement of locomotive-hauled trains by slam-door diesel-electric multiple units. To a casual observer these looked just like normal Southern Region electric stock, but the loud throbbing sound of their English Electric 4SRKT diesel engines gave the game away. It also earned the units the nickname 'Thumpers'.

Interior of a 'Thumper'

Despite this half-hearted attempt at modernisation, traffic declined. Most of the stations on the line were rather inconveniently located for the places they claimed to serve, and private car ownership was high in this prosperous corner of England. British Rail made little effort to reduce operating costs: level-crossings were still manned, the line remained double-track throughout, and most station ticket-offices were still fully-staffed even though they sold only a handful of tickets daily. It was no surprise when the line was listed in the infamous 1963 *Beeching Report*.

The closure of the railway was dependent on the provision of an adequate replacement bus service. Fortunately for the line, the local roads that meandered across Romney Marsh would not permit the operation of a bus that could serve the same villages as the train and achieve similar journey times. There were also vigorous campaigns against the proposed closure by the local authorities and many residents. In the late 1960s a group of protestors was photographed on Platform 1 of Ashford station holding aloft a large pair of female undergarments with a banner reading 'No more bloomers, Marsh!' (This was not a reference to Romney Marsh but to *Richard* Marsh, then Minister of Transport).

The branch line to New Romney closed in 1967, being retained as far as Dungeness as a siding to serve the new nuclear power station. The Rye Harbour branch, out of use for several years, was lifted around the same time; the narrow-gauge tramway to Camber had been obliterated during the Second World War.

The *Railway Magazine* reported that the Ashford - Hastings line would close in 1969, yet it was still in service in July 1971, when the front page of the *Kent Messenger* stated that the line would close by the end of the year. It didn't. On July 31, 1974, the Ministry of Transport announced that the line was one of those that were being considered for closure, *on which services would continue indefinitely*. This can hardly have sounded reassuring to the railway's regular users, and closure rumours persisted for the rest of the decade.

My earliest memories of this railway are of a double-track, apparently main line that had largely escaped modernisation, with manually-operated level-crossings, semaphore signals, gaslit stations and lineside structures painted in the old Southern Railway colours of green and cream. Departure from Ashford was something of an adventure; while the four other lines, to Maidstone, Canterbury, Tonbridge and Folkestone, all ran parallel for some distance either side of the station, the 'Thumper' to Hastings would suddenly veer off to the south, passing some redundant railway buildings before burrowing into a tunnel of trees. Alas, the construction of the new A2070 road and a great deal of new housing has completely spoiled this part of the journey, as now the busy modern road runs directly alongside the railway. However, the tall white windmill at Willesborough can now be seen from the train if you look to the left a mile after leaving Ashford. A magnificent smock mill, it dates from 1869 and was restored by Ashford Borough Council in the 1990s.

Special train at Ham Street

By Ham Street, things look a lot better. The pretty village station is nicely-maintained and is still staffed at peak hours. The station's platforms are 'staggered' rather than opposite one another, a typical feature of the SER. In 1991, a set of stamps was issued to commemorate the bicentenary of the Ordnance Survey; these showed square-inch pieces of Ordnance Survey Maps from 1816 to 1991, centred on the village of Ham Street. The railway and station appear prominently on all but the first stamp in the set.

From Ham Street the delightful rural ride begins. The trees are left behind as the railway passes through the village of Warehorne, where no station was ever provided. The church at Warehorne overlooks the line; it has a most unusual tower, partly medieval stonework and partly later brick. The track then crosses the Royal Military Canal. Built in the early 1800s as a defence against Napoleon, the canal was opened to general freight traffic after the end of the war with France. From 1851 it fought a losing battle with the new iron road, and the last *bona fide* barge paid its toll in 1909.

The railway is now crossing the vast expanse of Romney Marsh, with pastures criss-crossed by drainage ditches. This is one of the best places in the UK to see grey herons from a train. You will also see vast numbers of sheep and, if it is an early morning train, plenty of rabbits. With the canal and the cliffs of the former shoreline now way over to the right, the train crosses the B2080 on the level and enters Appledore station, which is marooned on the marsh a mile and a half from the village whose name it bears.

Taw Valley crosses the canal

As recently as the mid-1980s, Appledore station was still staffed, and had a delightful waiting-room with cosy chairs, a carpet and a selection of books and magazines. It is now an unmanned halt, although the boarded-up station building and goods shed remain intact. The signal box has gone. Beyond the station, a rusting single-track bears off to the left. This is the old Lydd, New Romney and Littlestone branch, which now ends just short of Dungeness nuclear power station, its principal *raison d'être*. Very occasionally a passenger train runs on this line; I travelled on a 'Hertfordshire Rail Tours' special on December 29, 1993. The most fascinating points of interest along this very flat and very straight line are the ruined church at Midley and the old station at Lydd, which is gradually falling into a state of picturesque decay. On November 4, 2006, a steam special hauled by *Tangmere*, a Southern Railway 'Bulleid Pacific' locomotive, visited this line and I watched the crew refuel the engine at Lydd. (See also rear cover photo).

The Hastings line, meanwhile, now also single-track, continues dead straight across the Marsh from Appledore to the outskirts of Rye. Almost halfway between the two, the tiny church of Fairfield can be seen on the left; it has a lovely Georgian interior with box pews and an enormous pulpit. It is dedicated to Thomas Becket, and during floods its parishioners have sometimes required a boat to attend services!

The Ashford - Hastings line is one of those where a fair proportion of the passengers are always looking out of the windows. There is no 'typical' traveller on this line; I have shared carriages with mindless, foul-mouthed teenage yobs, and with members of the twin-set and pearls brigade making their way across country from Rye to Glyndebourne. I remember an elderly gentleman once boarding a train with a large ginger cat, which slept on his lap all the way to Hastings. I have even occasionally taken groups of foreign tourists on the train and given a commentary en-route. On one very recent journey I was sitting opposite a little girl and her grandfather, who appeared to be playing some sort of complicated game in which they scored points when seeing certain species of animal. This terminated in victory for the child when she screamed "Look, granddad, a HORSE!" at the top of her voice, just as we were coming into Appledore.

Tangmere's driver

On another occasion I was travelling on the last train of the day from Hastings to Ashford when a passenger boarded the train at Doleham. This was unusual enough, but what was even more surprising is that she was a stunning blonde of about seventeen and I overheard her asking the guard for a ticket to Ham Street. I saw her take a window-seat about two rows ahead of me and then fall into deep slumber. When the train started slowing for Ham Street, the gorgeous maiden was still fast asleep. What could I do? I went over and tried gently nudging her, to no avail, so I then shook her until finally her beautiful eyes opened, rather aghast at this stranger who was molesting her. "Excuse me, but I think this is your station!" I said. She beamed with gratitude as she stepped down onto the platform of Ham Street.

The railway crosses the Kent - Sussex border and then an extraordinary thing happens: the busy A259 coastal road, nominally part of a trunk route from Folkestone to Honiton, zigzags around the line, making two level-crossings necessary within three-quarters of a mile. I cannot understand why nobody has ever considered relocating the road to the south of the line.

The last of Romney Marsh's special churches is passed just before the second level-crossing. East Guldeford Church, another quaint relic with Georgian box-pews and a charming interior, has, like the railway, survived numerous attempts at closure. One Sunday I drove over from Hythe to attend Holy Communion here and boost the congregation.

The train crosses a steel girder bridge over the River Rother with a tremendous clatter and reaches Rye. As might be expected in a beautiful and historic town, the station is well-maintained. The signal-box is freshly-painted and the former parcels office is now a café called 'The Fat Controller'. Sadly for me, I once lost a girlfriend at Rye station: after passionately kissing her goodbye on the train, the next thing I heard from her was a letter telling me it was all over. The train on which we had our last kiss was an old diesel-electric multiple unit with the magic number 1001, which is now privately preserved. It really should have a plaque on it somewhere. Funnily enough, when the new Southern Railway operating company had teething troubles with its state-of-the-art Turbostar trains in 2004-5, unit 1001 was sometimes hired from its owners and pressed into service!

Rye is an ideal place to break one's journey, but is so well-known that I have no need to give a full account of its beauties here. The cobbled streets, half-timbered houses, antique shops, 'Olde English' tea rooms and the fine parish church are all worthy of exploration. The little Ypres Castle with its 'gun garden' is one of my favourite places in Rye, and in the 1990s I was frequently greeted here by a lovely silver tabby cat with a magnificent stripy tail.

Rye Station

However, Rye also has its sinister side, with the ghosts of Turkey-Cock Lane, the memories of smugglers brandishing their pistols in the Mermaid Inn, and the skull of a murderer that is still preserved in gibbet irons in the town hall. The town was raided and burnt by the French on more than one occasion, and I suspect that dark secrets still linger behind its picturesque façades.

The Church Clock, Rye

Leaving Rye, the train passes a rebuilt windmill on the right and the grassy remains of a Martello Tower on the left - one of the 74 small forts built in the early 1800s as a defence against Napoleon. Beyond it are the ruins of an earlier fortification - Camber Castle. Nowhere near the village of Camber, this was one of King Henry VIII's coastal fortresses, built to protect Protestant England from Catholic Europe.

The railway has now left the Marsh and entered the valley of the River Brede. The next station is called Winchelsea, although it is about a mile from that village. When the line was 'singled' in 1979, the former station building was left stranded on the disused 'down' platform, all passengers now using the 'up' platform that has just a simple shelter.

Winchelsea is a remarkable place. When the former Saxon port was destroyed by the Great Storm of 1287, King Edward I had the town rebuilt on its present site, on a high bluff above the sea. It was a walled town, built to a regular grid plan with a magnificent parish church at its centre. Like Rye, Winchelsea suffered from French raids, but the sea was its worst enemy. It had destroyed Old Winchelsea by violence, and it ruined New Winchelsea by treachery. By the sixteenth century the harbour was silted-up and useless, and now only the population of a village dwells on the site of a town. The medieval church is but a fragment, albeit a splendid one.

A 'Turbostar' at Rye

Winchelsea formerly had a windmill, visible on the left as the train pulled away from the station, but it was a victim of that other great storm, seven hundred years after the one that laid waste to the old town. Fortunately, Icklesham's windmill still survives, and can be seen in the distance on the left, about a mile further on. A black post-mill with white sails (or 'sweeps' as they are called in Sussex), it dates from the eighteenth century and is maintained in excellent condition.

The railway unfortunately passes about a mile to the north of Icklesham, which is quite a large village. Beyond the village is the site of Snailham Halt, which closed in 1959.

The line is now descending towards Hastings, through pleasantly leafy countryside. There is the first curve of any description since Rye, and the train reaches the tiny halt of Doleham, which doesn't really serve anywhere in particular. There is a further descent through leafy cuttings to the similar halt of Three Oaks, located about midway between the biggish villages of Westfield and Guestling, but not especially convenient for either.

After a last glimpse of rural Sussex, the train plunges into Ore Tunnel, which is nearly a mile long. In the days of the 'Thumpers' you could open the windows and listen to the water dripping down the tunnel walls, which seemed to have been lined with corrugated iron.

Ore station today is a disappointment. In the late 1970s it was a typical Victorian SER station with a neat wooden clapboard building and decorative canopies. This was demolished in Network South-East days and replaced by a small glazed shelter. Within months this had been badly vandalised and every pane of glass was broken. The station has been tidied up since, but is hardly a welcoming place to wait for a train, especially at night.

From Ore the line becomes double-track again and is electrified. The third-rail electrification was extended to Ore in 1935 so that electric trains terminating at Hastings could be serviced and maintained at a depot here (now closed). Beyond Ore the railway goes through the short Mount Pleasant Tunnel and enters Hastings, with the old town, pier and beach spread out below on the left.

Unit 1001 at Hastings

The old Hastings station I remember was a 1930s brick building with a cavernous ticket hall, a circular waiting room and a buffet. It had been rebuilt by the Southern Railway in the last great days of seaside holidays. This station has recently been demolished and replaced by a state-of-the-art steel-and-glass structure that is the centrepiece of an £8.6 million redevelopment scheme for the whole area. I still preferred the old station, but the new one is seen as an important element in the regeneration of this rather down-at-heel resort.

The first time I ever went to Hastings by rail, I got lost when walking around town and actually had to ask directions to find my way back to the station. Perhaps the new station will not be as shy as its predecessor.

Nowadays most of the trains continue to Brighton, but I will finish my journey here. I have travelled on this wonderful 26-mile railway many times in the past 30 years, by 'Thumper', by modern 'Turbostar' and once, on June 6, 1992, on a special steam train hauled by 'Bulleid Pacific' *Taw Valley*. Since I first rode these rails the stations at either end of the line have been rebuilt out of all recognition, and many other features of the journey have changed, not always for the best. But the centre portion across the Marsh remains the same as ever and the line's future now seems reasonably secure.

40. The Little Train That Takes Me Home Past Many a Garden Gnome

1976 - 2007: Riding on the Romney, Hythe and Dymchurch

Steam railways are quite special; narrow-gauge railways are even more special. Yet when one lives very close to one it can become commonplace. My parents had taken my brother and myself for a ride on the RH&DR when I was very small, but my first memories of the line are from the mid-1970s when my parents purchased a bungalow in Dymchurch. From our front lawn you could see the trains crossing Romney Marsh, and if you sat outside chatting on a summer afternoon your conversation would be punctuated by steam whistles.

The RH&DR is firmly established as part of the local community, although the only local residents who use it regularly are the children who travel on its daily school train. But it generates business for the local area, its miniature locomotives are familiar to everyone, and there was a serious outcry in 1981 when there was speculation that the railway might rip up its tracks and transfer operations to a more scenic location. It was built primarily for pleasure, a rich man's plaything, yet it also fulfilled a local transport need. When Captain J E P Howey decided in the 1920s that he would like to build a large miniature railway, he considered several sites before settling on Romney Marsh. The countryside was flat, there were no major natural obstacles, the area was a flourishing holiday destination and it was not served by the main line: the Southern Railway had stations at Hythe, New Romney and Dungeness, but there was no railway along the coast.

'Hurricane' on the turntable at Hythe

Opened in 1927 between Hythe and New Romney, the railway was extended to Dungeness a year later. It was built very much as one piece, with Henry Greenly, the chief engineer, designing the locomotives, stations and rolling-stock. The railway proved an immediate hit with summer visitors, although its great days came during the Second World War, when it took on the dual role as a troop transporter and as a line of defence, with what must surely have been the only armoured train ever built to the 15-inch gauge! Reopened in 1946, the RH&DR had its busiest seasons in the immediate postwar period, carrying vast numbers of holidaymakers and even a substantial amount of freight: shingle from Dungeness was taken by hopper wagons to Hythe and New Romney.

There are many railways that can be enjoyed irrespective of what type of motive power hauls the train. The RH&DR is one that should ideally be sampled on one of the ten one-third scale steam locomotives that were originally built for it. With their evocative names: *Green Goddess, Southern Maid, Typhoon, Hercules, Samson…* they are inseparable from their native line. The blue engine named *Hurricane* is said to have been Captain Howey's favourite, and he often took turns at driving it. In the mid-1980s the souvenir shop at Hythe station used to sell a car window sticker with a picture of this locomotive above the words *I've seen a Hurricane in Kent!* The stickers quickly disappeared after the notorious Great Storm of October 1987.

Since the closure of the old British Rail New Romney branch in 1967, most visitors to the RH&DR have joined the train at Hythe. The station here has an impressive overall roof, whilst there is a picturesque signal-box, an array of semaphore signals and a much-photographed locomotive turntable. The visitor facilities now comprise a ticket office, waiting area and a well-stocked gift shop, although these were added only in the 1970s; before then there was virtually nowhere for passengers to wait except on the platforms themselves.

'Winston Churchill' leaving Hythe

The train always leaves Hythe with a whistle and gradually picks up speed. The line is flat but far from featureless. To the right is the Royal Military Canal and beyond it are the wooded hills that marked the Kent coastline in Roman times. On the hills can be seen relics of other conflicts: a huge concrete dish that was used as a listening post for enemy aircraft (before the invention of radar); and the shattered walls of *Portus Lemanis,* the old Roman fort now known as Studfall Castle.

On the left-hand side the train passes the rear gardens of the houses along Dymchurch Road. This is a theme that will be repeated for nearly fourteen miles, and fascinating it is. All rail travellers are used to looking into people's rear gardens, but most standard-gauge trains are too fast and too far away for the would-be Peeping Tom to see anything of great interest. With the RH&DR you pass so close that you can almost touch the garden furniture, and so slowly that you can observe blue-tits on a coconut, ginger cats strolling on the lawn or families enjoying a fine afternoon. Some of the railway's neighbours have put up such tall, solid fences that you see almost nothing, but many of them seem to like the little trains, and will wave at you as you go by. A favourite hobby of mine when travelling on the RH&DR is seeing how many garden gnomes I can spot!

The railway runs between the suburbs of Hythe and the canal for a couple of miles. Then it curves to the south, passes a large flooded gravel-pit that is now a watersports centre, and enters open countryside. This is the same Romney Marsh that is crossed by the standard-gauge Ashford-Hastings train a few miles to the north, and there are usually plenty of sheep visible. The narrow-gauge line crosses several of the Romney Marsh drainage ditches, known locally as 'sewers', and at Botolph's Bridge it bisects one of the major roads across the Marsh. In my early teens I would sometimes walk down here during the summer holidays and wave at the trains, and when visiting my mother I sometimes still do! If visiting the area in the autumn, there are some great blackberry bushes along Botolph's Bridge Road near the level-crossing.

Dymchurch is the first station. The village straggles along the A259 coastal road for about three miles, almost merging with Hythe, but on the railway there is a real sense of open countryside between the two settlements. The station is inland, but only a short walk from the beaches and amusement arcades. It is a 1930s country station in miniature, complete with a tiny ticket office.

The train continues past postwar bungalows to St Mary's Bay, and then comes out again into open countryside, passing through a short tunnel under the A259 road. The next stop is the railway's headquarters and largest station, New Romney.

'Green Goddess' at New Romney

New Romney has a large station with a roof over the platforms; there is a shop, ticket office, café and a museum with a model railway exhibition. The locomotive sheds and coachworks are on the left before the train pulls up at the platform. When two trains are leaving in different directions the station really evokes memories of a British main line in the days of steam.

Leaving New Romney, the train passes through a tunnel under Station Road, and then the double track reduces to single. A development of neat modern warehouse units on the right marks the site of the old standard-gauge New Romney & Littlestone-on-Sea station. Opened by the South-Eastern Railway in 1884 and served by a branch from Appledore on the Ashford - Hastings line, this station was closed by British Rail in 1967, despite the heavy seasonal traffic brought by the RH&DR.

The RH&DR, meanwhile, goes through a small wood, giving passengers a last glimpse of Romney Marsh before curving away to the coast. The remaining five miles are entirely on shingle. At one time there were request stops at Greatstone, Lade and The Pilot, but now the only intermediate station is at Romney Sands, which formerly served a holiday camp known as Maddieson's. There are only occasional glimpses of the sea, as modern houses have been built along the coastal road, their back gardens running down to the railway. The gnomes, rusting barbecues, plastic chairs and other paraphernalia are much the same as elsewhere along the line, but what distinguishes the majority of these gardens is the shingle. Although some householders have had lawns installed, at great expense, most families here have no need for a lawnmower.

Approaching Dungeness, the surroundings become wilder. Very few new buildings have been erected here since the War. On the left-hand side one can see fishermen's boats pulled up on the shingle, some of them with their own little narrow-gauge railway tracks! On the right are old weatherboarded bungalows, one of which, Prospect Cottage, belonged to filmmaker Derek Jarman. He created his own garden out of scrap metal, driftwood and other debris he found on the beach. Despite the looming bulk of the two nuclear power stations, Dungeness is still an exciting and remote place.

The Old Lighthouse at Dungeness

Dungeness station is built on a loop, so trains do not have to reverse; they simply continue around a great circle of track and rejoin the line towards Hythe. The station has a pleasant and friendly cafeteria that has changed little over the years and where one can still purchase excellent fish and chips. Outside the RH&DR station a crumbling platform and empty trackbed are all that survives of the South Eastern Railway's erstwhile Dungeness branch. Closed in 1937, it never had more than the most basic of facilities.

I have travelled on this great little railway so often that it is impossible to single out one journey for special attention. I have taken friends of my mother's - a visiting University professor from Texas and his wife - to Dungeness and back; I have also taken friends from South Africa, Zimbabwe and France. I have got off with a friend at Dungeness, visited the old lighthouse and then walked along the shingle to Romney Sands to rejoin the train there. I have probably travelled behind every one of its locomotives except *The Bug*, the small Krupp contractor's engine that seldom appears on 'main-line' service!

So after a delicious meal at the Dungeness cafeteria, I board the train and hear the steam whistle blowing as it curves around the loop and heads along the coast, delaying countless motorists at level crossings as it screeches across the Marsh to New Romney. Children with buckets and spades board at St Mary's Bay and Dymchurch, and householders wave from their back gardens as we run alongside the Royal Military Canal for the final mile into Hythe.

At Hythe station I wait to watch the locomotive being detached from the train and turned around in preparation for its next journey. The turntable at Hythe, incidentally, came from one of England's great lost railways, the Lynton & Barnstaple. This makes me remember that the RH&DR itself could so easily have become a lost railway.

Leaving Hythe station I cross Scanlon's Bridge Road and take the footpath along the canal bank to the centre of the ancient Cinque Port. Hythe is another perfect little 'railway town', with its oldest houses clustered on the hillside around St Leonard's Church, which is a magnificent piece of architecture in its own right but is best known for the macabre ossuary in its crypt.

It is but a short walk from the High Street to the long shingle beach, and here I might buy an ice-cream or a cold drink, if the kiosk by the public swimming pool is open. I continue past the slightly faded grandeur of the Imperial Hotel towards Battery Point, where I made friends with a bottlenose dolphin called Davina during the wonderful summer of 2007. First christened 'Dave the Dolphin' by the local media, she patrolled the coast from Folkestone to Hythe during two summers. Coincidentally, the world's most famous 'interactive' dolphin, Fungi, has since 1983 made his home in Dingle Bay, very close to the former terminus of another narrow-gauge railway - the late, lamented Tralee & Dingle.

'Captain Howey' at Dungeness

Davina has gone now, as has the old standard-gauge line that once ran from Sandling Junction through Hythe to Sandgate: the old 'Sandgate' station was located high above Battery Point and was not very convenient for the village centre. Further to the east, the old Folkestone Harbour branch has just breathed its last. Much has changed, but the RH&DR continues to give pleasure to holidaymakers and to provide a regular passenger service for the schoolchildren of Romney Marsh. And long may it continue to do so.

The Ethereal Railway

It was mid-afternoon when I tramped along the main street of Carsac-le-Château in the southern Loire Valley. The SNCF station was quite a distance from the town centre, and it had no left-luggage facility. I had struggled up the long, tree-lined Avenue de la Gare to the medieval castle that gave the town its name. Luckily the custodian let me leave my backpack under her desk while I made a leisurely exploration of the old fortress with its towers, battlements and dungeons.

Apart from the château, the rest of the town had little to offer. A typical square with a few cafés flanking a Renaissance Hôtel de Ville, a heavily-restored Gothic church and a handful of old houses.

I consulted the pocket timetable that I kept in the back pocket of my jeans. Train services to Carsac were very infrequent, and varied from day-to-day: it was vital to check the times correctly. But, no, I had made no mistake - the next train to Clairebourg was not until 6pm, and then I had a wait of over an hour at the junction before my connection to Bonneville, where I had booked a small hotel for the night.

Pondering on how to kill a few hours in Carsac, I followed the main street for a few hundred yards. There was a Pharmacie, a bookshop, a down-at-heel Boulangerie/Patisserie and a shop selling television sets. It was a typical little French town.

I don't know what made me take the turning on the right. The street looked no different from any other. There was a pet shop with a few caged white rabbits and some tanks containing bored-looking tropical fish. I put down my backpack and watched them for a while before continuing down the street.

I passed through the detritus of a street market: a few potatoes and squashed tomatoes were lying in the gutters. I then heard something that sounded exactly like the whistle of a train. But how could that be? I was on the opposite side of town from the railway station, and in any case I knew that no train was due for a couple of hours.

I continued around a corner and found myself face-to-face with a little, red-and-cream painted railcar. It was standing on rails that ran along the street like a tramway. The building behind it was a small station with a goods shed alongside. On its wall I could see a stucco plaque incised 'CHEMIN DE FER DE CARSAC A BONNEVILLE'.

A hand-painted sign by the railcar stated 'Autorail pour Bonneville - Départ 16h00'. The sliding door was open. I eased myself in, unstrapped my backpack and placed it on one of the vinyl seats. The interior of the railcar was Spartan but serviceable. After taking in the notices (Défense de Fumer, Défense de Cracher) and the luggage nets above the seats, I settled by the window. The station-master raised his starting-flag and the railcar was off.

After running for a while on tramway-type rails, we left Carsac behind and started heading across open country. The diesel engine was so noisy that I found it hard to catch anything more than the occasional word from the conversations of the other passengers - and there were not very many of them. I watched the telegraph poles go by as we passed vineyards, farms and fields where I could see a team of horses ploughing. At a level-crossing a wizened old woman lowered the barriers and a ruddy-faced man waited in an ancient Citroën *Traction Avant*.

I took out my *France-Vacances* Pass, but no-one seemed bothered about checking it. We stopped at a small country halt where a girl in a floral print dress kissed goodbye to a tall young man in a military uniform, who joined the train. At another station a middle-aged woman got out, carrying three enormous cauliflowers in a large wicker basket. I wondered what she was going to do with them: I have hardly ever seen cauliflowers featured on French menus!

I took another look at my timetable. It showed no direct service between Carsac and Bonneville. The schematic map of the regional rail network on the cover omitted the line. Why was this? It couldn't possibly be a preserved tourist railway: it was obviously being used by local people. And for me it was ideal: this little train was cutting across the foot of a triangle, getting me to Bonneville far quicker than I had expected.

We paused at a vine-clad village station, where the soldier got off and an elderly man got on. Another old car - this time a Renault 4L - was waiting in the station forecourt. An early 2CV was parked behind it. Perhaps a classic car rally was taking place somewhere.

The countryside seemed to be in a time warp; we passed haystacks that looked just like those that used to feature in children's picture books, and there was another team of horses, and a single, old tractor.

A final level-crossing, and the railcar started to slow down. We were running along a street again. A few minutes later we stopped at Bonneville station, which looked like an exact replica of the one at Carsac. I pulled my backpack off the seat, stepped out, and took one last look at the little old railcar before heading up the street in what I thought must be the direction of the town centre.

I reached a T-junction and realised I was in the main shopping street. A shop selling CDs and DVDs had a large film poster in the window showing Gérard Depardieu. There was a sudden blast of rock music and an electric blue Peugeot 206CC came by with the roof down, an attractive blonde at the wheel.

I found the Hôtel de la Poste without too much difficulty. As its name suggested, it was right next to the post office, and I was pleased to have got there rather earlier than I'd expected. I checked in and dumped my backpack on the sagging single bed, and had a quick wash and brush-up before heading out again to explore the town and find something to eat. I returned to the hotel around nine-thirty and went up to bed, where I read for an hour or so before turning out the light.

The next morning I was in no particular hurry, as my train was not until half-past eleven. I went downstairs to the breakfast room and took a seat. A man in his late sixties, evidently the hotel proprietor, brought me a wire basket containing a croissant and some slices of baguette. He reappeared a couple of minutes later with some little packs of butter and jam on a saucer.

"Tea or coffee?" he asked.

"Coffee, please!" (I never trust tea south of Calais!)

"You're English, aren't you?"

"Yes. I'm on holiday".

"But you haven't got a car, have you? How are you travelling?"

"By train. You have excellent trains in France."

"Yes, we do. But not around here. I suppose you came via Clairebourg. I hate changing there - that awful station!"

"Well, no, I didn't. I came on that little railway, the narrow-gauge railway, the one from Carsac."

"What?" The hotelier's jaw dropped.

"You know - the little railway. I think it's called the Chemin de Fer de Carsac à Bonneville."

"Mais cette ligne…" My host dropped the tray he was holding. "Sylvie, viens ici!" he shouted.

His peroxide blonde wife appeared from the kitchen.

"This young man" he started (I love the way the French still refer to me as a 'jeune homme' even though I am now well into my forties)… "this young man says he came here yesterday on the train, the train from Carsac!"

"It's happened again, Henri!" she exclaimed. "You remember, the Irishman. It must have been all of ten years ago!"

"Of course. At the time we all thought he was drunk!"

"But it's impossible!"

By now I was asking myself what it was all about, and wondering when I was going to get my coffee. "What's the matter?" I asked.

Sylvie pulled up a chair and sat opposite me. "That railway line was closed fifty years ago!" she said. "Henri, get the old map!"

Henri disappeared and I heard the sound of drawers being pulled open and papers rustling in another room. Sylvie meanwhile returned to the kitchen and brought me my coffee.

Henri reappeared with a tatty old Michelin map with a yellow cover. He unfolded it across an empty table. "Look, there is Bonneville!" he pointed with a greasy finger.

I bent over the map. I could see the inverted 'V' made my by the thick black main lines from Bonneville to Clairebourg and from Clairebourg to Carsac. And there was a thinner, cross-hatched line meandering between Carsac and Bonneville. I even recognised the name of one of the stations I had passed through the day before.

"But I didn't dream this. How did I get here yesterday?"

Sylvie smiled. "There are some things, young man, that we will never understand."

I checked out of the Hôtel de la Poste, walked down the main street past the record shop and found my way down to where I thought the narrow-gauge station was located. The building was there, clearly recognisable. The incised plaque at first-floor level read: 'CHEMIN DE FER DE CARSAC A BONNEVILLE'. It looked in good repair but the shutters were tightly closed: it was not possible to determine its present function.

The old station yard appeared to have become a car park. There was no platform, no passengers and no awning to protect them from the weather. But then I noticed something shiny on the ground, and looked down to see that in places the tarmac had worn down to reveal two parallel rails below.

A disused station in France

241

A Journey from Ashford to Hastings in 1980

At Ashford Station, Platform One, the little band of travellers come
To cross the Marshes once again aboard the ancient Hastings train.
The three-car unit stands forlorn; the London train looks on in scorn
As it awaits on Platform Two the duties that *it* has to do.

"To Ham Street, Appledore and Rye…" we all hear the familiar cry,
"Winchelsea, Doleham and Three Oaks" the loudspeaker recording croaks…
"… and Ore and Hastings, Platform One!" - the time for departure has come,
And twenty passengers, like me, are on the Slow Train to the Sea.

At Appledore nobody waits beside the level-crossing gates,
And, lurching over rusty points, the ageing train creaks in its joints.
Three coaches of a dirty blue go round the curve and into view
Of fat Marsh sheep who do not care about the train that's running there.

Across the Marsh the diesel train sounds out its whistle once again.
Through Ham Street, Appledore and Rye the three blue coaches rattle by.

From Rye to Hastings our train grinds: the single-track line twists and winds
Past Winchelsea - a Gothic gem built by King Edward and his men.
But Doleham's wooden platform's bare: no passenger is waiting there.
The diesel engine gives a roar, goes through the tunnel, into Ore.

And Hastings town is soon in sight, its beach and pier are a delight
And our small band of travellers leave. Their custom won the line's reprieve
But the receipts have seen a fall and now the writing's on the wall -
The small blue train upon its track may leave one day and not come back.

Yet back in Queen Victoria's time when Wellington surveyed the line,
The great steam locomotives gleamed as across Romney Marsh they steamed.
The folk of Winchelsea and Rye would gaze in awe as they went by.
But now this line is one of those that British Rail wants to close.

Across the Marsh the diesel train sounds out its whistle once again;
And, if they close this line to Rye, a little part of me will die.

A Word About PRAYAS

Helping the 'railway children' of New Delhi

PRAYAS is one of India's largest non-profit-making organisations. Its name means 'endeavour', and its goal is to protect the rights of marginalised children, women and young people. It has projects in seven states across India serving an estimated 100,000 people.

In New Delhi, the local PRAYAS group works with the Railway Protection Force to help improve the lives of young children who live and work at the railway stations.

The capital city has an estimated half a million street children, many of whom live in desperate and dangerous conditions on the railway lines. To help these children face a better future, a drop-in shelter has been created at Lahore Gate station where children receive food, clothing and emotional support in a place of safety. Social workers provide 24-hour support and the children have access to health care and counselling as well as informal education and vocational training. Computers have also been installed, to help with literacy and IT skills.

Some of these children may have travelled to Delhi from other parts of India and where appropriate, they will be reunited with their families or settled into residential care.

If you would like to make a donation to help this valuable work, please contact:

Saga Charitable Trust. The Saga Building, Enbrook Park, Folkestone, Kent CT20 3SE, England.

Web site: www.sagacharitabletrust.org   Prayas web site: www.prayasonline.org

The Saga Charitable Trust is a UK registered charity (No: 291991) founded by Saga Group Ltd.

PRAYAS in New Delhi

Appendix One - Elongated Coins

Elongated coin collecting is a hobby that owes its very existence to the introduction of railways. No-one knows who the first person was to lay a coin on a railway track to see what would happen to it after a train had passed over it, but it is said that people placed 'pennies' (American cents) on the track in front of the funeral train that carried Abraham Lincoln's body across the USA in 1865, and kept the squashed coins as a souvenir. My mother recalls putting halfpennies on the Cambridge - Sudbury railway line (closed 1967) during her childhood.

It is generally accepted that the first machines designed to squash coins and stamp a design on them were installed at the World's Columbian Exposition in Chicago, Illinois in 1892. This exhibition was held to commemorate the 400th anniversary of Columbus's discovery of America.

Since then collecting 'squashed pennies', as elongated coins are commonly known, has become a very popular hobby in the USA, and many museums and other places of interest have a machine where you insert an American cent plus two quarters and receive an elongated cent with a commemorative design. The machines have gradually spread to other countries, although in some places they have fallen foul of laws that prohibit the mutilation of currency.

Coin-squashing machines are a relatively recent introduction in the UK. I have not yet obtained any British elongates with railway designs, although I understand that machines have recently been installed at the National Railway Museum in York and at Bressingham Sream Museum in Norfolk. Overseas I have found machines at Interlaken-Ost and Spiez railway stations in Switzerland (only the latter had a train design) and at George Railway Museum in South Africa.

The USA, where squashed pennies originated, has the widest selection of railway-themed elongates, although the majority of these just show the generic outline of a steam locomotive. I have obtained examples from St Louis, Missouri, where the vast former Union Station is now a high-class shopping mall, and the handful of Amtrak passenger trains make do with a tiny halt nearby. I have also got specimens from Durango in Colorado and a rather nice one showing a cable car from San Francisco.

Strangely enough, although there are numerous postage stamps showing trains, there have been very few non-squashed coins depicting them, although most fortunately these include the £2 coin issued by the Royal Mint in 2004 showing Richard Trevithick's first locomotive, and the two £2 coins issued in 2006 to commemorate Isambard Kingdom Brunel. The Isle of Man has illustrated its own steam railway on a 50p piece, and Canada issued a quarter-dollar showing a steam locomotive in 1999. The 'Golden Spike' ceremony in Utah was featured on a US quarter issued in 2007. Other than that, most coins showing railways have been high-value commemoratives in precious metals, not issued for normal circulation.

A souvenir 'squashed penny' from George Railway Museum in South Africa

Appendix Two - Songs for a railway journey

In the old days the railway traveller who wished to listen to music had to inflict it on other passengers, as in the famous scene from *A Hard Day's Night* (1964) featuring the Beatles with their transistor radio and the long-suffering Richard Vernon. That all changed in the early 1980s with the appearance of the Sony Walkman. The portable compact-disc player and the iPod or mp3 player have now become so commonplace that in some carriages it is rare to see a single passenger who isn't wearing earphones.

This forward march of technology has reduced the chance of having an interesting conversation with a stranger, but it does provide the traveller with the opportunity to create his or her personal soundtrack. What could be more appropriate than to listen to *The City of New Orleans* while travelling on the train in question, or lulling oneself to sleep in a couchette to the sound of the Seekers' *Morningtown Ride*? If you can remember the TV advertisement a few years ago for Nescafé 'Alta Rica' coffee, then you just cannot visualise a train journey in Latin America without *La Colegiala* as a soundtrack - even though there is nothing in the song's lyrics to suggest that it is about railways! And Abba's *Another Town, Another Train* would be ideal for anyone backpacking around Scandinavia on a EuroDomino ticket.

There are, of course, hundreds of songs about railways. Many of these are children's favourites, and others are obscure Country and Western tracks. Whole CDs are available devoted purely to railway songs: the Bear Family label has issued a series under the title *Sentimental Journey*, while John Denver's last CD (apart from posthumous compilations) was *All Aboard*, an anthology of railroad songs. Of course, the musical *Starlight Express* was all about trains, and included the whimsical *U.N.C.O.U.P.L.E.D.* - a parody of the Tammy Wynette song *D.I.V.O.R.C.E.*

Some songs refer to specific lines and stations, others to the pleasure of travelling and others to events that happened on a railway journey. In some the songwriter is using the train simply as a metaphor.

Surprisingly, despite the vogue for 'protest songs' in the 1960s, I am only aware of two songs about the Beeching Cuts. The first is the wonderful *Slow Train* by Michael Flanders and Donald Swann, which combines a portrait of branch-line travel with a roll-call of some of Britain's more unusual station names. The second, Keith West's *Sam*, is the story of an engine-driver who rides away at night on his locomotive when he is told that his line is going to close. The Bruce Phillips song *Daddy, What's a Train?* (recorded by Joe Glazer and John Denver) is about children growing up in a part of the USA where railways have disappeared: with minor revisions to the lyrics it could equally apply to parts of post-Beeching Britain.

Specific locations

Chattanooga Choo-Choo - Bing Crosby
Canadian Pacific - Hank Snow
Last Train to San Fernando - Johnny Duncan and the Bluegrass Boys
Last Train to Clarksville - The Monkees
Last Train to London - Electric Light Orchestra
Last Train to Trancentral - KLF
City of New Orleans - Arlo Guthrie
The Good Old E. A. R. & H. - Roger Whittaker
Take the 'A' train - Duke Ellington
Rock Island Line - Lonnie Donegan

Up the Junction - Squeeze
The Atchison, Topeka & the Santa Fe - Judy Garland
Down in the Tube Station at Midnight - Jam
Night Train to Memphis - Jerry Lee Lewis
Midnight Train to Georgia - Gladys Knight and the Pips
Ballad of Casey Jones - Johnny Cash
Finchley Central - The New Vaudeville Band
3.10 to Yuma - Frankie Laine
Canadian Pacific - Chet Atkins

Railway closures

The Slow Train - Michael Flanders and Donald Swann
Sam - Keith West
Daddy, What's a Train? - Joe Glazer

French train songs

Caliñ-Caline - Alain Souchon
L'Autorail - Alain Souchon
Allo Maman Bobo - Alain Souchon
Tchou Tchou Le Petit Train! - Dorothée

Spanish train songs

Balada para un Viejo Tren - José Luis Pérales
La Colegiala - Son Caribe
Spanish Train - Chris de Burgh

General train songs

Morningtown Ride - The Seekers
Love Train - The O'Jays
Railway Hotel - Mike Batt
Choo Choo Chi Boogie - Louis Jordan
Slow Train Coming - Bob Dylan
One-Way Ticket - Eruption
Night Train - Visage
Jeannie dreamed of trains - John Denver
Another Town, Another Train - Abba
The Day We Caught The Train - Ocean Colour Scene
Freight Train Blues - Trixie Smith
Waiting for a Train - Flash & The Pan
Sentimental Journey - Billy Vaughan
I'm a Train - Albert Hammond
Choo Choo Train - Doris Day
Freight Train - Nancy Whiskey
King of the Road - Roger Miller
The Last Hobo - John Denver
Shimbleshanks, the Railway cat - The cast of CATS

Bibliography

Poetry

Ever since William Wordsworth put pen to paper about the building of the Windermere line, poets have been writing about trains. One of the earliest railway poems is *The Spiritual Railway*, engraved in 1845 on the tombstone of William Pickering and Richard Edger in Ely Cathedral. John Betjeman is undoubtedly the champion of railway poets, and his best poems, such as *Monody on the Death of Aldersgate Street Station* or *Great Central*, paint a picture of railways in decline that is touching, colourful and, at times, very amusing.

Adlestrop by Edward Thomas and *The Night Mail* by W H Auden are probably Britain's favourite railway poems; my personal favourite as a child was *From A Railway Carriage* by Robert Louis Stevenson, which was intended to be read to the rhythm of a moving train.

It is this built-in rhythm that distinguishes many railway poems and explains why there is so little blank verse about railways. It also means that there is quite a bit of railway doggerel. When this gets really bad it can unwittingly slide into genius: who could forget William Topaz McGonagall's classic, *The Tay Bridge Disaster?* Even Commander A B Campbell, a retired naval officer and founding member of the Brains Trust, showed that he could do it if he really tried: his children's book *Fun with Trains* tells the story, in glorious rhyming couplets, of Dick and his sister Sue going on a train journey to an idyllic English seaside resort, with Valerie Landon's accompanying line drawings showing immaculate stations, nicely-dressed children and a railway free from weekend engineering works, graffiti and litter. Perhaps one day Andrew Lloyd-Webber will turn it into a musical, although it wouldn't have quite the drama of T S Eliot's *Shimbleshanks the Railway Cat* that became one of the most exciting parts of *CATS* in the West End.

Many of the best railway poems have recently been put together into one volume, *Railway Rhymes*, edited by Peter Ashley. This means the railway traveller no longer needs to carry large numbers of poetry books!

Prose

Large numbers of railway books, although superbly written and researched, are very dull for the non-specialist: the same applies to many books on technical subjects. At the same time, the large, coffee-table books on 'the greatest steam locomotives' or 'the world's most beautiful train journeys', while lavishly photographed, are often inaccurate or sadly lacking in technical detail.

One writer who succeeded in making his books both informative for the specialist and interesting for the layman was Bryan Morgan. *The End of the Line* in 1955 set a standard against which other railway books may be judged. The David & Charles *Railway Holiday* books in the mid-1960s had a similar blend of technical and historical detail and amusing anecdotes, and Paul Theroux is a master of the art.

More recently, H P White's *Forgotten Railways* and its companion regional volumes gave a nostalgic look at the past, while Christopher Somerville and Hunter Davies wrote the definitive guides to exploring disused railways. *The British Railways Past & Present* series are fascinating books. They contain pairs of photographs, taken from the same angle 30, 40, 50 or more years apart, displayed side by side. Here you can see how a former branch line terminus has been replaced by a supermarket, how a sleepy halt with timber platforms has become a busy modern suburban station, and how some parts of the railway system have remained almost unchanged for decades.

Although their books could not be more unalike in content or style, Lisa St Aubin de Terán's *Off the Rails* and Muriel V Searle's *Down the Line to Dover* are both classics and prove that women *can* write some of the finest railway books! Of course E Nesbit proved this with *The Railway Children* way back in 1906!

Almost all British preserved railways produce their own guide books, and many of these are very well-written and superbly illustrated. Overseas railways are not so well endowed, but a number of highly evocative books have been produced on French lines, often using old postcards to illustrate stations and trains in days gone by. Sadly these are often local publications and tend to disappear from the shelves a year or so after publication.

Most little boys' introduction to railway fiction begins in the nursery with the Reverend W H Awdry's *Thomas the Tank Engine* series - I know mine did! The railway novel became a work of literature with Emile Zola's *La Bête Humaine* and Graham Greene's *Stamboul Train*. Agatha Christie established herself as a master of the genre with her *Murder on the Orient Express* and *The 4.50 from Paddington*. David Beaty's *Electric Train* is a very readable thriller with a fantastic sense of suspense and a wholly believable scenario and characters, but the ultimate railway novel has to be John Hadfield's *Love on a Branch Line*.

Periodicals

Magazines about railways can be very dull to those who are not enthusiasts, but the best can also be quite interesting even to the layman. The doyen is *The Railway Magazine*, which celebrated its centenary in July 1997 by printing amusing contributions from readers that predicted what rail travel would be like 100 years hence. Its main rival, Ian Allan's *Railway World*, also has fascinating articles and superb photographs. The French preservationists' magazine *Voie Etroite* manages to be informative and yet retain an element of humour, while the American magazine *Railfan and Railroad* even has a regular comic strip! Many preserved railways issue their own magazines: the Kent & East Sussex Railway's *Tenterden Terrier* is superb.

Film / Video / DVD

If you cannot get to travel, then watching a film or video is the closest you can get to experiencing a real train journey. One of the first movies ever made by the Lumière brothers (in 1895) was of a train entering La Ciotat station. Many 'cab rides' are available on DVD, and these are often sold with little in the way of commentary, so they are certainly not just for the hardened enthusiast: just sit by and enjoy the scenery! Vast numbers of railway DVDs are available these days, including a set of the *World's Greatest Railway Journeys* by Musicbank. Of course, the real classics are Buster Keaton's *The General* (1927), Will Hay's *Oh Mr Porter!* (1937), David Lean's *Brief Encounter* (1945) and the Ealing Studios' *The Titfield Thunderbolt* (1952). The latter, about a group of villagers who re-open their local branch line, is arguably the all-time greatest British railway film and heralded the preservation movement. The greatest American railway film is perhaps Cecil B De Mille's *Union Pacific* (1939); the French equivalent, albeit directed by an American, is *Le Train* by John Frankenheimer(1964), about resistance fighters preventing the Nazis from taking a train loaded with works of art to Germany. A superb recent 'international' train film is Wes Anderson's *Darjeeling Limited* (2007).

General books to take on a train journey

Railway Rhymes - Peter Ashley (editor), Everyman's Library (2007)
Fun with Trains - Commander A B Campbell, Epworth Press (1954)
The Railway Children - E Nesbit, T Fisher Unwin (1906)
Off the Rails - Lisa St Aubin de Terán, Hodder & Stoughton (1990)
Thomas the Tank Engine (Complete Collection) - The Rev. W Awdry, William Heinemann (1996)
La Bête Humaine - Emile Zola, Penguin Classics (1977)
Stamboul Train - Graham Greene, William Heinemann (1932)
Murder on the Orient Express - Agatha Christie, Collins Crime Club (1934)
The 4.50 from Paddington - Agatha Christie, Collins Crime Club (1957)
Electric Train - David Beaty, Secker & Warburg (1975)
Love on a Branch Line - John Hadfield, Hutchinson (1959); Penguin (1994)

The following are recommended for those who wish to find out more about some of the great railway journeys featured in *Single Track Obsession.* In addition to these, most preserved tourist lines have their own guide books.

The End of the Line - Bryan Morgan, Cleaver-Hume (1955)
Minor Railways of France - W J K Davies, Plateway Press (2000)
Essential Guide to French Heritage Tourist Railways - Mervyn Jones, Oakwood Press (2006)
Vivarais Narrow Gauge - John Organ, Middleton Press (2001)
Le Chemin de Fer d'Alais à Bessèges - Thierry Malnuit, Association Terre Cévenole (1991)
Switzerland by Rail - Anthony Lambert, Bradt (1996)
Railway Holiday in Spain - D Trevor Rowe, David & Charles (1966)
Great Railway Journeys of Europe (Insight Guide) - Tom Le Bas (editor), APA Publications (2002)
Canadian Rail Travel Guide - Daryl T Adair, Fitzhenry & Whiteside (2004)
The Atlas of Train Travel - J B Hollingsworth, Sidgwick & Jackson (1980)
America's Railroad - Robert T Royem (2002)
The Old Patagonian Express - Paul Theroux, Houghton Mifflin (1979); Penguin (1980)
Great Railway Journeys of the World - Max Wade-Matthews, Lorenz Books (1998)
Australia and New Zealand by Rail - Colin Taylor, Bradt (1996)
Rails to the Top End - Robin Bromby, Outback Books (1992)
Rails across New Zealand - Matthew Wright, Whitcoulls (2003)
The Beaten Track (by Tranz Scenic through New Zealand) - Graham Hutchins, Grantham House (1999)
The Wellington to Johnsonville Railway - Geoffrey B Churchman, Industrial Publishing (1988)
The TranzAlpine Express - Roy Sinclair, Grantham House (1995)
Forgotten Railways - H P White, David & Charles (1986)
Country Railways - Paul Atterbury and Ian Burgum, Weidenfeld & Nicholson (1996)
Stopping-Train Britain - Alexander Frater, Hodder & Stoughton (1983)
On the Settle and Carlisle Route - T G Flinders, Ian Allan (1981)
Branch Lines into the Eighties - H I Quayle and Stanley C Jenkins, David & Charles (1980)
London Underground Stations - David Leboff, Ian Allan (1994)
The Railways of South-East England - Andrew Knight, Ian Allan (1986)
Down the Line to Dover - Muriel V Searle, Bloomsbury (1988)
The Bluebell Railway (Past and Present Companion) - Terry Gough, Nostalgia Collection (1998)
The Kent & East Sussex Railway (Past and Present Companion) - Terry Gough, Nostalgia Collection (1998)
South Coast Railways: Hastings to Ashford - Vic Mitchell and Keith Smith, Middleton Press (1987)
Narrow-gauge Railways (England and the Fifteen Inch) - Humphrey Household, Alan Sutton (1989)

Periodicals

La Vie du Rail No. 969 8 November 1964 (Etaples - Arras and Flåm - Myrdal lines)
Rail No. 315 8 October 1997 (Stockport - Stalybridge line)
Railway Magazine No. 1023 Vol. 132 July 1986 (Amtrak; Spanish narrow-gauge); No 1036 Vol. 33 August 1987 (Costa Rican railways)
Railway World Vol. 35 No. 408 April 1974 (Corsica); Vol. 37 No. 430 February 1976 (Ashford - Hastings line); Vol. 43 No. 503 March 1982 (Vivarais); Vol. 54 No. 639 July 1993 (Bluebell Railway)
Steam Railway No. 14 June 1981 (Paraguay)
Today's Railways No. 5 February 1995 (Brünigbahn; French Alps); No. 41 May 1999 (Harz Mountains); No. 75 March 2002 (Cannes - Grasse line); No. 90 June 2003 (Bilbao - León line)

Index

A20 road, Kent, England 58, 214, 217, 219
A21 road, East Sussex, England 221
A259 road, East Sussex, England 230
A272 road, Sussex/Hampshire, England 210
Aare Valley, Switzerland 66-7
Adelaide, Australia 175, 177
Aérotrain monorail system 7
Agra Fort station, India 148
Ajaccio, Corsica 55
Alajuela, Costa Rica 118
Albi, France 47
Alcázar de San Juan, Spain 81
Alès-Bessèges line, France 37-43, 249
Alexisbad, Germany 91, 93
Alice Springs, Australia 175-7
Alicedale-Grahamstown line, South Africa 166-9
Alloa-Stirling line, Scotland 11
Amtrak 11, 106-11
Andrew's House, Tyne and Wear, England 192-3
Animas Valley, USA 103-4
Annemasse, France 61
Anvin, France 17
Apple Express train, South Africa 170-2
Appleby, Cumbria, England 196
Appledore, Kent, England 226, 229-30, 237
Arahura ferry, New Zealand 183
Archers, The 67, 93
Arras, France 17-8
Arthur's Pass, New Zealand 185
Ashford-Hastings line, Kent/Sussex, England 72, 88,
    221, 226-33, 236-7, 242, 249
Ashford-Maidstone East line, Kent, England 214-8
Ashford station, Kent, England 215, 227
Ashford, Kent, England 216-7, 225
Asunción station, Paraguay 134
Atherstone, South Africa 168
Attractive fellow passengers 8, 40, 42, 86-9, 109-10,
    115, 154-5, 198, 219, 224, 230
Auckland, New Zealand 179-81
Austen, William H 221
Automatic train control 208
Bad Sachsa, Germany 94
Balmaseda, Spain 79
Bangkok, Thailand 153-5
Barming, Kent, England 214, 218-9
Barog Tunnel, India 151
Bastia, Corsica 55-56
Bearsted station, Kent, England 214, 218
Beaune, France 27-8, 30
Beechbrook Farm, Kent, England 215
Beeching, Dr 7, 10, 11, 37, 227
Begona (locomotive) 75
Bellinzona, Switzerland 73
Benson, EF 226
Bergen-Oslo railway, Norway 83-5
Berlin, Germany 90
Berner-Oberland-Bahn, Switzerland 68
Bern-Lötschberg-Simplon Railway, Switzerland 70-1

Bertholène-Espalion line, France 47
Bessèges station, France 39-43
Bessemer, Miss 209
Béthune, France 17-20, 44
Betjeman, Sir John 247
Bickley, Kent, England 220
Biguglia station, Corsica 56
Bilbao, Spain 74, 80-1, 249
Bingham, Hiram 126
Blaenau Ffestiniog, Wales 197
Blake Hall station, Essex, England 205
Blanc-Argent railway, France 21-6
Blea Moor Tunnel, North Yorkshire, England 195
Blenheim, New Zealand 183
Bligny-sur-Ouche, France 27-30
Bluebell (locomotive) 211, 213
Bluebell Railway, Sussex, England 43, 193, 209-13,
    249
Bodiam (locomotive) 222
Bodiam, Kent, England 224-5
Bolivia 123, 134-5
Bonaparte, Napoleon I 228
Bonaparte, Napoleon III 226
Books about railways 247-9
Botolphs Bridge, Kent, England 236
Boucieu-le-Roi, France 33
Boulogne, France 15-6
Braintree-Dunmow line, Essex, England 11
Brias, France 18
Bridge on the River Kwai 153, 155
Brienz Rothorn railway, Switzerland 68
Brig, Switzerland 71
Brocken Mountain, Germany 92
Bromley South station, Kent/Greater London,
    England 194, 215, 220
Bromley, Kent/Greater London, England 12, 194,
    215, 220
Brunel, Isambard Kingdom 153, 206
Brünig railway, Switzerland 63-8, 249
Budd dome cars 98
Buenos Aires, Argentina 130, 136-7
Bug, The (locomotive) 238
Bushman Sands, South Africa 169
Butch Cassidy and the Sundance Kid 103
Buzançais, France 21, 25-6
Calais-Dunkerque line, France 15
Calais, France 15, 17
Calonne-Ricouart, France 19
Calvi, Corsica 53, 56-7
Camber, East Sussex, England 226, 228, 232
Cambridge-Ipswich line, Cambridgeshire/Suffolk,
    England 12
Camedo, Switzerland 72
Canadian Pacific Railway 97
Cannes-Grasse line, France 49-52, 249
Caravelle railcars 20, 38
Cartago, Costa Rica 113, 115
Casamozza viaduct, Corsica 56

Cascade Canyon, Colorado, USA 104
Cat, ginger, on train 229
Cat, pure white 58
Cat, silver tabby 231
Cat, Stasi 93
Cat, three-legged 22
Cats, Corsican 53-7
Causey Arch, Tyne and Wear, England 191-3
CD player, see Personal Stereos
Centovalli Line, Italy/Switzerland 69, 72
Cèze River, France 38
Chabris, France 23-4
Chamonix, France 59-60
Channel Tunnel rail link 215
Charing, Kent, England 215-6
Chelsea, South Africa 170
Chicago, Illinois, USA 111
Chips, best in France 19
Chocolate, taking to Cordoba 81-2
Christchurch-Greymouth line, New Zealand 184-6
Christchurch, New Zealand 184
Cidad-Dosante, Spain 74, 79
Cistierna, Spain 76
City of New Orleans train, USA 109-11
Class 37 diesel locomotives 199
Class 47 diesel locomotives 196, 199
Clochemerle 32
Closures of railways 11-2, 25, 31, 35, 37, 45, 49, 97,
    112, 135-6, 164, 175, 179-80, 203-5
Coastal Pacific train, New Zealand 183-4
Colombier-le-Vieux, France 32
Columbus, Christopher 53
Cordoba, Spain 80-2
Corsica 53-7
Corte, Corsica 54
Costa Rican railways 112-9, 249
Cuckoo Trail, Sussex, England 12
Cuzco-Machu Picchu railway, Peru 126-9
Cuzco, Peru 126, 129
Dan-Air 48
Davies, WJK 21, 249
Death Railway, Thailand/Burma 153-5
Delhi, India 150, 152, 243
Denton station, Greater Manchester 201
Denver & Rio Grande Western Railroad, USA 102
Deviationists 198
Dickens, Charles 7
Didcot, Berkshire, England 8
Disused railways 11-12, 33-4, 36, 44, 83,175, 238
Docklands Light Railway, London, England 8
Doleham, East Sussex, England 227, 230
Dolphins 184, 238
Domodóssola, Italy 71
Douce-Plage, France 32
Drei Annen Hohne, Germany 92
Dungeness, Kent, England 229, 234, 237-8
Dunières, France 31, 34-36
Durango-Silverton railway, Colorado, USA 102-5,
    249
Durango, Colorado, USA 102
Dymchurch, Kent, England 22, 236, 238

East Grinstead, Sussex, England 58, 209, 213
East Malling, Kent, England 219
Eastern & Oriental Express (train) 154
Edwin Fox ship, New Zealand 183
Eiffel, Gustave 54
Eisfelder Talmuhle, Germany 92-3
El Gran Capitán (train) 130-1
El Paso, Texas, USA 108
Embalse del Ebro, Spain 78
Emett, Rowland 221
Encarnación, Paraguay 131-2, 135
Enya 139
Epping-Ongar line, Essex, England 203-5
Espinosa de los Monteros, Spain 79
Etaples-Béthune line, France 15-20, 249
Etaples, France 15-16
Eurostar train 7, 52
Eynsford station and viaduct, Kent, England 220
Fairlight, New Zealand 187
Farrer, Richard 113
FART (Domodóssola-Locarno line),
    Italy/Switzerland 69-73
Female enthusiasts, lack of 7
Ffestiniog Railway, Wales 31, 196-9
Films 248
Finse, Norway 85
Fitterman, Charles 45
Flåm Railway, Norway 84-5, 249
Florac station (disused), France 44
Folkestone Harbour branch line, Kent, England 238
Food on trains 76, 87, 114, 125, 130, 146, 176
France-Vacances railpass 22, 239
Garden Route, South Africa 162-163
Gatwick airport, Sussex, England 48, 58
General Urquiza Railway, Argentina 130-1
Geneva, Switzerland 58, 60-2
George, South Africa 70, 164-5
Geyserland train, New Zealand 180
Ghan train, Australia 176-177
Ghosts and Ghost Trains 200-2, 218, 239-41
Gièvres, France 23
Giswil, Switzerland 65
Glacier Express train, Switzerland 63, 69-70, 73
Glenbrook Vintage Railway, New Zealand 181
Glenelg, Australia 177
Graceland, Memphis, Tennessee, USA 110
Graffiti 9, 16, 40, 58, 80, 180
Grahamstown, South Africa 166-8
Grasse station, France 52
Great Brak River, South Africa 165
Green Goddess (locomotive) 235-6
Greenly, Henry 235
Greymouth, New Zealand 186
Guácimo to Guápiles line, Costa Rica 117
Gunn, David 10
Gwynne, Andrew, MP 202
Hakone, Japan 144
Halberstadt, Germany 90
Ham Street station, Kent, England 228, 230
Hamilton, New Zealand 180-1
Harrietsham, Kent, England 214, 217

Harry Potter 97, 149, 176
Hartenbos, South Africa 164-5
Harz Mountain railways, Germany 90-4, 249
Hastings station, East Sussex, England 234
Headcodes on trains 219
Headcorn, Kent, England 221
Hellifield station, North Yorkshire, England 195, 199
Helsinki-Moscow line, Finland/Russia 86-9
Henley branch line, Berkshire, England 206-8
Hercules (locomotive) 235
Heredia branch line, Costa Rica 118-9
Hertfordshire Rail Tours 229
Hesdigneul level crossing, France 16
Hesdin, France 17
Hitch-hiking 28, 30
Hollingbourne, Kent, England 214-5, 217-8
Holman F Stephens (locomotive) 222
Holman Hunt, William 226
Hop pickers 221, 223
Hornby, New Zealand 185
Horsted Keynes station, West Sussex, England 211-3
Hothfield, Kent, England 215
Houston, Texas, USA 108
Howey, Captain JEP 234-5
Humewood, South Africa 169, 172
Hurricane (Great Storm of October 1987) 217, 235
Hurricane (locomotive) 234-5
Hythe, Kent, England 58, 235-8
Icefields Parkway, Canada 97
Ile-Rousse, Corsica 57
Imberhorne viaduct, West Sussex, England 213
Indian railways 148-52
Interlaken, Switzerland 59, 65, 68
iPod, see Personal Stereos
Irauregui, Spain 79
Jabalpur, India 148-9
Japanese railways 143-7
Jarman, Derek 237
Jasper, Canada 98
Johnsonville branch line, New Zealand 182-3, 249
Jones, Casey 111, 246
Joyeuse, France 44
Juan-les-Pins, France 51
Juliaca, Peru 125
Jungfrau Mountain, Switzerland 68
Kaaimans River Bridge, South Africa 163-4
Kaikoura, New Zealand 184
Kalka-Shimla railway, India 150-2
Kanchanaburi, Thailand 154
Kandaghat, India 151
Kanha National Park, India 149
Kankakee, Illinois, USA 111
Karen (locomotive) 199
Keith, Henry M 112
Kelburn funicular, Wellington, New Zealand 182
Kemsing, Kent, England 219
Kennedy half-dollars 104
Kent & East Sussex Railway, England 221-5, 248-9
Kimberley, South Africa 162
Kingscote station, West Sussex, England 209, 211-2
Kingston Flyer train, New Zealand 187

Kinki Nippon Railway, Japan 146
Knysna, South Africa 162-5
Kuala Lumpur, Malaysia 157-60
Kyoto, Japan 145-6
La Raya, Peru 125
La Robla Railway (Bilbao-León), Spain 74-80, 249
La Tour de Carol, France 26
Laissac, France 45-6
Lake Louise, Canada 97
Lamastre, France 31-4
La-Roche-sur-Foron, France 60
Laura 86-9
Lausanne, Switzerland 58
Lavatory on Peruvian train 125, 129
Le Châtelard, France/Switzerland 59
Le Cheylard, France 31, 34
Loughborough, Leicestershire, England 7
Lenham, Kent, England 217
León, Spain 76-77
Les Arcs-Draugignan line, France 50
Limon, Costa Rica 115-6
Litter 9, 148
Little Kenton, Abton & Bletchley railway 8
Liveries 10, 21, 34, 159
Liverpool, Costa Rica 116
Locarno, Switzerland 72-3
London Underground 203, 249
London, England 194, 203, 249
Loop, the (railway), Chicago, Illinois, USA 111
Los Angeles, California, USA 106-7
Lötschberg Tunnel, Switzerland 71
Lowry, LS 201
Luçay-le-Mâle, France 24, 26
Lucerne, Switzerland 59, 64-5, 68-9
Lugano, Switzerland 73
Lumio, Corsica 56-57
Luzern-Stans-Engelberg line, Switzerland 65
Lydd, Kent, England 229
Lynton & Barnstaple Railway, Devon, England 238
Lyon-Nîmes line, France 32, 36
Machu Picchu, Peru 128
Machynlleth, Wales 199
Madrid, Spain 12, 80-1
Madrid-Atocha station, Spain 81-2
Maggie 219
Maidstone East line, Kent, England 19, 215-20
Maidstone East station, Kent, England 218
Maidstone, Kent, England 58
Major, John 10, 199
Malaysian Railways 157-9
Mallet locomotives 32-4
Maree, Australia 149, 175
Marley Hill, Tyne and Wear, England 193
Marsh, Richard 227
Martigny, Switzerland 58-9
Mataporquera, Spain 74-5, 77-8, 93
McBride, Canada 99
Meiringen-Innertkirchen line, Switzerland 66-7
Melbourne, Australia 175, 177
Melling branch, Wellington, New Zealand 179, 182
Memphis, Tennessee, USA 110-1

Meyzieu Tourist Railway, France 31
Mid-Kent Railway, Kent, England 220
Mikado (steam locomotive type) 147
Military railways in France 29
Miranda de Ebro, Spain 80
Mitterand, François 45
Monchy-Cayeux, France 17
Monkeys 151, 149, 159
Mont Blanc, France 60
Montfaucon, France 36
Montreuil-sur-Mer, France 16
Montreux, Switzerland 58, 63, 68
Montreux-Oberland-Bernois, Switzerland 8
Morgan, Bryan 16, 21, 31, 35-6, 66, 70, 249
Moscow Metro, Russia 89
Mouans-Sartoux, France 51-2
Mould, George 74
Mount Floien funicular, Bergen, Norway 83
Mount Fuji, Japan 144
MRT (Singapore transit) 157, 160-1
Myrdal, Norway 84-85
Nara, Japan 146
Network South-East, England 206, 217, 219-20
New Orleans, Louisiana, USA 107-9
New Romney, Kent, England 226-7, 229, 234-8
New York subway, New York, USA 10
New Zealand railways 179-87
Nordhausen-Northeim line, Germany 94
Nori, 143-4
North British 2-6-0 locomotives 132-4
North Island Main Trunk, New Zealand 181
North Weald station, Essex, England 204-5
Northiam station, Kent, England 223
Norwegian Mogul (locomotive) 224
Ongar, Essex, England 204-5
Ore, East Sussex, England 232-3
Orient Express train 7, 129
Osaka, Japan 146-7
Oslo, Norway 85
Otford, Kent, England 219
Otira Tunnel, New Zealand 186
Outeniqua Choo-Tjoe train, South Africa 162-5
Oviedo, Spain 74
Palmerston North, New Zealand 181
Panoramic Express train, Switzerland 63
Paraguayan Railway 130-5, 249
Paraiso, Costa Rica 115
Paris, France 9, 12, 16, 22
Pernes-Camblain, France 18-9
Personal Stereos 9, 99, 159, 178, 245-6
Picton, New Zealand 183
Pilatus Railway, Switzerland 65
Pilgrims' Way, Kent, England 217, 219
Poetry about railways 247-8
Ponte Brolla, Switzerland 72
Ponte-Leccia, Corsica 53-5
Port Elizabeth, South Africa 162, 167, 169-72
Porthmadog, Wales 199
PRAYAS 152, 243
Prince George, Canada 99
Prince Rupert, Canada 98, 100-1

Privatisation 10, 199
Provence Railway, France 49
Puente Ruinas station, Peru 128
Puno-Cuzco railway, Peru 123-6
Puno station, Peru 124
Puntarenas, Costa Rica 113
Q1 class locomotive 210
Queenstown, New Zealand 186-7
Raffles Hotel, Singapore 160
Railway Development Society 11
Railway Magazine 228, 248-9
Ranguin, France 50-1
Raurimu Spiral, New Zealand 181
Reddish South station, Manchester, England 201
Redhill-Tonbridge line, Kent/Surrey, England 12, 48
Renault Espace 23
Renault railcar 57
Rex, George 163
Ribblehead Viaduct, North Yorkshire, England 194-5
Rice, Anneka 223
Rigi rack-railway, Switzerland 63
Rio Frio, Costa Rica 117-8
Robertsbridge, East Sussex, England 221
Robiac, France 37-8
Rocky Mountaineer train, Canada 97
Rodez-Séverac line, France 45-7
Rolvenden station, Kent, England 223
Rome Metro, Italy 9
Romney Marsh, Kent, England 226-31, 234-7
Romney, Hythe & Dymchurch Railway, Kent,
   England 138, 234-8
Romorantin, France 21-3, 72
Rother Valley, East Sussex, England 221-5
Rotorua branch line, New Zealand 180
Route 66, USA 106
Royal Military Canal, Kent/East Sussex, England
   228, 235
Rye, East Sussex, England 226-7, 230-1
Saarinen, Eliel 87
Saga Charitable Trust 243
Salbris, France 21-22
Samson (locomotive) 235
San Francisco cable cars, California, USA 147
San Isidro, Argentina 136
San José, Costa Rica 112-5
Sandhurst, Kent, England 224
Santa Maria Maggiore, Italy 72
Santander-Bilbao line, Spain 79
Santander, Spain 74, 78
Santander-Mediterráneo railway, Spain 74
Sardou, Michel 30
Sato 144-5
Schools class (locomotives) 227
Sedgefield, South Africa 163
Settle-Carlisle Railway, England 194-6, 249
Sevenoaks, Kent, England 219
Sharpthorne Tunnel, West Sussex, England 211
Sheffield Park, East Sussex, England 210
Sheffield, New Zealand 185
Shimla, India 150-1
Shinkansen (bullet train), Japan 144

Shoreham, Kent, England 219
Shosholoza Meyl, South Africa 166
Silverton, Colorado, USA 104
Simplon Tunnel, Switzerland/Italy 71
Singapore 157-8, 160
Singapore station 157-8
Siquirres, Costa Rica 93, 116-7
Sissy 176-7
Skeena (train), Canada 97-101
Snailham Halt, East Sussex, England 227, 232
Snow 83-5, 97, 99, 216
Solan brewery, India 151
Songs about railways 245-6
Sony Walkman, see Personal Stereos
Souchon, Alain 21
South African Railways 162-72
South Island Main Trunk, New Zealand 183
Southern Maid (locomotive) 235
Southwest Chief train, USA 107
Spiez, Switzerland 68-70
Springfield, New Zealand 185
Squashed pennies 68, 70, 104, 110, 244
St Mary Cray, Kent, England 220
St-Agrève, France 34
Stagshaw (locomotive) 192
Stalybridge station, Greater Manchester 202
St-Ambroix, France 37-40, 42
Stamps showing railways 179, 228
Staplehurst, Kent, England 7
Stephens, Colonel Holman Fred 153, 221
Stephenson, George 7
St-Etienne, France 36
St-Geniez-d'Olt, France 44
St-Gervais, France 59-60
Stiege, Germany 93
Stockholm, Sweden 85-6
Stockport-Stalybridge Railway, Greater Manchester, England 200-2, 249
Stockport viaduct, Greater Manchester 201
St-Pol-sur-Ternoise, France 16-7
Streetcars, see trams
Sunset Limited train, USA 107
Swanley, Kent, England 220
Swiss Railways 58-73
Swiss Railways June 2005 power failure 63
Sydney 175, 178
Tadpole trains 12
Taeri Gorge Railway, New Zealand 184
Takayama branch line, Japan 144-5
Tanfield Railway, Tyne and Wear, England 191-3
Tangmere (locomotive) 229
Tan-y-Bwlch, Wales 198
Taw Valley (locomotive) 229, 233
Telegraph poles 12, 16, 26, 145, 159, 183
Tence, France 34-6
Tenterden, Kent, England 58, 222-3
Terrier tank locomotives 222
Thai railways 153-5
Thomas the Tank Engine 7, 12, 248

Thornhill, South Africa 170, 172
Three Oaks, East Sussex, England 227, 232
Thumpers (diesel-electric multiple units) 227-8, 232
Tibetan travelling to Zurich 61-2
Tickets 113-4, 135, 139, 160, 172, 179, 182, 197, 205
Tierra del Fuego, Argentina 137-8
Titicaca, Lake, Bolivia/Peru 123, 125
Tolstoi train, Russia 87
Topless sunbathers 32
Toulouse, France 9, 44-8
Tournon, France 31-2, 185
Train Control Point, Singapore 158
Tralee & Dingle Light Railway, Ireland 238
Trams 61-2, 67, 86, 109-11, 134-5, 147, 177, 184, 200
Tranz Alpine train, New Zealand 184-6, 249
Tren de la Costa, Argentina 136-7
Tren del Fin del Mundo, Argentina 137-9
Trolleybuses 65, 182
TSS Earnslaw ship, New Zealand 186-7
Tunbridge Wells, Kent, England 23, 58, 209
Turner, J M W 7
Twyford, Berkshire, England 206-8
Tyler, Bonnie 199
Typhoon (locomotive) 235
Urubamba River, Peru 127
Ushuaia, Argentina 137-8
Vainikkala, Finland 87
Valençay, France 24-5
Vallée de l'Ouche railway, France 27-30
Van Stadens River Bridge, South Africa 171
Vandalism 9, 205, 233 (also see 'Graffiti')
Velay Railway, France 34-6
Via magazine 59
Viaduc 07 Association 39
Viaur Viaduct, France 47
Vivarais Railway, France 7, 31-6, 249
Vivario, Corsica 54-5
Vizzavona, Corsica 55
Voie Etroite magazine 7
Voss-Granvin line, Norway 83
Vyborg, Russia 87
Wealden Pullman (train) 224
Wellington, Duke of 226
Wellington, New Zealand 182
Welsh Highland Railway, Wales 199
Wernigerode, Germany 90-2
West Hoathly, West Sussex, England 210-2
West Malling, Kent, England 19, 219
Wilderness, South Africa 163-4
Winchelsea, East Sussex, England 232
Windermere branch, Cumbria, England 7
Windmills 90, 224, 228, 231-2
Winston Churchill (locomotive) 235
Wittersham Road station, Kent, England 223
Wordsworth, William 7
Wrotham, Kent, England 219
XPT train, Australia 177-8
Yamanote line, Tokyo, Japan 143
Zurich, Switzerland 61-4

Printed in the United States
By Bookmasters